"...is th

water board?..."

Alan Smith

Thank you for buying this book.
You have donated £2 to Water Aid, the international charity that is
committed to providing clean water and sanitation to the World.
Every minute a new born dies from an infection caused by lack of safe water
and an unclean environment.
1 in 10 don't have clean water close to home and 2 billion people – 1 in 4 –
don't have a safely managed water service at home

www.water-people.com

Published by:
Alan Smith
TQ7 2RY
UK

*This book is dedicated to Rachel, Maxine, and the rest of my family
who often had to play second fiddle whilst I worked long hours trying to get the
water mood music sounding better*

*There were high notes and bum notes but loads of harmony at home
Thank you for all your love, patience, and listening ears*

ALBANY COUNTY JUNIOR SCHOOL STAPLEFORD NOTTINGHAM

SCHOOL REPORT AGE 8 YEARS 1953

...thanks for all your support Mother....
(it did get better...)

GENERAL REPORT		
ATTENDANCE	CONDUCT	GRADING AVERAGE
Regular Frequent short absences Long Absences	Fair.	B A +

Alan is a very youthful 8 years. He is still very much dependent on his fellows and does not take kindly to working on his own. His report is a result of an unsatisfactory term in which Alan has not got down to it.

Victor Maslin

Form Master
Mistress

I am afraid Alan is not moving quickly enough from the Infant Stage. He must exert himself if he is to make the progress necessary to keep up with his fellows

Thompson

Headmaster

Parent's or Guardian's remarks :—

I am of the opinion Alan needs more discipline at school & should be punished in some form for his silly behaviour. As a matter of interest, all his playmates (who are in the same class as Alan) seem to act in the same silly way.

Date 29/7/53   Signed D. Smith.

v

"...is that the Water Board?..."

Introduction

"Alan's writing is very neat, but he is very slow," said the teacher when I was 7 years old. 70 years later nothing has changed. I did speed up in the decades in between but for some reason have now returned to neat and slow.

In the meantime a lot of water has gone under the bridge, and I thought I would capture, neatly and slowly, how water, as well as keeping me alive, has influenced my life. Cold water, hot water, and no water.

This watery tale is the story of a Derbyshire lad, born into post war poverty, raised in a working-class community, who failed his 11 plus, left school at 15, no qualifications, first paid job £200 per year, and went on to work in America, the Caribbean and Europe.

From talking to local primary schools about Willie the Waterman, Sam the Sewageman, and Ronnie the Riverman, to presentations to US Congress on Capitol Hill, Washington DC.

From junior clerk to water company director. Meeting and greeting politicians, royalty, and setting up his own UK and international business, working on many continents and with many nationalities, along the way.

Most importantly working with the many unsung heroes who provide the most precious commodity on earth – safe clean drinking water.

Along the way incidents and anecdotes; serious lessons in the art of simple communications and dispensing one of the rarest attributes known to man, common sense. An increasingly vanishing commodity in a world of would-be smart arses.

"...is that the Water Board?..."

Contents

Yorkshire Water/Kelda Group

Water-people

Facts v fiction

Today and tomorrow

Chapter 1. In the beginning

My instincts are that if you are doing an autobiography the more you talk about early life; the more the reader is tempted to say, 'so what?' – unless of course you already command a compelling public interest borne out of current fame or notoriety. Neither gifted to me. Anyway tempting fate with the reader, here goes with a brief scene setter.

Born in the mining community of Heanor, Derbyshire on 15th May 1945 to Dorothy and Edward Smith. Father worked on the local railway, Mother an office worker. They "had to get married," at the time a common phrase to describe a rapid civil ceremony because of imminent childbirth (me). I must also be one of the few who knew where they were conceived. Bluntly highlighted by my Mother in her late 80's during a visit to a very proper Aunt's home in the village of Awsworth, near Nottingham.

There is no blue plaque, but the corner of the field, used to consummate early passionate feelings, remains; a testament to cupid and natures resilience, fortuitously preserved despite the Common Agricultural Policy. Nine months later we settled into a damp, two-up, two-down, rented terraced house; no bath and crude outside loo. A simple, basic, but happy life, supported by post-war rations, staying for the best part of a decade before graduating to a posh council house. There began my real education that would lead to working in Europe, US, Caribbean, and other parts of the world. I started by failing my 11 plus examination which meant a secondary modern, as opposed to grammar school education. Essentially in with the chaff rather than the wheat elite.

The secondary modern experience proved to be fundamental to the progress I was to make in life. Mixing and understanding kids who had narrowly failed the exam, to kids who had narrowly failed to go to borstal. And everything in between.

Approaching 15 years of school-leaving age, Mother and Father asked what I wanted to do for a living. I hadn't got a clue, no idea. Mother scratched her head.

"You are good at English", she said. Mother was a secretary so ensured my spelling and writing skills kept up.

"How about an office job?"

"Alright," I said, eager to retreat from a boring conversation and go to football practice. A slight digression here but worth mentioning before we continue Mother dialogue.

Football was my passion. I played in the Bramcote Hills Secondary Modern School for Boys first team and ached for Saturday match-day mornings to come around. Aged 14 years of age and a seasoned team veteran, I was approached one Saturday morning by Mr Gregory, sports teacher, and team manager.

"Alan," he said, putting his arm on my shoulder, "if you don't mind I am going to give a trial to one of the second-year boys this morning, so you will be a reserve today. Is that alright?"

I struggled to choke out, "of course," whilst wanting to vomit in my sports bag. Fancy, I thought, a little second year runt wearing my shirt, and playing in my position. The humiliation of it.

That little second year runt was Dave Watson who went on to play 65 times for England, including captain, played for Manchester City, and won an FA Cup winners medal with Sunderland. But crucially he never experienced a career in the water industry. Envy? Jealousy? Of course there was bound to be, but I think Dave has come to terms with it.

Anyway back to the conversation with Mother…how about an office job?….alright I said…

"Coal Board, Stanton Ironworks or Trent River Board?" she persisted, pointing out potential employers in the local newspaper. "Shall I ring them?"

"Alright," I said.

Mother rang all three. "Trent River Board are looking for a Junior Clerk" she said a couple of days later. "They want you to go in for an interview next week. They pay you when you are off sick and the man sounded nice."

"Alright," I said. Note my unrestrained enthusiasm at this point.

One week later, with heavily brylcreamed hair, best school blazer, and second new pair of long trousers, I sat in front of Mr Hooley, a loud speaking authoritative Trent River Board office manager with an RAF moustache which twitched every time he bellowed. After trembling through a series of innocuous questions, basically quizzing my spelling, writing and hobbies, the oak panelled door of his room suddenly burst open. In came a spindly youth with big NHS spectacles pushing an office mail collection trolley. The intrusion surprised both of us.

The youth apologized for the disturbance before looking at me and exclaiming "turd, turd, how are you turd?" I immediately recognized him as George Noon, an older and former pupil from my secondary modern school. He had once pinned me down with other seniors in a school stock room and applied biro ink all over my testicles for being cheeky. "Hello George," I said, trying to retain my composure and manners, whilst keeping my legs together. Mr Hooley exploded.

"Get out George. Do get out," he barked.

Retreating quickly with trolley George yelled a final "he's a good lad Mr Hooley. Turd is a really good lad."

To this day I have no idea whether the George intervention gave a positive impression – unlike those on my testicles. Anyway I got the job and was duly appointed Junior Clerk to the Trent River Board on 25th July 1960 on an annual salary of £210 per year .

And the nickname Turd? Not sure but it was used extensively in my secondary school as an expression of affection. Little did I know then that both real and imaginary turds were to play such a large part in my future career.

TRENT RIVER BOARD

IAN DRUMMOND
SOLICITOR
CLERK OF THE BOARD
TELEPHONE: 42807

IN ANY REPLY PLEASE QUOTE
MY REFERENCE
KH/CB 119.
YOUR REFERENCE

206, DERBY ROAD.
NOTTINGHAM.
18th July, 1960.

Dear Sir,

Appointment of Junior Male Clerk.
Clerk's Department.

With reference to your application for the above appointment and to your recent interview with my Assistant, I am directed to offer this appointment to you. The appointment is subject to the provisions of the Scheme of Conditions of Service for Staff – subject to the terms of Condition No. 5 of the Scheme as set out on the back hereof. The salary for the post is within the General Division and your salary will commence at £210 per annum, payable monthly. The maximum of this Division is at present £465 per annum, but upon production by you of appropriate educational certificates your salary will rise by annual increments – again subject to satisfactory service – to £595 per annum. The appointment will be determinable by one month's notice on either side and will be subject to any conditions or regulations now or hereafter to be made by the Board respecting the appointment. In particular I would call your attention to a Resolution passed by the Board on the 9th May, 1951, details of which are set out on the back hereof.

The post is subject to the Local Government Superannuation Acts, 1937 to 1953 but these will not apply until you reach the age of eighteen years.

Please let me have your Certificate of Birth. This will be returned to you after notation.

I have received a satisfactory Medical Certificate from the Board's Doctor.

I shall be obliged if you will let me know that you are prepared to accept the appointment upon the terms and Conditions set out above and at the same time confirm that you will commence your duties on Monday, 25th July, 1960.

Yours faithfully,

Clerk of the Board.

Mr. Alan Smith,
124, Stanton Road,
Sandiacre,
Notts.

5

Chapter 2. A goggle eyed junior in a River Board start 25th July 1960

[UK Number 1 – Good Timin' - Jimmy Jones]

My very early days of working at the Trent River Board (TRB) were extraordinary, odd, and humorous. I had no real-life work experience whatsoever and so activity, behaviour, issues, and incidents were all new as I witnessed the good, the bad, and the ugly.

Sub consciously I think I tried to remember the good and jettison the bad and ugly. My very first weeks recollection was sitting at a desk in a restricted and rather dark uninspiring back office with two other administrators opposite carrying out general clerical work including filing, mail, and stationery services. The more senior administrator was a small fellow nicknamed Ken-Ten who seemed to pre-occupy himself with duties not necessarily connected with the work we were supposed to be doing.

The minute the office door opened he would scramble for another piece of paper from underneath his blotting pad that may have been more fitting for what we were being paid to do. After a few days I soon became aware of his extra-curricular blotting pad activities. He would quietly sidle up to my desk and produce an artistically excellent pencilled sketch of a very fat nude lady, or ladies, with enormous boobs and bums, and often in compromising positions. He was intrigued to look at and ogle at my shocked and naive reaction, bursting out in a sniggering, creepy way to the youthful surprise on my face.

The other administrator in the office was younger, and obviously liking and liked by the ladies. In those early weeks I also witnessed regular visits by a typist to the office asking for stationery items. Very regular visits. 'KP' would open the tall stationery cupboard door and they, the typist and he, would disappear behind the hidden protection of the open door, supposedly looking for said items; whilst I could not help noticing below the gap at the bottom of the cupboard door, the stiletto heels and brogues closely intertwining. There were long silences with occasional sighs. Obviously taking stock. Of what I will never know.

Idiosyncrasy abounded. For example, as I scurried around doing my post and other menial duties, I would occasionally catch sight of a very tall, gaunt figure, who looked, walked, and talked, like Basil Fawlty. His name was Cecil Quartermain, a solicitor, who had such a long nose, you

6

could hang him by it on a coat rack. The long, marble lined, office corridors would echo at the faintest noise and having espied me, he would bellow down the corridor, " had your bowels open this morning boy?" My regular (pardon the pun) answer was Yes, which seemed to pacify his curiosity. I didn't like to offer the opposite in case he was prone to suppository, as well as legal administration.

There were many more anecdotes in those early days, too many to go into but a few stick out in the memory. In the hustle and bustle of a busy office, and people paper chasing, it was not uncommon for an office door to be sellotaped to the frame whilst closed. Any unwitting paper chaser in a hurry would burst through the door to be greeted by an almighty explosion as door and frame cracked apart.

Another ruse, very popular leading up to Bonfire Night, was small deposits of gunpowder dropped into an ash tray. A junior administrator in the Treasury Department applied this trap on a colleague who he thought smoked in the office far too much. Unfortunately a senior manager entered unexpectedly into the office, and after a few minutes of conversation walked towards "loaded" ash tray to extinguish his cigarette. Despite the best efforts of the junior to offer the senior manager an alternative ash tray, the manager went ahead and stubbed his cigarette in the doctored ash tray. There followed a very large bang, flash, and scorched finger nails. The inaccurate conclusion of the later inquiry was the presence of discarded Sellotape in the ash tray and an internal memo to refrain from such deposits.

Those early days of settling in to working, and my second pair of long trousers, was an overriding impression of many men chasing paper documents, agendas, and minutes. Looking and acting busy, lots of overblown and flurried activity, puffed cheeks, homage to status; "yes chairman – what was the question?," beaurocracy and many meetings, committees, and sub committees.

On the other hand I had come from a working-class family who called real work physical, sweating, muscle sapping. A Dad who for 50 – 60 hours per week satisfied the appetite of a demanding coal boiler on a grimy, monster railway engine. Stoking and shovelling for a living.

Yet, despite the River Board administrative beaurocracy, the hard work at the sharp end of their responsibilities was really impressive. Land drainage, fisheries, and river pollution prevention, all had seen big post war improvements. The environment was beginning to matter.

Flooding mattered because food mattered, and farmers and land owners dominated the strategy and direction of River Board activity. However, looking back, only a fragment of a complicated water environment jigsaw. The significant and much-needed environmental gains also came at a price. As with all post war public authorities there was a beaurocratic and lumbering decision-making process and costly overheads.

Change was afoot and in 1963 River Authorities replaced the River Boards; taking on existing River Board powers, but importantly, adding the key areas of river water quality and water resources planning and policing, which were both urgent and critical national issues.

Recognition that water usage in the home and industry was rising dramatically, but at the same time the appetite for flooding picturesque valleys for large-scale reservoir storage was becoming more difficult to justify. However taking more water from other sources, including likely polluted rivers and depleted underground aquifers, had to be managed, both in terms of quality and quantity, hence the greater powers of the new river authorities.

So where was our hero during this period of change? Well, by now free from the daily diet of boob and bum sketches, I was given more responsibility.

Transferred to the Engineers Department from the committee dominated Clerks Department and running the filing and mail office. Boring, yes, but very different.

Previously the professional animal I had supported as a humble junior, was packed with committee clerks and legal executives. Now I was providing clerical services to engineers. From a culture of 'Yes chairman what was the question' to 'tell the Chairman to f**k off – I'm an engineer"

What career?

Throughout the 1960's and early 70's my principal focus was getting to Friday, playing football on Saturday and Sunday, and joining the local village factory mates on an alcohol dominated trip to either the Nottingham Palais or Derby Locarno.

Late on one of those boozy evenings I was encouraged by mates to swim across the local Erewash Canal in Sandiacre town centre. This followed a challenge from bleary-eyed factory lads bound for the local fish and chip shop.

The nonsensical rationale of the challenge was based on the fact that I worked in the water sector – questionable but whole heartedly endorsed by the rest of the inebriated rabble.

So, after agreeing a five-pound bet with each of the gathered, I disrobed behind a nearby advertising hoarding and, wearing only my birthday suit, dived into the filthy and stagnant canal waters; swimming frantically until climbing out on the other side with algae-topped hair and canal weed dangling from numerous other parts.

Behind a convenient bus-shelter I carefully peered out and signalled my fist pumping triumph to the canal bridge onlookers. However they were already chip shop bound and, worse, they had deposited my clothes on top of the traffic lights by the canal bridge.

My trousers were now glowing red, and then red and amber, before getting the green light. I had no alternative but to venture forth and scale the ever-changing lights to the astonishment of waiting traffic. Yes, Derbyshire folk had seen the streaking craze at Lords, Wembley, and Wimbledon, but not in Sandiacre Market place.

Still I did make £25 on the night and considered the exercise a further career experience of immersing myself in the water industry. What I hadn't planned was so much exposure so early.

The General Office

From the boring and tedious filing and mail room activity, broken only by the occasional buttock clenching realisation that the monthly stamp book reconciliation would not balance, I was eventually "promoted" to the general office. Here I was asked to do something even more boring. Filing suddenly seemed positively sexy. I will keep the explanation simple. Because it was. The boss said it could lead to better things. It certainly could not lead to worse.

100,000 stores items in four geographically placed Midlands stores. Each item with a stores code number. OK so far? All stores code numbers in four huge hand-written stores ledgers. OK? Enter new technology. Get a private company to type out an index card for each individual store code item. We now have about ten drawers full of index cards in numerical order. Now, thanks to a strategic management decision, it was decided the cards should be in alphabetical, rather than numerical order.

Who shall we ask to mind-numbingly shuffle the 100,000 index cards from numerical to alphabetical? And call it promotion? Alan Smith. Thoughts of the canal loomed again – this time with entry only.

Even more so when I would come across confusing cock-up's on index cards from an obviously equally bored outsourced typist. 'Delmag Hammer' typed as 'Delming Buzzer.' Unsurprisingly none in stock.

Meanwhile life in the large all-male general office was unsympathetic. Often cruel, mickey taking from senior clerks. You quickly had to learn to look after yourself. The hard-working facts of life. During this time I was under the management of an uncompromising, elderly, senior character called Mr Burke. Full title Lewis George Bugg-Burke. If Mr Burke didn't like you, your employment time was both short and uncomfortable.

Fortunately he did like me and often used me as his stooge for humour. For example in a packed general office he would come in and ask how I was and then suddenly declare to the gathered, "Do you know that when young Smithy leaves home in the morning to come to work, his mother cries?" Sympathetic and participative audience response …really?...arrr…shame…

"In case he should ever return," was his punch line. Followed by obligatory laughs from the gathered, although they had heard it many times before. If Mr Burke laughed, we all did.

On regular occasions he would request that I go into his office to change carbon paper as part of his daily order signing ritual. He suffered from diabetes and would regularly take insulin to control his blood sugar levels. Unfortunately this resulted in frequent, obnoxious, and foul smelling passing of wind, from him not me, which he was fully aware of but insisted that I stay to enjoy the moment. He saw it as a test of character.

Prima donnas were not tolerated. If jobs had to be done you did them – without question. During this time I was designated temporary deputy chauffeur and on one occasion requisitioned to take Board and committee members to and from the authority's annual inspection.

These were largely unnecessary ceremonial events – and an excuse for an expensive alcohol binge. I was asked to transport a select few members from Nottingham to Owston Ferry – a small North Lincolnshire village close to the mouth of the Trent and the edge of the world, where signs of life were difficult to come by.

Here they boarded the grub and alcohol laden 'MV Trisantona' vessel which would take them on an inspection of the lower reaches of the River Trent before disembarking in Newark. Collecting them later in the day, they were all pie-eyed and away with the fairies.

Very few could walk or talk straight. This was, in large part, a snapshot of the rather idiosyncratic life of a River Authority board member.

Compromised on the crossing

Back to life in the general office. As I previously said no prima donnas and taking your turn on the mid-morning snack run was mandatory. On one of my turns a surreal experience stood out. I was aware that the West Indian community in the Nottingham city district where we worked was growing fast but little did I realise how I might be asked to play a modest part in that growth.

I was walking from the office across the busy A52 road on the snack run when a rotund West Indian lady approached me in the centre of the Zebra crossing. Grabbing my arm she said that she wanted to have a baby. My mind however was still fully occupied with ham sandwiches, crisps, Mars Bars, a packet of KP nuts, Fanta, and the need to avoid being mown down by fast moving traffic either side of us.

Certainly sperm donorship was not something I had previously considered or could contemplate for the first time on the busy A52. Above the noise of the traffic she repeated, "I want to have a baby NOW." And then, glancing down at the desperate lady, I could see that her wish was about to be granted. She was heavily pregnant and was going to have a baby NOW. Holding her hand, and with a babble of nervous reassurance, I quickly reversed direction back to the office and into the main reception.

"Rita, she is going to have a baby NOW," I blurted to the receptionist. The ambulance duly arrived from the nearby hospital, and she gave birth later that day. Later the general office lads moaned about the late snack delivery and found my alternative delivery story hard to believe.

Meanwhile I continued to impress my general office boss whilst finally beginning to wake up to something called a career. From the successful tedium of card shuffling to the fulfilment of a promise. Promotion to Senior Administration Assistant and managing all purchasing for the four river authority area stores in Nottingham,

Tamworth, Gainsborough, and Keadby. A hectic role related to procurement of essential materials for the capital river engineering and operational management schemes across the East and West Midlands.

Here I learned to think, as well as do, which was a step up in terms of responsibility. However the elevation was to be jolted by an annual personal review conversation carried out by the Deputy Engineer, Mr John Cyril Rowley Cook. Strange that most river authority luminaries had posh long names – William Stratford Dugdale, Cecil Quartermain, Lewis George Bugg-Burke, Ian Ruxton Drummond, John Cyril Rowley Cook….A Smith?...I digress…

He asked about my academic intentions going forward and said I would not progress if I didn't buckle down and study for appropriate Local Government qualifications. Failure to do so would mean I could not earn any more than £500 per year he said. Little did he know in later life I would go on to earn more than that in a day. I came out of the room despondent but motivated to prove him wrong – and determined not to study for what I thought were meaningless and irrelevant qualifications.

Belton House Grantham
The posh name curiosity continued that same week. We had decided to change our car. In the Nottingham Evening Post I came across an advertisement for a Mini 1000, 800 miles only, and rang the local number.

"Portrasus," came the reply in a baronial tone.

"Hello?" I said,

"Portrasus," came the irritated repeat.

12

"You are advertising a Mini 1000 in tonight's Post," I continued "That's correct, it is Mi' lady's," was the rather upper lip retort.

"Could I come and see it? " I said, opting to side-step the MI' lady' reference.

"Certainly – do you know the whereabouts of Belton House?"

Portrasus gave me the directions and we journeyed to the ancestral home of Lord and Lady Brownlow from our two-bed flat in Nottingham. Down the vast drive whilst gazing in awe at the "Brideshead Revisited" style stately mansion.

On arrival at the servants entrance, Portrasus, ushered us to the stable block, explained that Mi' lady thought the car too small, whereupon we agreed the price and completed the purchase. Vehicle ownership changing from Mi' lady's car to Mi 'duck's car. The thick, green log book then read:

1st Owner: Lord Brownlow Belton House, High Road, Belton
2nd Owner: A Smith Flat 3 Lenton Ave The Park Nottingham

Chapter 3. Change in the air

It was now the early 1970's and the country's economy was booming. The post war austerity years were behind us, and the country was enjoying significant growth and prosperity. House building was at record levels and industry was rapidly expanding. All of which was giving the water industry a big headache. Habits on water use were changing – and in a big way.

With housing development came huge leaps in domestic water use; washing machines, dish washers, garden ownership; not to mention the massive thirst of industrial manufacturing. More clean water demand meant more dirty water and sewage treatment. Treating sewage was always a Town Hall after-thought and it was always said that there were no votes in shit.

Post war there were over 1000 local authorities treating and distributing drinking water supplies in England and Wales. As the demand grew local authorities reduced this number by creating local Water Boards in some parts of the country, sharing funding, and managing resources to wider geographic areas.

By 1970 providing water was carried out by around 200 largely local authority-controlled water undertakings. Demand however was continuing to outpace the ability to provide in spite of these changes. Furthermore, experts predicted that public water supply demand would double by 2000.

The equally critical activity of taking water away after use and treating it, sewage treatment, was suffering real neglect. Sewage treatment was much more parochial than water supply with over 1400 local authorities deemed to be "sewerage undertakers." Many were unable or unwilling to urgently invest in upgrading sewage treatment works and the sewer network.

This neglect had a significant and detrimental effect on river discharges, leading to poor river water quality and as a consequence increasing the difficulty of treating raw water abstracted from rivers for drinking water, as well as damage to fisheries and the natural environment. A cruel irony was that many of the local authorities causing pollution were the same authorities facing increased drinking water treatment difficulties further downstream.

It became obvious that the fragmentation of different organizations dealing with different aspects of the water cycle; water resources, water treatment and distribution, sewers and sewage treatment, river water quality, pollution, and flood control, could not go on.

These fragmented organisations had served the earlier 20th century purpose well, but with massive society and environmental changes afoot, and a nation rapidly expanding, they were no longer fit for purpose. Something big had to happen. And it did. Very big. A regulatory and legislative reorganization so profound it would lead the world in integrated water catchment management.

The Water Act 1973 decreed that the duties currently carried out In England and Wales by over 1600 public sector bodies, should be reduced to ten Regional Water Authorities.

The ten Water Authorities

These duties would include water, sewerage, and environmental responsibilities. The water cycle. The new regional water authorities boundaries would be based on major river basins or catchments.

The 1973 Act did not have a significant impact on the 29 existing relatively small privately owned statutory water only companies who provided around 20% of drinking water needs in England and Wales e.g. Bristol, South Staffs. Mid Kent, Cambridge, York, Essex/Suffolk, and others. Many were formed well over a century ago and were already subject to Government controls including dividend and interest restrictions.

So what did this monumental reorganization mean for A Smith, the humble River Authority purchasing clerk based in Nottingham? It was a significant career changer. From slowly plodding along in a River Authority for over 10 years, and more interested in football than the future, things began to happen. Initially not to my liking.

I received a letter (as thousands of others did across the country) confirming my future in the newly constituted Severn Trent Water Authority. Job title: Purchasing Clerk in the Nottingham Divisional HQ on less money than I was currently receiving. What a blow. I had just turned down a job offer at Anglian Water on more money, but the charm and allure of Peterborough did not appeal. Now to find I was going backwards.

And then, as life often does, I got a break that would send my career path into overdrive. I was fortunate to meet a man that I went on to greatly admire and respect, and someone who saw life and decision making in much the same way. Not long after receiving the disappointing news of the new assignment, a rather small, inconsequential looking man wandered into our general office. A latter-day Ralph Richardson lookalike. Nothing unusual in strangers suddenly appearing. Reorganisation had served up people changes, building use changes, people moving in and out, rooms being sized up for new occupants. Generally all hell let loose for the impending industry shakeup.

The man glanced around. He asked if Alan Smith was around. He said he would like a private conversation. We moved to another room. He said he was Cyril Moore, former Deputy Engineer to the Nottingham Water Department, and he was going to head a design team of 80 plus civil engineers who would be engaged in the delivery of much needed capital improvement schemes to drinking water, sewage treatment and river infrastructure across Nottinghamshire.

He said he had little time to "f**k about" but needed a senior administrator to manage an admin team providing support and building maintenance management for a large new team of project engineers who were to be based in the former river authority building we were standing in. He had heard about me and thought I could do a job for him. Was I interested? Yes – was the reply. This was a man I thought I could do business with. It would keep me away from the Divisional HQ beaurocracy a few miles away and importantly it was more money.

We went on to establish a great working relationship. Cyril would let me get on managing the admin activities, supporting any common-sense suggestions, and often telling me that if Divisional HQ interfered, I should tell them where to go. Although not quite in those words. Meat and drink to my ears and we progressed for two years forging into an effective and well-respected support team for the busy technical group.

Not that working with engineers was easy – most will tell you that, generally, they don't like administrators, thinking they get in the way. Building things not paper shuffling things. At times they can be arrogant, bloody minded, high handed and obtrusive, but I enjoyed the thrill of the chase when quick-thinking rapport was a must and thick skin a blessing.

The traits of secondary modern man. I always thought that the engineering bark was bigger than the bite and went on to have the greatest respect for the animal and his/her technical commitment and achievements. However to this day I still believe PR for the engineering profession has been crap. Ask an accountant.

Chapter 4. Out of the trenches to Mansfield

Two years flew by. Doing most things right kept Divisional HQ at bay and allowed us to introduce procedures which suited us if not always corporate beaurocracy. Little did I know but Cyril was talking positively at HQ about me and in the early part of 1976 I was summoned to talk to the Divisional Finance/Admin Manager for an informal chat. He asked me if I had seen a post advertised on the notice board for a Senior Admin Manager for the Mansfield Operational and Billing Office – the former Central Nottinghamshire Water Board.

"No," I said

"I want you to apply," he said, "You've done good work for Cyril but this will be stepping out of a relatively orderly engineering professional culture into the cut and thrust of a sharp end, and busy, day-to-day operations centre. It will be like coming out of the trenches. You will be responsible for a 20 strong team paying out a work force of about 200 manual employees including water distribution repair and maintenance gangs and also operatives from the many sewage treatment works in the area." Seeing my obvious surprise he said think about it and added, "of course there is no guarantee you will get the job."

So I did think about it. I would miss Cyril and the awkward engineers. Also what did I know about "manual workers' wages and conditions" and "bonus incentive schemes" and large-scale billing operations. Add to that a sprawling operational centre of modern offices, stores, workshops, garages, and depot.

A week of brown trousers, rubber underpants, and bike clips went by. I applied and got the job. Mansfield, although only 14 miles away from Nottingham, is a world away in terms of history, personality, culture, and towns people. A gritty, honest attitude to life, harder edge and more outspoken compared to Nottingham. Coal mining dominated the economy and employment for much of the 20th century with pits scattered across the area. Mine workings that caused significant subsidence and regular burst water mains and fractured pipes.

So here I was – the lad from poncy Nottingham, being introduced to the team I would manage. I knew what they were thinking. What does he know about wages and bonus, disputes, dealing with unions? All good points. The answer was nothing. But on my first day I met one of the nicest guys I was to work with in my career. He was to be my assistant,

Joe Jarman. He had been in the Mansfield office for donkeys years and was well liked and respected by the local team, and I strongly suspected they would have wanted him to get the job. There was very little that Joe didn't know about wages and bonus pay and conditions and that was to my good fortune, particularly during the early months of settling in. Joe was in his 50's and I in my 30's but in every way 100% supportive and we went on to make a great team. So where to start? It was a high-profile job and I needed to win confidence early. Part of the routine of a typical week was the arrival of a Securicor vehicle, armed with the delivery of cash wage packets and simultaneously, the gathering of gangs of distribution operatives to sign for and collect their wages.

Union influence in the Depot was strong across most activities and wage discrepancies were often taken up by the union steward who was himself part of the distribution workforce. Joe let me know that the "payout" took place in the depot canteen and that he joined the Securicor guards to ensure correct individual pay-packet signing and handover. This had been the tradition and my senior position attendance was not necessary.

I disagreed and from week one I attended with the specific aim of getting to know all of the operatives by their first names and to be on hand if any had wage pay queries. My rationale was that if I could get individual trust, then the operative would ask me to sort out any problems, rather than the union. In turn this would de-escalate a potential union led grievance and profile. It worked and over the months I struck up a healthy relationship with most operatives. I know in their eyes I was still seen as "management", but I hoped with a growing trust and approachable demeanour.

I had another break not long afterwards. A local water main burst very close to my Lambley, Nottingham home. On a cold winters evening our domestic water supply was suddenly shut off. Soon afterwards we were informed that a local burst main was being repaired and the water would be back on by morning. In the distance I could see the arc lights of the gang repairing the burst.

Around midnight I drove into Nottingham and got fish and chips for the gang and drove back to the scene of the burst. To my surprise it was a Mansfield water distribution gang, and not from the nearer Nottingham Depot. I knew them all from the weekly pay-out exercise, and they knew me, but were unaware that I lived nearby. Not a lot was said but I could tell they appreciated the gesture, and I knew that talk of my appearance would circulate at the Depot. I knew I was seen as an outsider, but depot pay-outs, fish suppers, and lady luck helped.

More bizarre was that most of the close working colleagues I had previously worked in the ex-River Authority general office were now looking at me as if I had crossed the line of being one of the lads to supporting and adopting management habits. Remember your station and all that. Absolute rubbish of course and disappointing but prevalent in some who decided five o'clock and retiring at fifty was their adrenalin rush. It didn't affect me one iota, other than increasing motivation.

Meanwhile life at Mansfield was never dull. The HQ boss was dead right about coming out of the trenches. Working with all character facets, from highly educated and academic brethren who had only seen the inside of an air-conditioned office, to the guys who worked in all weathers to keep water supplies flowing, it was a compelling and frenetic atmosphere.

Not for the first time, and probably not the last, I really appreciated failing my 11 plus. Priceless. The secondary modern basic education had given me a fantastic insight into almost every conceivable character I was coming across; and how to communicate, adjust, and manage very different and often difficult working relationships in a claustrophobic environment.

'Russell'

One of the characters at Mansfield was Russell, a cheerful distribution operative, who signed for his weekly pay packet with a kiss, whilst smiling broadly and revealing two remaining brown molars. His vocabulary was limited and his language colourful. He was however one of the best performing operatives on the Mansfield operational gangs and often sent out to difficult water main repair jobs. Getting it fixed was his focus, the man for the moment, but not necessarily customer service pleasantries.

On one such occasion he was sent out as part of a repair gang to fix yet another subsidence-caused burst water main on a local industrial estate. The routine of repair was tried and tested. Locate point of burst; shut off mains so that a repair can begin; simultaneously inform local businesses by tannoy loud-speaker van that the water supply would be shut off; fix and complete repair. Turn supply back on. Russell and mate were at shoulder height in the mudded repair trench, digging aggressively through the tarmac, loose earth and gravel to locate the cracked water main below.

Russell became aware of a pristine apparition figure dressed in pure white garb; white plimsolls, tunic, trousers, and hat, gazing down on them. "You've cut my bakery off," exclaimed the indignant apparition. "F**k off – we don't buy your bread anyway," advised Russell. The burst was duly repaired but it took a little while longer to repair our reputation with the bakery.

Meanwhile my job was going well. Local relationships were good, and we had a great team. There were hiccups occasionally. On one particular occasion I was awaiting a visit from a Senior Manager from Divisional HQ who was over an hour late and I had a solicitors appointment in Nottingham. I left and asked Joe to give my apologies if he turned up. He did and I was summoned the next day to Divisional HQ for what I knew would be a rollocking.

It was carried out by a friendly soul called Leo Titman, the Divisional Administration Manager who was very close to retiring. After platitudes of how well I was doing he addressed the issue and was disappointed I showed no remorse. He then came out with a piece of advice.

"Alan, despite doing well, you have to learn to swim with the tide, and not against it," a phrase I have not forgotten and used as a career motivator to do exactly the opposite as and when I judged the need. As I closed the door, I felt sorry for him. I could tell he had been pressured to discipline me against his better judgement. So, knowing that it would get back to the retiring Leo, I made a beeline for the aggrieved managers office and apologized. However I did it with the sincerity of Russell's bread procurement declaration.

In a career, as in life, some episodes you win and some you lose. Either way you learn. Midway through my four-year stint at Mansfield, one of the wages team professionals came to me and asked whether I was aware that the six office cleaners were leaving at around 7 00 pm each night but were completing approved timesheets that said they were working until 7 30 pm. Apparently, this had been going on for some time. Not a huge issue but a sensitive one and needed to be handled carefully, particularly as one of the cleaners was the depot union stewards wife. Equally when a respected employee dealing with many pay and timesheet issues, raises a legitimate area of concern and irregularity, it obviously had to be followed up.

I decided to see for myself. Sure enough I witnessed the same practice. The cleaners had departed approximately 30 minutes early and the timesheets showed the approved, but incorrect, departure time later that week. With that I talked to the supervisor and the cleaners and said this was not to continue and that, for the actual night I had witnessed, I would retrospectively deduct 15 minutes from their wages.

Needless to say a very big storm in a very small cup erupted. Next day the union steward marched into my office and demanded that the 15 minutes be reinstated otherwise it would be reported to "higher authority." I refused and explained why. The practice had been going on for some time and was a false claim, albeit aided and abetted by the supervisor. The 15 minutes deduction was an in-principle action. The reality of previous time incorrectly claimed was much greater, but I had decided to overlook in view of the supervisors' approval signature.

The upshot was that it was discussed at a later Joint Consultative Committee meeting at Divisional HQ and I was instructed to reimburse the 15 minutes. To say the least I was disappointed that senior management had not supported me. Hung out to dry comes to mind. Ironically the experience did bring me closer to my Mansfield team.

They strongly disagreed with the outcome and respected my standpoint. Lesson? Never trust a back-scratching Consultative Committee. A few months later came another show of union strength and, thanks to my brother many miles away, good sense prevailed.

Hot reception

It was the late 1970's and Union frustration; the so-called winter of discontent and a weak Labour Government, showed its local impact with an organized Union-led demonstration in the main Mansfield office and reception. I was told by the Union that sixty or so operatives from the local water distribution gangs were to gather in the Depot at the end of their day shift and march to the main office building and monopolise the main reception area.

A peaceful but potentially embarrassing gathering in a busy location often used for bill paying by the general public. There was little I could do to stop it or plan to control it. Any seemingly provocative act would have inflamed the situation, leading to potential local media attention and further confrontation. A Union godsend. So it was suck it and see.

Divisional HQ was aware but offered little (again).

The appointed hour arrived with operatives filing in, full of chatter and relatively good humour, with mud-clad trench boots and protective clothing adding to the general chaos of the scene. Rent-a-crowd was now well packed in, a clamour of anticipation and awaiting a reaction. The union steward asked the receptionist to contact me. I knew the game. He wanted to address the guys whilst I was there, and for me to see the impressive turn-out and surreal untidy reception occupation, more than to say anything significant.

I was in my office on the 1st floor when the call came. I slowly descended the open plan, two-tier stair case and caught sight of the gossiping throng, through the carcinogenic cloud of roll-your-own tobacco smoke. I talked earlier about luck and sometimes it happens and sometimes it doesn't. Today was my day.

As I got to the bottom stairs and the waiting union steward, the receptionist shouted through the hubbub that my brother was on the phone. "Shall I say that you will ring him back?" she said through the noisy din.

"No," I said, "I will talk to him. Acknowledging the steward whilst brushing passed him, I asked him to hang on. "I'll take this call and come back to you."

My brother began by remarking about the noisy background but going on to say that it was just a quick call to confirm what time we were meeting later that night. I responded by asking a series of questions, how was he? was the new job going well? how were his children? had he seen Mother lately? did he go to the match last week? what do you think of Forest's latest signing?

"Are you OK?" he interrupted.

"Keep talking – will explain later," I said.

As our anal conversation continued from five to ten to fifteen minutes, although I had got my back to the mob, I could see from the reflection on the reception security glass that in one's and two's, the operatives were slowly drifting out, bored from the anti-climax, and more importantly ready for something to feed the inner man after a hard day's graft. Within 20 minutes the mud strewn reception was empty. My secondary modern calculation was right. These guys get bored just as quickly as they get excited. Thanks brother and lady luck. Your timing was impeccable.

About Jack Twort – the heartbeat of the industry

Jack was an ex-military sergeant. Over 6' 4" tall and an imposing

figure. A hard man who was responsible for all operational activities of the water distribution repair and maintenance gangs at Mansfield. An ex Central Notts Water Board veteran who managed with carrot and big stick. Well respected by his staff and workforce. Could be warm and generous but equally like granite when it came to

keeping order with senior and junior employees. Jack must have been in his late 50's when I entered the scene at Mansfield and he was intrigued to get to know me and tell me how it was and, subtlety, where I should keep my nose out of his domain. He was a stickler for demarcation lines of responsibility – all no doubt from his military days.

He called me into his office on my first day. I knew he was sussing me out and I guess I was returning the compliment. His reputation was larger than life and he knew it. Loved by the girls in the admin wages office and always, with a glint in his eye, massively helpful in solving operatives worksheet queries and other wage-related issues.

Such a strong personality, we were bound to argue and argue we did. Always the job won however, and he was also fair and magnanimous. If he wanted to tear a strip off anybody it was best if you were not present. It was very ugly. By watching and observing him he showed me how you manage operatives; a minority of whom could be reckless, opportunistic, and untrustworthy. In many respects like a boardroom.

Jack was a man of stature and uncanny character. There was one day in particular I remember very well. We had chewed the fat over an area of disagreement and when the emotion had subsided, he said, " you know you are going to progress from here at some point don't you – come off it, you know you are?" I was taken aback. I had never, either been far-sighted enough, or ambitious enough, to have given his suggestion any thought. My main aim had been to keep my head above water and not to fail in this job.

Jack's pronouncement was a shock. I was now almost four years into the job at Mansfield and loving every minute of the cut and thrust of the sharp end. Little did I realise that Jack's prediction would soon come true, and my Mansfield adventure was about to come to an abrupt end.

24

Chapter 5. On the move again – a new boss and changes

It was now 1980. The massive national water industry re-structuring of 1974 was settling well and generally the multi-functional water authorities were seen to have made progress. Moving from 1500 disparate bodies to ten had created significant disruption but made a positive impact.

However there was still a critical lack of funding and under investment with Government priorities in health, education, defence, transport, way ahead of the relatively low political profile of water supply and sewage treatment.

Ironically at around the same time as the 1974 water restructuring had happened, the UK had joined the European Community (EC) and that ironic coincidence was to play out positively in lifting the priority status of the water industry with the UK Government. More about this later. Meanwhile, in the early part of 1980, I was busy in the Mansfield Office when my phone rang. A secretary of the newly appointed Divisional Finance and Administration Manager, Brian Duckworth, said that her new boss wanted to talk to me.

The next day he arrived at the Mansfield office. I shook his hand and almost before sitting down, he asked me what I was doing at the Mansfield office. I told him that, with the support of an admin team of around twenty I was providing wages/bonus calculations/payments to approximately 200 personnel, also typing services, billing reception collection payments, building maintenance etc.

He asked the question again. I was puzzled as to what he didn't understand about my answer. I repeated it. By now I was beginning to wonder whether he or I were not familiar with the same language. Seeing my obvious discomfort he added a further phrase to the original question. "What are you doing at the Mansfield office because I want you at Divisional HQ?"

I finally twigged that, in some laconic way, which had escaped the comprehension of a secondary moderner, he was inferring that he believed my presence was more important at Divisional HQ in Nottingham. Confusion over, he explained he wanted me to start the following week at the Nottingham office on a six-month secondment to manage the admin teams in Nottingham, Mansfield, Gainsborough, and Keadby.

A daunting task with over 100 employees carrying out similar admin services to those we were doing at Mansfield. My immediate boss was going to regional Severn Trent HQ in Birmingham for a six-month stint, and I would carry out his management position at Divisional HQ during his absence. A week later, a hasty goodbye to the Mansfield team and a promise of a Schwarzenegger "I'll be back," I was off on another very different challenge. I was never to go back.

A Mansfield epilogue.

Mansfield was unique. As I have said before its people, culture, behaviour, history, is completely different from its noisy neighbours in Nottingham just down the road. They work harder. Mansfield operatives regularly out-performed similar distribution gangs in Nottingham, drink harder, play harder and the sense of community is stronger.

My time there was fantastic and taught me so much. Most importantly I learned at first-hand how unbelievably hard the lads at the sharp end work, often in the most difficult and hazardous weather conditions and unsocial hours. All to make sure that we get that cuppa in the morning. We have a lot to thank the Russell's of this world.

The six months of secondment at Divisional HQ in Nottingham flew. All about managing budgets, more senior people, making sure that area support teams functioned, addressing issues, communicating new ways of working as a result of operational changes etc. Time to go back to Mansfield. One week before the return date, the mercurial Brian Duckworth called me in to his office.

"Are you looking forward to going back to Mansfield," he asked? Now there was a question.

"No," I said,

"Well, I have another six months project for you", he said casually. But the next words made me want to don brown trousers, rubber underpants, and the obligatory bike clips again

" We are going to introduce and install, for the first time in the UK, a digital switching system linking voice and data across all of the five area offices you have been dealing with," he said.

I tried unsuccessfully to look intelligent, and to respond equally casually with an "oh really" – as if I completely understood the technology. The "oh really" came out more like a yodel.

"Yes," he went on, "Plessey will be the providers and you will also have to work closely with the GPO (General Post Office) and of course

26

internal departments, both before and during installation. Go and see David Orton. He has the project budget, and you will be working for him," he concluded. I exited the brief meeting. Project Manager for a UK first-time digital voice and data switch? This really was way out of my league and cerebral understanding.

I needed help. And I got it. David Orton was charismatic, humorous, professional, and to the point. An accountant who did not suffer fools lightly. In the "digital" briefing he shed more helpful light on my ignorant understanding and forthcoming challenge. At its most basic, the finished project would mean one master digital telephone switchboard at the Nottingham office (replacing 5 area office switchboards), capable of handling all internal and external calls across all area offices.

Additionally, with the rapid advent of digital data technology, it meant that data could be crunched across the same digital lines. But who decides what local, national, and international calling status each telephone should have? After all there were nearly 500 extensions. "You do," said David. "Oh really," I said, reverting to the utterly false casual gait of a day earlier.

"But before that, next week you are going on a five-day course to Plessey who will educate you in the practicalities and issues of a first time state-of-the-art digital switch installation. You will also shortly be meeting the Project Manager of Plessey and the Project Manager of the GPO who you will be working very closely with over the next 6 months."

"I should warn you" he went on "the relationship between these two organizations is not good". *[Until the early 1980's the GPO was a monopoly supplier of switchboards, telephones, and the like]* "Plessey are the new interloping kids on the block. So integrating and marrying the Plessey kit and GPO landlines will be critical to the success of the project. You will be piggy in the middle and making sure they do!" he said with a wry if not meaningful grin.

Well, that's OK then I thought. A client Project Manager thrust into a digital world with zilch product knowledge and managing warring factions whose cooperation was critical to the project success. Managing Russell suddenly seemed a lot easier.

So the next week, bright eyed and bushy tailed, I arrived for my one-week indoctrination at Plessey, Nottingham. I looked at 'Les the lecturer,' stood before us during the introductions. Little did he know that I was about to bleed him dry of every last drop of technical knowledge in him, becoming the class pain in the arse that he would talk about during fag break to similarly wired colleagues.

Up until this time in my modest career, I thought courses were lukewarm affairs, with smatterings of boring lectures and syndicates, along with the obligatory after-hours alcohol, but generally not memorable. This was altogether a different ball game. Not to over exaggerate, but the success of this week could make or probably break the next 6 months of my digital adventure and project delivery, and even my career. Bleed Les dry I had to.

I was always first there and last out of the classroom. In the early evening peppering Les with a myriad of queries and questions about issues I had not understood during the day. I said earlier that sometimes you are lucky in life. In Les I had found a great professional with unbounded knowledge and patience. So enthusiastic about his specialist subject that he was always prepared to further explain.

The course made me confident and the project successful. I went back to work knowing more than David and Brian about the essential detail needed for a successful project delivery. Over the coming 6 months I was also blessed with working with two consummate project managers from Plessey and the GPO.

Both rose above the angry politics and back biting of national telecoms reorganization and were equally responsible for the projects ultimate successful implementation. And as for those 500 new extensions? I was told six months after the system went "live" that none had to be changed from the original designation from yours truly. Trumpet blowing?

No. Just experience of knowing what water industry professional actually did what, at every level, and what he or she needed to carry it out. So obvious but how many employees these days know what Harry and Freda do down the corridor or in their own company's neighbouring departments and offices?

Installation complete, I was scheduled, yet again, to return to Mansfield. Uncannily two weeks before Auld Lang Syne another potential opportunity cropped up – this time permanent and, again very different.

Chapter 6. Water Consumer Relations Advisor – a new animal – and a changed organization.

Leading up to the 1974 reorganisation and the creation of the 'big ten' companies, it was generally acknowledged that after decades of local authority stewardship of water and wastewater responsibilities, capital spending had been nowhere near enough to keep pace with current and future demand. Critical additional investment was needed in many infrastructure areas, replacing and upscaling of rusting and inadequate Victorian water mains, crumbling under-sized sewers, poorly performing treatment works, and more. Yet, in the ten-year period through to the early 1980's, capital spend actually dropped further.

A new, more efficient engine, but lack of fuel to drive it. The Government was battling inflation and would not allow the water authorities, either to borrow more, or raise consumer bills to tackle the infrastructure deterioration and historic under investment.
In 1982 total capital investment by the water authorities was less than half that of 1974. Something had to give, and it did.

The Water Act 1983 was introduced. It changed the way water authorities were run. Even though 1974 had wrested much of the operation and management of water and wastewater away from local authorities, the large water authority boards were still dominated by local authority representatives and councillors. The new Act did away with local authority Board representation and the overblown committee structures and talking shops, and replaced them with new, slimmer and commercially minded Boards.

Also for the first time, the Act allowed the authorities to borrow from the capital markets rather than solely from Government. Two significant caveats to the changes. The long arm of Government continued to control and appointment Board members. Government also continued to exercise control over total water authority borrowing, which ironically suppressed access to much-needed alternative private borrowing. So still the issue of critical under-funding to renovate and expand treatment works, water mains and sewers, remained.

OK, so where did that leave our modest digital hero? Yes, you've guessed it. A call to go and see Brian Duckworth. Entering his office and before Brian spoke, I commented, "No, before you ask, I am not looking forward to going back to Mansfield."

"Well in that case you should look at the new job on the notice board," he said, " It's come from HQ Birmingham. The successful candidate will be based here but report to Birmingham." Later I took a look. The vacancy read, ***Water Consumer Relations Advisor.***

As a counter to the shake-up of the water authorities new Board structures, and the perceived lack of local representation, the Government had legislated that new local water consumer consultative committees would be established, based on divisional (almost county) boundaries. In our case Nottinghamshire.

As well as being responsible for setting up the committee and providing the secretariat services, which looked dry and uninspiring, the Consumer Relations Advisor (CRA) would also be responsible for talks and presentations to local groups and managing local press and media relations. The latter looked really interesting. Enough to live with committee administration.

I threw my cap into the ring. After all "new " for me was becoming par for the course, I thought pompously. However I didn't know many of the hierarchy at Birmingham HQ so reputation, good or bad, would not hinder or help. One week later I got a call from HQ to say that I had not been successful. A blow which brought me back down to earth.

Mansfield and Russell beckoned. A day later Brian stopped me in the corridor and asked if I had heard anything.

"Didn't get an interview," I said in a monotone.

"That's a pity," he said.

Two hours later, whilst packing my things in the office I had used for 12 months, the phone rang. HR from Birmingham HQ.

" We've had a potential interviewee drop out and would like to know if you are still interested? If so could you attend an interview in Birmingham next week? he said.

" I would be delighted," I said. Later that day I bumped into Brian again. "I was going to come and see you tomorrow, Brian," I said. "A Human Remains Advisor from HQ has been on this afternoon, and they now want me to attend an interview for the CRA role next week.

"Good," he said, climbing into his car.

It was never confirmed if someone had dropped out or someone had made an intervention. But I knew.

Being a Consumer Relations Advisor (CRA)

My interview at Birmingham HQ went OK. Nothing sensational but no clangers. I was offered the Nottingham role and accepted. The following months were tedious and mind-numbingly boring although the status felt good. Managing the administration behind setting up a water consumer consultative committee was busy but underwhelming. But with membership nominations coming from local authorities, agriculture, commerce, industry, and household representatives, a chance to meet a new set of characters and contacts. HQ Birmingham kept a tight control on the committee's scope and influence.

Agendas were largely set by HQ and minutes approved by HQ. Did they achieve anything? No. A shop window to democracy? Yes. Did anybody buy anything? No. I always sensed that members knew this, and no one particularly ruffled feathers or caused problems. Membership, after all, looked good on the CV.

Much more interesting was the other half of my job description, talks, exhibitions, and press and media relations. Little did I know it, but the latter was to fashion and profile the rest my career. I tolerated the work of the Committee but with only around four meetings a year, there was plenty of time to pursue and develop local customer and media communications. Many talks to myriads of different groups, from tots to tottering and in-between. A travelling and unwitting 'Mori-like' researcher, learning and understanding different groups perceptions of what we did and what they wanted us to do. All whilst honing and shaping public speaking experience and learning the art of building and managing press and media relationships.

Severn Trent Birmingham HQ, who were now my paymaster, initially decided at the outset that the new clutch of eight CRA's were to be sent on intensive speech and media training courses in the Lake District, followed quickly by real time exposure in the local patch, in my case Nottinghamshire. We were now up and running and responsible. All sharp as a tack and looking forward to what the media and his wife could throw at us. And throw they did. A curved ball that I did not see coming.

A baptism of fire.

I took my first media call from a reporter at Central Television in Nottingham. At the time we had a hosepipe ban in the East Midlands and he was looking for a Severn Trent spokesman to be interviewed on a ban infringement story at Kimberly, near Nottingham. The essence of the story was that a young married man had been ticked off and warned by a patrolling Severn Trent Water Inspector for using a hosepipe to water his thirsty garden plants. Fair enough.

However the young man had explained to the Inspector that he was actually conveying used bath water in the hosepipe which he was siphoning from his upstairs bathroom down to his thirsty plants below. The jobsworth Inspector had pointed out that "the Water Act 1945 does not allow either fresh or used water to be conveyed by means of a hosepipe" but that on this occasion he would let him off with a warning.

I checked and confirmed with Operations that the story was accurate from our perspective. As a sanity check I rang HQ and they advised that we "put someone up" for TV interview. If not the Divisional Manager, then I should do it. I went to see John Brown, Divisional Manager, a lovely man who had great faith in me (he said), and quickly suggested that I should do it. "Good experience Alan, good experience" he said, with a wry smile. I got the distinct impression that my volunteering was not stepping forward but others stepping back. Exposed but naively enthusiastic.

As I drove to meet the TV film crew in the young man's back garden in Kimberley I knew I was in a no-win situation. Technically, and in law, the Inspector was correct, but the court of public opinion would say this lad was an environmental hero for re-cycling used bath water. As I pulled into his drive and the scene of the crime, I had decided that I would have to explain, with a friendly face, that, technically, the Inspectors stance was the law, but we applauded the young man for the public-spirited way in which he was trying to save water, and it would go no further. There were enough media trucks around to suggest the scene of a recent assassination. Rubber underpants territory.

I met the young man in his back garden. He seemed bewildered by it all, cameras, boom operators, reporters. He smiled and apologized for all the fuss, but the story had seemed to be interesting to the press and he had agreed to cooperate, he told me nervously. A minute later, when the cameras were rolling and questions being asked, he grew metaphoric horns and growled his indignation. Aided and abetted of course by the reporter. Such is fame. A little un-nerved I then took my place in the two-minute spotlight and faced the reporter's questions. Later as I drove back to base, I thought I had achieved the right balance between the law and applause for the young man's environmental approach and well-meaning actions. I watched the coverage later that night. As expected it was awful. Goliath rapping the knuckles of a well-meaning David.

One winner. What made it worse was that they had edited out my empathetic interview ending bit and just showed me stating that technically it was a breach of the law. I came across as an understanding Hitler before the Poland invasion. The following day all hell broke loose. A local news agency had fanned the story far and wide. Local, regional, national. The editorial comment in the 'Daily Star' national tabloid, ran with the headline 'Drip of the Drought'. That was me. It ended...*as far as Mr Smith was concerned the technical breach might have been etched in tablets of stone and so we nominate Mr Smith the Drip of the Drought."*

During the next 24 hours the coverage was high, wide, and handsome. I had made a mark. The next challenge was to make the right one. My Mother did say I spoke up clearly. A lesson learned. Looking back, and with a lot more experience, we should not have put anyone up and instead given a statement. Acquiescing to the thrill of the media chase only prolongs the story.

In the meantime I was kept busy with many talks to schools, WI's, Rotarians, Guilds, Pensioners, and many more, including the Ashby De La Zouch Parakeets Society. I think it was about bills. Schools were a delight – particularly at primary age. Talking them through the water cycle with tales of Willie the Waterman, Sam the Sewageman, and Ronnie the Riverman; followed by a rousing all-together chorus of a 1950's Max Bygrave's hit:

> *If you didn't have rain, then you couldn't have flowers*
> *You couldn't have flowers if you didn't have showers*
> *Nowhere to swim, there'd be no babbling brook There'd*
> *be no fish to catch on the end of a hook*

> *You'd be so awful dirty, there'd be an awful stink*
> *All day you'd face the barren waste looking for a nice cool drink So*
> *you gotta' have rain every now and then*
> *To make the whole world shine then every day will turn out fine*

And I was getting paid to do this. I would tell the kids that I had been to a nearby school, and the other school had sung it louder – so a re-run would result in the school hall full of bellowing tots, determined to win the neighbourhood water rant.

All good stuff and showing the human face of a largely unpopular water company. As part of the talks to adult groups, I was contacted by the Nottingham Society for the Deaf wanting a local water cycle presentation.

I was taken aback simply because of what I thought might be the practicality or otherwise of communications. I was still not sure but departed into the city of Nottingham on a miserable December evening and eventually located the venue. A second-floor meeting room with no lift and narrow staircase. A struggle to get all the kit, projector, screen, and the like into the room. .

A dozen or so eager Society members greeted me and whilst doing so, I had a quiet word with the Secretary of my concern of members being able to hear me. Not a problem she said. There was an electrical loop which encircled the audience chairs. This clever device supported the members ability to hear. Two hours of successful and satisfying communications later I was heading home.

Several days later a surprise contact from the Chief Executive of Severn Trent. The Secretary of the local Deaf Association was a personal friend. She had contacted him to say how much they had enjoyed the talk and he passed on the message and his congratulations. The experience reinforced two key essentials. Never prejudge an audience and give everyone the same level of consideration.

Meanwhile my determination to get closer to the press following the Central Television debacle continued. I got to know Richard Harris, Assistant Editor of the Nottingham Evening Post well, and we agreed to work on a double page feature of how the water cycle worked for his readers and the good people of Nottingham.

To understand more I insisted that he come on a conducted tour of Stoke Bardolph sewage treatment works which treated the "wastewater" of over 500,000 people. He reluctantly agreed. We arrived at the works. The workforce were made aware he was coming. Shortly after entering the gates, a Severn Trent operative appeared from one of the sewage sludge reception tanks.

Polite introductory words were exchanged. Richard enquired how long had he worked here? Did he enjoy it? The operative smiled wryly, "It may be shit to you but it's our bread and butter," he said, and then pronounced proudly that he had been asked to take us on a works tour.

Richard was impressed with his style and obvious passion for the job. As we looked at the different processes, the humour continued.

"We get all sorts coming down here," said the friendly operative, as we peered over rails to look at the massive sewer inlet belching forth Nottingham's excrement at a formidable pace, on its way to the first stage of treatment. "On those screens below we get wage packets, sex toys, false teeth, and once even a 6-foot python" he said.

To Richard and his journalistic "sniff" for a story, this was too much. He needed to know how, when, where, and why. The operative went on, "well, for a start the wage packets generally arrive over a weekend. You see many of the lads get paid on Friday afternoon at the likes of Raleigh, Boots, and other big Nottingham employers. Just before going home they visit the loo and in the hasty dropping of trousers, the wage packet in the back pocket slips out, unbeknown to the poor wage earner and he flushes a cash deposit with his unwanted deposit."

I was beginning to think that Richard's focus and interest was shifting toward anecdotes rather than the subtle art of anaerobic digestion and tertiary treatment. I wonder why? The tour through the processes and the anecdotes continued. "So," said Richard, " how the hell did a 6-foot python arrive down here?"

"One day we got a call from a distressed pet lover to say that his pet python, Monty, (it just had to be) had slipped down the loo whilst he was taking a phone call. Apparently he was just giving him some recreational slither time in the bath when the phone 'coil' came. And as you'll appreciate Richard we always advise that you never leave a python in the bath unattended when there is a nearby WC with the lid up."

"No," interjected Richard, "I never do."

" Anyway, trying to be helpful, we said we would keep an eye out for Monty and sure enough, two days later, he did surface in the inlet sewer over there. That was the good news. The bad news was he was in three parts. Cut up by the pumps in the sewerage system which support the flow on its way here."

"Oh dear," lamented Richard, "did you tell the owner?"

"A bit at a time," said the operative. By now I was concerned that this was becoming a double act and the serious business of treating business was altogether secondary. However I persuaded myself that this was good PR and part of relationship building with one of the most influential local newspapers.

"And the false teeth? " enquired Richard.

"Oh, that one's pretty obvious," said our operative entertainer, "usually jettisoned into the porcelain after a good night out along with re-cycled pie and chips or vinda-loo."

In fact, he went on, "one day we took a call from an embarrassed chap who explained that he had awoken to find he had lost his teeth, probably as a result of the birthday celebrations the night before. Apparently he had further many happy returns during the night, this time rendered in a kneeling position. Incredibly he did say that if we saw his gnashers, could we let him know and he would come and fetch them - despite their journey through thousands of litres of prime, fresh, Nottingham No 2's. One thing was for sure, he certainly didn't need Fixodent."

Our conducted tour over, and a much more enlightened journalist on the complexities of sewage treatment with free entertainment thrown in. Richard later remarked on the obvious dedication of the people that operated the treatment works at Stoke Bardolph. A real eye opener.

Papplewick Pumping Station Nottingham...

There are times in life when you fail, there are times in life when you succeed , there are times in life when you succeed and fail at the same time. Such was the case on a beautiful summers day in 1984.

If you have not been to the most magnificent and preserved Victorian pumping station at Papplewick near Nottingham you have not lived. I had not. Until Brian Duckworth said you should go and see it and ask them if they want to do a joint open day with Severn Trent. But first about Papplewick.

A majestic Victorian water pumping station, about nine miles north of Nottingham, and set in a tranquil landscape and gardens. Designed and built in the early 1880s to pump millions of gallons of clean fresh water every day to the then rapidly increasing population of industrial Nottingham. Thanks to the tireless endeavours of The Papplewick Pumping Station Trust, and the enthusiasm of the volunteer members of the Papplewick Association, you can experience the most spectacular, preserved, and working, Victorian water pumping station in the UK.

Advertisement over. My first visit confirmed what a fantastic location for an Open Day. The old alongside the new. Exhibitions, demonstrations, talks, balloons, rides, the whole nine yards (8.23 metres). There followed weeks preparing, drawing offices creating larger-than-life information boards, all ready for the big day. A chance to test free advertising and new found media relations contacts. Live local broadcasting from site. Interviews with Radio Nottingham, Radio Trent, and day before coverage from my friend at the Nottingham Evening Post.

Dawn of the day and rubber underpants donned. Would anybody come? Reputation at stake. Good bowel movement Mr Quartermain. A reported drift of the occasional car and then more, a good sign, particularly an hour before opening.

Went inside the various tents to make sure all was looking good. Quick coffee. Chat with Papplewick grandees. 30 minutes to go. I was then accosted by a worried Severn Trent car park attendant who asked if I had seen the queues? Looking over to the toilets it looked pretty clear.

"No, I mean the cars," he said, frog marching me down to the entrance parking field. I was taken aback. As far as the eye could see, line upon line of cars. Like the London Marathon on wheels. Had we overdone the publicity?...probably, had we underestimated the attraction of a freebie day?...probably, was it the lure of a pristine Victorian working pumping station?…probably…was that a policeman making his way over to me?…probably.

"Are you in charge?" he said from underneath the brimmed scrambled-egg hat of an Inspector. I briefly thought about a grab for the nearby car park attendants armband but too late. "Yes," I said.

"Well, you'd better do something about these bloody cars then," he rapped. "They're back-to-back all the way to the A 60 (over a mile away)."

The rubber underpants were a wise garment of choice. Thankfully a local farmer came to the rescue with two more fields to stack the automobile swarm. Our day was a steaming success. Moral of the story? Never underestimate the public's interest in a freebie day in the country.

Monday 4th June 1984

A day that will always live in the memory. In nearby Derbyshire, Severn

Trent's contractors were close to finishing the construction of a massive earth dam that would form a vital part of the new Carsington Reservoir, bringing much needed extra water resources for the East Midland areas of Derbyshire, Nottinghamshire, and Leicestershire. Located between Wirksworth to the north and Ashbourne to the south, the resource strategy was simple. To take water from the plentiful River Derwent winter flows and store in Carsington Reservoir before releasing water back into the river during dry summer periods for treatment further downstream. Planned in the 1960's, and the subject of much planning and political debate, leading to long delays, the construction eventually started in 1979 and by June 1984, the completion of the huge earth dam was in sight.

What had that got to do with me? I was not an engineer. It was not in my area. Other than a personal interest in a major Severn Trent project, and the occasional question at local talks, I had not been involved.

On the fateful day of 4th June 1984, I was minding my own business in the Nottingham office, when an excited colleague came into the room and said that the HQ Regional Board meeting, this time being held in the Nottingham office, had suddenly, and unexpectedly, broken up. All members, he said, were hot footing their way to Carsington. Something had happened. And something big. Within hours came the news that on a routine inspection on the crest of the dam, a site engineer had spotted a 50 mm crack in the crest of the dam.

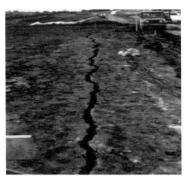

Crest of Carsington Dam 4th June 1984   Crest of Carsington Dam 7th June 1984

By the time others were alerted, the crack had widened to 40 cms and by Thursday 7th June, three days later, to 15 metres revealing a catastrophic collapse stretching over 500 metres in length. All work stopped. It would not start again for 5 years.

In the meantime there were significant detailed investigations from national and local technical and civil engineering specialists as to what had happened and why, and if a dam could ever safely be built on the site. The most significant, The Coxon Report, two years in the making, reported to the Secretary of State in 1986 and concluded that "a replacement embankment (dam) could be designed and safely constructed on the Carsington site." The technical boffins had given their view. But they had said the same in the late 1960's and early 1970's, before the go ahead and ultimate collapse of the dam.

Try saying that "everything will be OK this time" to the local Derbyshire folk in the picturesque villages dotted around the reservoir site. A tall order was an understatement. An impossibility would be more realistic. Scepticism and widespread objections were loud and clear.

After Coxon and the technical go-ahead, I was asked to get involved. I got a call from HQ to say that they wanted me to work with others on local communications. I should meet the newly appointed Seven Trent Engineering Project Manager for Carsington and liaise with ST's Engineering Director. We discussed the obvious need for local public meetings, production of information materials, leaflets, and other intensive local communication initiatives. All explaining the case and aiming to give much-needed reassurance to anxious residents of nearby villages and communities close to the reservoir site.

After many months of political, technical, and public debate and argument, in 1989 the reservoir dam embankment re-construction began, and the £100 million Carsington Reservoir project was completed and opened by Her Majesty The Queen in 1992. Thirty long years of controversy, delays, and setbacks since the initial plans were originally mooted. Today Carsington Reservoir sits in majestic countryside as one of the country's most picturesque recreational and conservation amenities, second only to its vital role as an essential and critical contributor to the East Midlands water resource needs.

John Jepson – Mr Carsington

I talked earlier about the biggest metaphorical mountain to climb. The understandable fear and concern of the local communities, particularly after the engineering disaster of the original dam wall collapse. How to pacify and persuade. Seemingly impossible. And yet, incredibly, it began to happen. The gradual, often fragile, and sceptical local endorsement was essentially achieved by one man. A retired Severn Trent Operations Manager called John Jepson.

John was persuaded to temporarily return from retirement to be the local liaison officer for Carsington. He had worked in the local water industry, man, and boy, all of his working life. I talk frequently in this book about unsung heroes who make the water industry tick. John is up there with the best. No he didn't work for 6.5 years and get a CBE for services to the water industry like some transient and overpaid directors who worked in the distant HQ ivory towers.

A qualified chemist, process expert, operations manager, and not many equals in water expertise. John knew the patch and knew the people. He lived and breathed Derbyshire. He knew the culture, understood the local concern, talked to them and not at them, and had a thick Derbyshire brogue that said he was one of us. John called a spade a shovel, sniffed bullshit from a hundred miles, and did not take prisoners. But his language, view, and emphasis, was listened to and respected.

He and I spoke numerous times and when we did, there was always an understanding, camaraderie, and trust. Carsington Reservoir and Severn Trent owe a massive debt of gratitude to John. Right place, right time, and right man. He will be remembered by many for his candour and honest approach. There is a memorial stone in his honour at the reservoir, paying tribute to his life and work, and particularly to his Carsington contribution.

More than fitting for a true, dedicated, professional who served the local area and the water industry so well.

John Jepson 1931 – 1998

Carsington memorial stone

40

Chapter 7. Getting on the front foot – at last

By now the reason for my role existence and activity in promoting Severn Trent's work to the world outside, was becoming well known internally. Not appreciated by all though. I recall one day we had a burst water main in Nottingham city centre which meant no water for a sizeable urban area, and, reasonably, the press wanted information. I went to see a long-standing senior operations manager for facts, repair time, water-back-on estimate etc. Tersely he turned around to me and said "what's it got to do with them (the press)? Just tell them it's our water network and we are dealing with it. We'll tell the locals when we are good and ready."

Sadly, even at senior levels, the acknowledgement that we had customers connected to the network still seemed almost irrelevant – a throwback to the mentality of local authority days. But that was becoming the exception. Different operational and engineering units were coming to me with potentially interesting stories to feed to the press and media. Even a begrudging respect from my former capital engineering colleagues who had found it hard to accept my recent high-profile reincarnation, following my departure to Mansfield.

One particularly huge and impressive local engineering feat that I was asked to support had a big and positive national media exposure but a bitter-sweet internal reaction. The biggest sewer in Nottingham's history was in urgent need of replacement. At the time, it was the largest sewerage modernisation scheme in the UK. The multi-million-pound plan was to upgrade and replace the seven miles of sewer that conveyed most of Nottingham's sewage from the city, across tricky built-up urban and rural areas to Stoke Bardolph sewage treatment works.

A potential nightmare in terms of disruption to traffic, sensitive woodlands, habitats, walkways, schools, and the digging up of many back gardens, most of whose owners had been blissfully unaware of the silent sewage flow underneath their prized tomatoes, sheds, and greenhouses. We blitzed every contact area of the local community with public meetings, talks, exhibitions, press coverage, and letter drops before work began. Once underway, time to alert the national press. And this is when the fun started. One of the most influential national magazines for the water industry was Water Bulletin, with wide circulation in England, Wales, Scotland, and Northern Ireland.

Enter Paul Garrett, Water Bulletin News Editor, fresh from the city of London, and persuaded to come out to the sticks, and see the huge and impressive construction project. I knew Paul well. A local tour was planned around the key areas but there was a last-minute hitch. The designated engineer scheduled to accompany us on the day and to take the lead role, could not make it at the last minute. So what? you may say. Well, how ironic. Here was an ideal opportunity for a professional civil engineer to get a well-deserved national profile for a major national civil engineering scheme. To take all the plaudits and enjoy the oxygen of publicity. So often a bee in the hard-hat engineering bonnet of supposed down-trodden engineers.

And where was he? Missing from action at the crucial time. Instead our reluctant hero (me) was given no alternative. I became tour guide, which was OK, until Paul asked me to pose for a photograph looking at the new works. I explained that this should really be the engineer who was managing the work.

"No problem," said Paul, "it's only a scene setter. You might not end up on the shot anyway by the time the editorial team have cropped it." So I obliged. A successful day over, and Paul headed back to the smoke promising to let me know the publication date.

Two weeks later the article was published. The News Editor had decided to make the story a front cover lead and a double-page centre spread. The front cover was dominated by our reluctant hero looking like a latter-day Isambard Kingdom Brunel and the story, for some reason, was biased towards public relations.

A brilliant, but unintended, piece of self-publicity. Needless to say the publication went down like a lead balloon with the engineering team. My understanding is that the absent engineer who should have been with me on the day was last seen entering the final phase of the sewer replacement, just before sewer flows went live. Clandestinely I pinned the front cover to the engineering notice board, adjacent to the existing Drip of the Drought press cutting.

He who hesitates…

Project Engineer Smith (?)…

Water Aid

The talks and presentations kept coming and growing in number. Groups seemed to like hearing about their local water cycle and how it worked. Source to tap and home to sea. Local water resources, treatment works, river discharges. The speaker-finder in the Group often thanked me and asked if I could give my office address so they could write formally. I would say don't write to me but to John Brown, Divisional Manager. So on a regular basis, positive thank-you letters would come across his desk. One day he called me in. "Are you enjoying the job?" he said. "Very much," I replied. "In that case can I ask you a favour?" he continued, "we don't have a Water Aid ambassador in the Division, and I wondered if you would consider taking it on. It will mean regular talks about the charity to similar organizations you are already talking to in the community."
I reacted positively and went on to learn more about the UK water industry charity. I knew it had been formed by the water companies around the time I got this latest job but little else. The following statistics horrified me, and I was more than pleased to add a Water Aid talk to whoever wanted it in the Nottinghamshire patch.

- Every minute a new-born dies from infection caused by lack of clean water and an unclean environment
- Diarrhoea caused by dirty water and poor toilets kills a child under 5 every 2 minutes.
- 771 million people don't have clean water close to home.
- 1.7 billion people don't have a decent toilet of their own.
- 2.3 billion people lack soap and water for handwashing at home.
- Around the world up to 443 million school days are lost every year because of water-related illnesses.

I began responding to requests for Water Aid talks. Little did I know what was to come. Just about getting in my stride on the new assignment when I was invited to Nottingham Rotary Club. They were very interested in Water Aid and decided to carry out a number of fundraising activities at the Club. Later a Nottingham Rotarian contacted me to see if I would talk to their 'Rotary District gathering at Sutton in Ashfield.'

He explained that this was their District organization which included almost seventy Rotary clubs from Derbyshire, Nottinghamshire, Leicestershire, Staffordshire, and South Yorkshire. They often joined together to raise funds for a "one off" adopted cause.

On a cold, rainy, winter, night I drove to Sutton in Ashfield where representatives from the 70 clubs were holding their annual get-together and talked for some time about Water Aid and its work. Their reaction was positive and a number of days later we agreed on an ambitious fundraising project which would be unique, and hopefully appealing, to would-be donors.

The initiative would be called "Running for Water" which meant that a flask of water would be filled at Biddulph Moor, source of the River Trent, near Stoke on Trent, and carried by relay runners from each Rotary Club bordering the Trent for almost 200 miles, to the mouth of the Trent at the Humber Estuary.

It would emphasise the plight of many people in the World who had to walk miles for their drinking water supplies. Each Rotary club involved would organize a run in their patch; from serious to fun-loving runners, before handing over the flask to the next club.

We talked to Matthew Parris, then a Derbyshire MP, keen Marathon runner, and later to become a well-known journalist and broadcaster and he agreed to run the last few miles. Much great organizing by the Rotarians, terrific publicity, fantastic public participation later, resulted in £9,000 (nearly £30,000 value in 2022) being raised over the two days of the event.

That amount was graciously doubled to £18,000 by the Rotary

Rotary District 1220 Annual Meeting
Scarborough October 1986

Foundation HQ in the US, and the UK's Overseas Development Administration (ODA) doubled that to a staggering £36,000 (over £100,000 in 2022) which went to support a much-needed safe drinking water supply for a Ghanaian hospital.

And all starting from a wet cold, night in Sutton in Ashfield.

Chapter 8. The industry, Severn Trent, and me, changing again?

The mid- eighties were seeing yet more planned change. The Conservative Government had embarked on a series of privatisations or "denationalizations." Gas, Telecoms, BP, Airways, Rail, and more, were already sold off. Speculation on potential water industry privatisation was rife but deeply unpopular.

Although the ten water authorities had made progress since 1974 in key quality and environmental areas, the pace of investment was nothing like sufficient to cope with the combination of increasing water demand and new European quality and environmental legislation. Capital spending was still being throttled by Government restrictions and far too modest slices of the public sector investment cake. UK political priority and pressure was not in water. But it was in the EU.

The irony of the UK's EU entry and the formation of the water authorities in the same year (1974), was to have a significant and mutually beneficial effect. By now the EU Commission was getting tough, very tough, on the need for compliance with EU law and Directives on water quality and environmental legislation.

It had been on the EU books for some time but few member states had paid more than lip service, including the UK. Brussels had decided that if the UK was to be made an example of on non-compliance, others would fall in-line. The EU began the real threat of legal 'Infringement Proceedings' with ultimate referral to the European Court of Justice. The political and legal noose was tightening on the Thatcher Government, and something had to give.

Meanwhile Severn Trent had decided it was time for an internal restructure. Eight existing operating divisions, based largely on the counties in the ST regional area was not efficient and too costly. The divisions, stretching from the Humber to the Severn Estuary, would be reduced from eight to four - with consequent reduction in the number of divisional management teams and other functions.

Also the administration of the local Water Consumer Consultative Committees would be managed from HQ in Birmingham. So my CRA post along with others was going. However Birmingham HQ had seen the value of improving press and media relationships and community contact in the local areas and decided to create four 'Information Officers' to be based in each of the new divisions.

46

I was appointed as Information Officer to the Eastern Division (Nottinghamshire and Leicestershire) and relieved to shed the water consumer committee skin which never really appealed but was a means to an end. The new divisional HQ was in Anstey, Leicester, and we relocated. Media relations work with local radio, TV, and newspapers, continued unabated, and local talks snow balled. I loved every minute.

Leicestershire tales - the talk

The old music hall saying, "a funny thing happened to me on the way to the theatre," did happen in my first few weeks working in the Leicestershire area. Bear in mind by now I had clocked up hundreds of talks to all manner of groups, so the routine of preparation was tried and tested. On this occasion a scheduled talk to a Women's Institute in a tiny village in the Leicestershire Wolds on a dark November evening.

Before departure, routine checking with our operational control centre to establish where the village drinking was sourced and treated and, where, after use, the "wastewater" was treated and discharged back into the local water environment. My trusty, heavy 16 mm projector and awkward, independently minded, projector screen were loaded in the car; clean white shirt donned, tie straightened, and off we go.

Travelling to the village in the Leicestershire Wolds was a nightmare but not untypical in the rural outback. Poor location details, no Sat Nav (in those days), no streetlights, horizontal sheeting rain. Peering frantically through full-on wipers and main beam headlights at bent-over village signs. I eventually located the village and then the village hall with welcoming indoor lights beckoning and floodlighting the lashing rain. I pulled into the gravel car park. Made it! Checked the watch - 30 minutes early - perfect.

Time to get heavy duty projector, and wayward screen set up, and share introductory pleasantries with Secretary on foul weather, when to speak, allotted time, Jerusalem, etc.

Quick dash from car and indoors to make initial contact. Polite shouts of hello as I entered the building but, as per usual, no reply. Absolutely normal and expected. Those already in the building are the worker-bee volunteers in the back room, making sandwiches, jam and cream scones, cranking up the tea urn for the interval break, when I will be asked to judge a one-night only members competition of objet d'art. This might be ladies evening handbags, pastoral paintings, or bakery offerings. Diplomacy skills absolutely essential.

47

By now I had erected projector screen at far end of the main hall room, whilst avoiding usual hernia threat when lifting heavy 16 mm projector on to stand at other end. Now in the process of looping film and adjusting image to actual screen size. It was at this point that I became aware of being watched. Someone had quietly entered the main hall behind me.

"Hello," I said continuing to look forward, squinting, to get the projector image to focus on the screen. No reply.

"Hello," I repeated, "I'm Alan Smith from Severn Trent Water." At that point from the corner of my squinting eye I could not help noticing that the male individual was in dressing gown and full ankle length pyjama bottoms.

Not an everyday outfit that a potential audience member would wear for a riveting speech about the water cycle, but bear in mind that it was a village hall and all manner of different events overlap, and he could have been rehearsing for the local Christmas play. In fact he looked remarkably like Noel Coward.

"Yes?" he said questioningly, in response to my "I'm Alan Smith from Severn Trent Water"

"So sorry," I said breaking off from my projector preparation. Turning round, with one eye still squinting, and stepping forward to shake his hand, I continued, "I'm Alan Smith and the speaker booked for tonight to talk about the water cycle.

Not impressed he said vigorously, "You're in my house."

At that exact moment the projector which I had left running boomed out the music and opening titles of "Water for Life" (the main feature). Somewhat clumsily I shouted over the noisy soundtrack, "is this not the village hall?"

"NO, it is not the village hall, it's my house," he reiterated, "and I was just going to bed!"

Humiliated and embarrassed I switched off the projector, humbly apologized and gathered my props as quickly as possible.

Mr Coward went on to explain that the village hall was a further 200 yards down the village main street. Amazingly he did manage a smile even though by my actions, I had unwittingly suggested that his expensively renovated ex school house looked like a village hall.

Driving home that night I recollected that I had addressed many audiences where I was aware that several had nodded off during my animated speaking presentation, but it was the first time that someone had attempted to go to bed before I had started.

Moral of the story? Never assume the obvious. It might not be. This transgression was read in full by Simon Mayo on BBC Radio 2 programme as part of his 'Confession' slot in April 2017. I was forgiven.

Leicestershire tales - stirring the sludge – and Tomorrows World

We were now cooking on gas when it came to working with the local press and media. Interviews on many watery topics were happening on Radio Nottingham, Radio Leicester, and Radio Trent (the aptly named commercial station) and regional Central Television. Around that time I was approached by an enthusiastic Leicester Operations Manager who came bustling into my room to enquire as to whether I had seen his 'shit' buggy?

"No, it's not in here," I replied quizzically, "have you lost it?" (I meant the plot not the buggy).

"No, I'm serious," he said, and went on to explain.

But just before letting you, the reader, know what he had to say, I will briefly interject so that you will be as wise as I was before his dramatic entrance and explanation. After treating sewage (*stay with me*) to whatever high treatment standard, you, or should I say we are then left with an awful lot of what is politely known as sludge, sewage sludge. Now the more you can reduce, or thicken, the liquidity of the sludge, (*are you still there…?..*) the more efficient and manageable it is, for onward transportation to farming land or other disposal routes. OK?

Back to the excited Operations Manager and his explanation.

" At Wanlip sewage treatment works, (*which treats most of Leicester's "wastewater"*) we have devised an innovative way to accelerate the sludge thickening process and that's where the sludge buggy comes in," he said.

"Come down and see it working – it's fantastic! Definitely worth a media shout!"

Two days later, and with an amount of scepticism, I arrived at the Wanlip site. I was introduced to Tony, the intrepid Seven Trent operative and driver of the nearby "sludge" buggy. With great enthusiasm he leapt into what looked like a converted golf cart, revved the engine and disappeared headlong down the slipway of a huge concrete lagoon, the size of a football-pitch, and full of "sludge." I had to rub my eyes. Was I really seeing this? A driver, or was it a sailor, motoring up and down this cavernous open lagoon, full of the finest Leicester excrement, with a tail surge of flying "sludge" behind. The operative would carry out this unenviable task for hours every day and it did the job, reducing the quantity, improving the quality, and making it easier to dispose of.

Over the next few weeks we got stuck in to exciting the press and media. The unique buggy was widely featured across local and regional media channels. The icing on the sludge cake was a national TV broadcast on the BBC 'Tomorrows World' programme. The outburst from the Operations Manager in my office had paid great PR dividends.

The 'sludge' had hit the fan in an incredibly positive way. And as for me, I was left thinking that I had met many shit stirrers along the way, but none as effective as this.

Sludge Buggy creating a stir on the Leicestershire sludge lagoon at Wanlip

Leicestershire tales – a big bag of fish – and Blue Peter

They say that big opportunities rarely come in two's but at this point in time it did. Again this was down to another enthusiastic ST Leicestershire manager who was responsible for recreation and conservation in the area. We talked about Cropston Reservoir, in the picturesque Charnwood Forest area, and the fact that it was slowly being drained to allow for urgent repair and maintenance work.

When most of the 3 billion litres of water, normally supplying nearby Leicester customers had drained, there was the task of netting and transferring around 8 tonnes of course and game fish into the safe waters of the River Soar. That time was almost arriving, and we would witness one of the biggest "catches" since biblical times. We knew it would provide spectacular, once-in-a-lifetime pictures. We also knew that getting local press and media interested would be an easy task. The question was who do we give the story to nationally?

After conversations we thought it fitted well with children and, in particular, the BBC Blue Peter programme. We were right. They were very keen. And so the Blue Peter team, film crew and all, including presenter Yvette Fielding, and Bonny the dog, descended on Cropston to witness and help in the netting of thousands of fish before their relocation to a new watery home in the nearby River Soar. Another positive national profile, but this time for all the family and the many keen anglers up and down the country. Blue Peter badge time for me? No, they said, but one for the kids who helped on the day. Career wise things were really happening, more by luck than planning.

Cropston helpers, Emily, Daniel, Abigail Smith with Blue Peter presenter, Evette Fielding

51

Chapter 9. Water privatisation - and me

By the mid 1980's EU political and legal pressure on the UK Government to comply with new and higher challenging water and environmental standards was mounting. Despite the national unpopularity of the prospect of privatising water, including some from within their own party, the Conservative Government finally decided on change. The result?

Plans for water privatisation were included in the Conservatives 1987 General Election manifesto. With the election won Mrs Thatcher called a weekend 'water' summit at Chequers, the PM's country residence. Invited were the leading regional water authority Chairmen of Thames, Severn Trent, Welsh Water and others, to discuss privatisation and seek their views. Was it feasible, practical, and would it work? She was given a ringing and positive endorsement from all attending.

From that moment, despite lively opposition from back benchers, a negative press and media, and unfavourable opinion polls, Mrs Thatcher gave the green light to progress with all speed to take the water industry in England and Wales into the private sector.

At the same time to enshrine, by legislation and tough regulation, urgent steps to comply with the significant, new EU water and environmental obligations, that had initially forced the issue. For political reasons, the water sector in Northern Ireland and Scotland would remain in the public sector. The Chequers decision was to herald the biggest shake-up the water industry in England and Wales had seen.

Meanwhile in downtown Leicestershire and Nottinghamshire all was going well when I received a call in the spring of 1988 from my boss, Colin Slater, at Severn Trent HQ Birmingham. He also of Radio Nottingham and Notts County commentator fame. His water career was short and sweet, but a nice guy.

He wanted to see me and went on to explain that an internal Severn Trent privatisation management team had been created which included some of the best brains in the business, representing engineering, operations, finance, law, and regulation.

At their early meetings they had decided that they also wanted someone on the team with communications experience, who would ensure that Severn Trent's 7000 plus employees would be kept informed of latest issues, activities, implications, as we progressed from public sector towards privatisation at the end of 1989. I listened with interest, thinking I had been summoned to be told who that communicator would be, when he paused and said, "I would like you to do it."

The next few sentences he uttered were lost on me. All I could remember on the drive back to Leicestershire was "the first meeting you will attend will be at HQ next Monday". So there I would be, every Monday morning for almost two years, with six or seven of the best brains in Severn Trent, listening and taking notes, as we deciphered complex Government edicts and their implications, from lawyers, bankers, and many other Whitehall mandarins. For my part deciding on the more important messages to communicate to employees on impact and change.

A lad who had failed his 11 plus, attained no academic qualifications, rubbing shoulders with the Severn Trent Brains Trust, and with a front row seat to one of the most controversial Government privatisations of our time.

I was to combine this latest role with my other communication activities in the East Midlands but as time went on and we got closer and closer to the December 1989 privatisation date, I spent more and more time on HQ privatisation projects and initiatives. Employee communications, press and media initiatives, corporate videos, London meetings with PR companies, other water company communications managers, and Government PR advisors.

At the Queen Annes Gate, London, meetings of the Water Services Association (now Water UK), I regularly bumped into Tim Bell, close confidant and PR advisor to Margaret Thatcher, and Tom McNally, who were advising the Association on privatisation communications and activities.

Both decent guys who went on to be Lord Bell and Lord McNally, but neither had a clue about the water industry and how it worked. Often the mantra of borrowing our watch, telling tell us the time, and sending us the bill. So often the case with externally employed PR companies – but Board rooms tend to use them as comfort blankets, rather than delivering anything substantial, apart from the bill that is.

Six months into the new and exciting chaos of privatisation preparation and my HQ duties, came another really significant career change. Internal management structures were changing to reflect the developing need for life post privatisation.

A belated but key initiative was the Thatcher Government decision to retain environmental responsibilities for monitoring and improving river water quality, safeguarding water resources, pollution control, land drainage, and flood prevention, in the public sector. The public guardian of the environment, heralding the creation of the National Rivers Authority (NRA).

Conversely the newly privatised water companies would focus on potable water and wastewater treatment, including water supply and distribution, and sewerage, sewage treatment and disposal. The NRA would have regional boundaries and HQ's based on existing water authority boundaries. So began the transfer of many former colleagues into the new NRA. Some were given a choice; to stay in the soon-to-be privatised water company or to opt for the NRA. Some had no choice.

I was called in by Colin Slater to say that Geoff Mance, who I knew, was to be the new General Manager of the Midlands based NRA. He wanted to see me with a view to offering me the role of PR Manager in his new structure. I quickly decided that it was not for me.

Geoff was a good man, and I could have worked well with him, but green wellies was not for me. Things were now moving fast. Severn Trent had a new Chief Executive, and I soon had a new boss.

And so to HQ...

Jim Oatridge was appointed Head of Corporate Affairs. A former west midlands Severn Trent divisional manager and with significant experience across the business including, operations, engineering, and finance. Jim was charged with the management of all corporate communications. Smart cookie who, as well as knowing the industry inside-out, was a shrewd, strategic thinker, and operator.

Jim quickly brought out a new HQ structure for the communications team and I was appointed Media Relations Manager to be based in Birmingham. A high-profile role managing TV, radio, and newspaper outlets from Gloucestershire in the South West to Humberside in the North East, and mid-Wales to Rutland. As well as all national news and media outlets.

With Severn Trent I had now relocated from Nottingham to Mansfield, back to Nottingham, Leicester, and now Birmingham. Exciting times for my career but more importantly at home a wife and three children to enjoy and care for. Domestic life was never dull but at times difficult with crazy, long office hours. Moving house regularly, kids making new friends, new schools, but all the family coped pretty well given the regular disruption.

However, at one point we had a really traumatic family situation. We almost lost our youngest daughter, Emily. Aged three years, she had suffered from Asthma from 13 months old and each time she had a cold or chest infection, it would more often than not lead to an Asthma attack.

Many parents with asthma-suffering children would recognize this. A really nasty condition and greatly underrated by the general public. We had nebulizers, steroids, inhalers, at home, as well as red card emergency authorization to go direct to the asthma ward of the local hospital if she should have a really bad attack.

On one particular late night of an extreme attack, Emily had regurgitated the steroids, and the nebulizer was having little effect. She had real difficulty breathing and we paced the living room hoping for signs of an upturn in her condition, but she was getting worse.

I will never forget her becoming increasingly limp in my arms. We raced to hospital, entered the asthma ward, and she was immediately put on a ventilator, whilst at the same time the duty trauma manager vigorously pumped her chest. All of the medical team treating her looked concerned which made us even more frightened and anxious.

We were told the next few hours were critical. My wife and I were at her bedside all night, watching Emily and her shallow, laboured, breathing. At around 5 00 am, she slowly turned her head, looked at us, and asked if she could have a cob (bread roll).

I was emotionally overcome and ran down the ward corridor of the hospital in tears, shouting cob, cob, cob, has anyone got a cob? Emily went on to make a full recovery.

A couple of days later I met old friend, Richard Harris, News Editor of the Nottingham Evening Post. During our conversation, I told him of our recent harrowing experience. Later that day he rang to ask if I would mind if he did an editorial story on our plight. He did. I thought it deserved repeating for its treatment, empathy and understanding.

Why it's not weak to weep

A friend of mine cried the other day. He doesn't mind admitting it. His three-year-old daughter had been desperately ill for a couple of days and he and his wife had been sitting beside her bed in hospital. The little girl slipped in and out of unconsciousness and there wasn't much he could do but sit there holding her hand and hoping and praying and fearing the worst, whilst trying not to let anyone know that deep inside he was scared to death. For all that time he managed, in best British stiff upper lip style, to keep his emotions under control. But then, suddenly, the little girl woke up. And he cracked.

She opened her eyes and smiled at him and said, "can I have a cob (bread roll) please?" and it was enough to send the tears streaming down his face. He told me about it because, I like to think , he knows that I don't think it odd that he cried, and I don't think any the less of him for admitting it. And he told me because he and I share the belief that the daftest thing a father can do is tell his young son to put on a brave face because "big boys don't cry."

The truth is that big boys do...and the world would be a better place if everyone learned to accept it. I admit that I cried when each of my children was born, and I cried when I heard that my Dad was dying, and I even confess to the odd lump in my throat while watching various tearjerking films on the telly. It's about time that we accepted that emotion, and, more importantly, the showing of it, is a pretty normal part of being human. Any doctor will tell you that you can't beat a good weep, or a good belly laugh, as a way of releasing tension.

So goodness knows how much harm we are doing to ourselves by trying to keep it all bottled up inside us. We were given eyes to cry with and mouths to laugh with...but most of the time we'll do our damnedest to go through life showing only the minutest variations of a poker face. We were given arms to hug with too...but give us the chance and we'll choose to greet our friends with a stiff handshake or a wave.

We will hug and cuddle our children while they are young...but once they grow up we'll get embarrassed about it and we'll end up showing them less affection than we show to the cat. It's too big a problem to be changed overnight. But maybe we can make a start. By telling our sons that it's alright if they cry. Because, secretly, their Dads do too.

Media, mayhem, and the movie

As a Media Relations Manager in a very unpopular privatisation, life for me and the press team was never boring. Incessant phone calls, easy journalistic privatisation stories for any politician, councillor or campaigner looking for profile and exposure. But we enjoyed it and soon television and radio interviews were second nature. We had to tread a careful line regarding our position. The decision to privatise was not a matter

for water authorities, but for Government of the day and politicians. Having said that John Bellak, our chairman, was a two-time Tory Parliamentary candidate, and close to Margaret Thatcher, and we certainly knew his thoughts and expectations. We held the neutral line, apart from the occasional provocative remarks and public statements from the Chairman. I had never met him prior to getting the new role but I quickly became aware of his

John Bellak Chairman

Severn Trent Water 1983-1994

no nonsense approach, confidence of purpose, and direction. He did not suffer fools lightly. And also had an obsessional dislike of split infinitives. As a newly appointed wordsmith I was soon made aware of it.

He was a good man, very colourful, never grey, and a shrewd operator. Born In Czechoslovakia and a Jewish refugee, his family were forced to flee from the Nazis to the UK in the 1930's, which made all the more remarkable his rise in UK business and other enterprises. Originally working in the wool trade in Yorkshire he was to become MD and Chairman of Royal Doulton in the 1970's and 80's before moving to Severn Trent. He spoke fluent **Spanish, German, and French as well as** English.

I liked him. When I first spoke with him he could sense that I was a bit apprehensive but was always kind and generous with his explanation of what he was looking for but beware if you wasted time with small talk.

As I got to know him better I remember a particular occasion when, in the heat of the political, privatisation debate, a Birmingham trade union official came out with a load of negative rubbish regarding Severn Trent. He had to be publicly corrected, but without leaning too far into political dialogue.

I put together a draft press release but knew that in itself it would not gain news-desk traction or coverage. So, knowing by now the Chairman's bent for thrill of the chase, I titled the press release, "TU official in Cloud Cuckoo land!" ...says John Bellak, Chair of Severn Trent. He liked it and said go with it.

We did and it grabbed news-desk attention and turned the story on its head. I think that one single issue gave each of us an understanding of where we were coming from, and the relationship grew from there. An important lesson for aspiring communicators – play to your senior man or woman's characteristics, not standard nothingness.

One of my early privatisation projects included producing a corporate video of Severn Trent's activities in treating water and wastewater across the Midlands. Intended to be pitched to all interested stakeholders, including would-be investors, customers, and employees, it should have broad appeal and be factual. The latter point was absolutely crucial, given tight legal requirements.

Leading up to privatisation and the sale flotation, we had Government lawyers and advisers from the likes of Herbert Smith and Schroders crawling over everything we did in terms of what went out into the public domain. Nothing should contradict, embellish, or lessen the words in the public prospectus being drawn up by Government as a critical part of the privatisation flotation process. "Facts and not bullshit" – as one adviser put it.

Publications, announcements, videos, and film material, all had to be vetted and approved by a London legal panel drawn from advisers in the Department of the Environment. The draft video script was provisionally approved but before release, the completed video had to be shown to the panel in London.

So I, and the accomplished director of the film, Mike Macleod of PurchasePoint, met them in Whitehall for the showing.

It was a bizarre meeting. We were ushered into a room to be greeted by three dour legal hooray-henry's. Introductory small talk over and I was about to press the "play" button when one of the legal beagles asked why we had called the film 'At the Heart of the Nation?'

I explained, what I thought was the blindingly obvious, that Severn Trent did sit at the heart of the nation, having borders in the east to Lincolnshire, and in the west, Mid Wales, and to the north, Humberside, and to the south, the Severn Estuary.

There then followed a twenty-minute esoteric debate between the panellists as to whether we could honestly call it "At the Heart of the Nation." Could we prove it? Beyond reasonable doubt? Why couldn't South Staffordshire Water (SSW) and East Worcestershire Water (EWW) also claim that?

I responded that SSW and EWW were not part of the privatisation – they were already in the private sector. The Panel knew that but argued that legally this was not the point. 'At the Heart of the Nation' as a phrase was referred to several times in the completed film and I had a horrific thought that we were going to have to re-edit and call it 'At the Heart of the Nation – including South Staffordshire Water and East Worcestershire Water.' Really catchy and box office.

Unbelievably one of the Inspector **Clouseau** panellists was intimating that this might be the solution. I asked if we might first see the film, hoping then that someone on the Panel might see sense – and see the creative nonsense of the suggestion.

The 12-minute showing completed, and the ploy worked. Their mood had softened, and after a couple of additional questions, they said they were OK with the content and, given the context, they could live with the title. We were leaving the room when the Head of the Panel pulled me to one side and quietly said it was the best water pre-privatisation film they had seen of the ten water companies.

It went on to win high awards in the UK Festival for Film and Video Communications, and the Annual International Film and Television Festival of New York, competing with nearly 7000 entries from 45 countries. At the Heart of the Nation or what?.....as the Yanks say, give me a break!

[the legal luddites later persisted in wanting a caption at the end of the film
"SWWCo and EWWCo also supply water in the area covered by Severn Trent Water Authority"]

Meanwhile back at Birmingham HQ more twists and turns as the press team got used to the media frenzy and my projects took on ever more different and interesting avenues. Jim the boss came to see me one particular Monday morning to say that he wanted to discuss two initiatives he would like me to handle.

The first; the Rt Hon Neil Kinnock, Labour Party leader (now Lord Kinnock), was coming to Birmingham and that Severn Trent and other Brummie businesses had been invited to a 'business breakfast' to meet him and his Labour team. At the time the Labour leader was riding high in the polls and trying to knock Mrs Thatcher off her perch. Jim explained that neither the Chairman nor the CEO were available, and that Jim was out of the country on the date in question, and would I go to represent the company?

I couldn't possibly comment on the fact that water privatisation was such a hot national topic, and that Labour Party outright opposition to the principle meant that their unavailability was more than a coincidence. Anyway the chance to meet and greet would be an interesting diversion.

The second initiative was more challenging and definitely different. Jim explained that the Chairman was going to Tokyo to present to analysts and interested parties of the Tokyo Stock Exchange. It would be a factual presentation of the work of Severn Trent, its size, location, and financials etc.

Would I put together the presentation and include the recently produced corporate video "At the Heart of the Nation"? Not a problem I said. Leave it with you he said. As he was leaving my office he turned and added,

"Oh and by the way it needs to be in Japanese."

"Right", I uttered in John Cleese teeth-together fashion. "And the video narration?" I enquired.

"Yes, that too."

With that Jim exited and I felt a slight tightening of the buttocks. OK, so I had gained RSA English Language Stage 1 Elementary, at Ilkeston College. That qualification had at least taught me that my inherited Derbyshire slang, like 'Ayup me duck' (hello) and 'scrating' (crying), 'maunging' (moping), and 'middling' (average), were just that. But fluent Japanese? A step too far. However where there's a will, and after a lot of work with a west midlands translation company specialising in Japanese, plus patience and understanding from the Chairman, we got there, and his trip was successful. Little did I know, after jousting with the London legal lot, that 'Heart of the Nation' would take on such a far-flung emotive tone, or as we multi-lingual Anglo Derbyshire/Japanese experts would say, Kokka no chūshin de 国家の中心で

Japanese education completed, the day to spruce up and meet Neil Kinnock quickly came around. Realistically, in a potential audience of over 200 suited and booted business 'brummies'' there was little chance of meeting him, but the experience was worth being there.

Early at home that morning, whilst abluting and competing for the bathroom with earnest school attendees, Daniel my 11-year-old son, asked what I was up to today. I told him that I was going to meet Neil Kinnock and he said, "no seriously Dad what are you doing today?"

I repeated same and he convinced Mum later at breakfast that Dad was up to the usual pulling the leg stint. Anyway off I went and listened intently at the breakfast to polite welcoming's by people with polished brass chains- of-office, before a speech from the main man. All very good and, whilst tucking into the freebie food, I struck up quite a respectable conversation with one of his aides sitting next to me about water privatisation, the industry, and my experience in it. Nice bloke and whilst also chatting about family and respective number of kids, I mentioned that one of mine was a doubting Thomas as to the validity of my "meeting" with Neil today.

Chuckle from both and after a few more pleasantries he was gone, and I turned my attention to a more boring individual sat on the other side. After about 5 minutes, I was aware of the chair shuffling next to me and, what I thought was a return of the aide. I turned around and was surprised to be greeted by Neil Kinnock.

"Hello," he said, "is it Alan?" looking down at my name badge.

"Yes," I said, before sharing a firm handshake.

"I understand that your son was doubting that you were meeting me today," said Neil

"Yes," I said, still shocked by the full frontal of the main guest.

"Well, we had better put that right," and with that he reached for a table menu and took out his pen. "What's his name?"

"Daniel," I said, as he scribbled a note to him which read, *Dear Daniel, I met your dad today and we had a good chat, and I enjoyed it very much. Look after yourself and take care, best wishes, Neil Kinnock.*

After a couple of minutes of small talk, off he went leaving me to address our family teatime later that day with a surprise validation of said meeting. I think it began with "oh ye of little faith" before handing over the special menu to a surprised son for safekeeping.

And as for Neil Kinnock? One of the more genuine political guys I have been fortunate enough to meet.

Press office diet – but beware indigestion

Much of press office work activity in a utility is mundane and routine. Journalists asking about day-to-day operational work, water mains laying, burst mains repairs, traffic diversions, incidents, sewer upgrades, and so on. However, from time to time, appears a relatively benign, press enquiry, which could potentially be a national blockbuster in terms of coverage. Spotting it is the art. Managing it is the key.

A local newspaper editor rang me on a relatively quiet day in the newsroom to say that he had been tipped off by a Severn Trent employee, who was also a local union steward, that we had infringed strict drinking water quality regulations at a water treatment works where he worked. I said I would get back. There followed a tried and tested internal information-gathering exercise.

Ring the works operational manager, talk to the HQ water quality experts, if need be elevate to Head of Water Quality, and then respond when we have a clear, transparent, and honest response position. Additionally, the press office was always made aware of any operational issues that required rapid communications and messaging to customers in a local community.

We had heard nothing in this case. The message came back to me that the News Editor was correct. There had been a 'minor exceedance' of quality standards at the treatment works, but that had been rectified in the treatment process in a matter of hours. I was told that there was absolutely no threat to the health and well-being of local customers.

Not good enough. I decided to elevate the issue to the highest level. Why? A few weeks before, Camelford, in Cornwall, had suffered a major water supply operational incident which had impacted on many local customers and the river environment of the Camel Estuary. That incident had generated massive national and international attention. Any complacency with our issue had to be eliminated and I needed 100% reassurance that the 'minor exceedance' was just that. Otherwise we were going to ride a similar wave of scrutiny, however unwarranted.

Don't let the facts get in the way of a good story.

Within an hour, gathered around my desk in the press office, we had the local operations manager, the top water quality expert in Severn Trent and arguably in the UK, the Head of Water Quality, and the Operations Director, along with my boss, the Head of Corporate Affairs. Question 1: Gentlemen: are we absolutely sure there was no threat to public health?

The Answer: Yes 100%

Question 2: why so confident?

The Answer: The compliance standard set by European and UK drinking water regulations is both precautionary and intentionally set at a very high level, to ensure that any short-term marginal exceedance does not cause a health threat. The number of hours in this case, relates to this criteria.

Question 3: Why was the press office not informed of this? The Answer: Because of the reasons given in the previous answer. The minimal amount of exceedance together with the minimal number of hours of that exceedance meant there was no reason to escalate.

Looking into the whites of the gathered eyes, particularly the renowned water quality expert, I was now prepared both factually, and with an honest confidence, to return the call to the News Editor. With the gathered internal audience staying and listening to my side of the conversation, and on the other end of the line the news editor asking the questions and listening to the responses, I picked my way through a balanced conversation. We came to the end of the conversation.

The News Editor decided not to run the story. His call not mine. I made my way home. Moral of the story? Threefold. First, make sure you have all the facts. Second, don't believe everything that is given to you. Make sure that you are sure before you put your name and reputation to it. Third, credible and honest relationships with press and media news editors go a long way. He/she has to believe and respect you. Essential when you need it.

Private matter and public concern

The cut and thrust of water privatisation preparation continued at a chaotic pace, both internally, regionally, and at national level. Long days and nights, press calls unabated, and still very much an unpopular nation-wide political initiative with hostility from all quarters. Despite this the honourable lady from Grantham and her Conservative

Government remained resolute and legislation was progressed through Parliament.

On 6th July 1989, The Water Act, enabling the privatisation of the water industry in England and Wales came into law. Reporting to the Secretary of State for the Environment, the Act also saw the establishment of (i) the National Rivers Authority (later to become part of the Environment Agency) with responsibility for river management, including land drainage, flood protection, and pollution control (ii) the Director General of Water Services (Ofwat) as economic regulator (iii) the Drinking Water Inspectorate with responsibility for regulation of drinking water quality.

This meant that my employer, Severn Trent Water Authority, was now a water and sewerage company and registered at Companies House, along with Anglian Water, Dŵr Cymru (Welsh Water), Northumbrian Water, North West Water, Wessex Water, South West Water, Southern Water, Thames Water, and Yorkshire Water.

On 22 November 1989 Schroders Merchant Bank, on behalf of the Secretaries of State for the Environment and for Wales, offered for sale 2,183 million shares in the 10 water companies at a price of £2.40 per share. At the close on 6 December, the offer was heavily oversubscribed; including 2.65 million applications from the general public in the United Kingdom seeking around 2,900 million shares.

Trading in water company shares began on 12th December 1989. We now had customers, rather than consumers, and shareholders, and regulators, rather than Government. I said to my team at the time that my belief was that the most successful water company would be the most anonymous, and still believe that today. Or as an analyst once said the best reputation would be gained by the water company that manages the wrongs.

Early in January 1990, with the dust still settling from the privatisation process, I had a very brief encounter with someone I hardly knew which was to change my life, and that of my family.

I had a meeting with the Severn Trent Group Finance Director and as I left his office, his secretary casually passed a copy of 'Water Bulletin' magazine to me.

"Surprised you are not interested in that," she said. "In what?" I replied. "the job advert on the back page," she said, and carried on typing. As I was going down the stairs, I glanced at the back page advertisement; *Public Relations Manager South West Water, Exeter base....*

During that day the magazine lay on my desk with no further attention. Driving home my thoughts briefly returned to it but not for long. Why would I be interested in yet another move? I was in a strong position with Severn Trent.

My reputation and profile in the company had grown through the privatisation exercise, great press team, family were settled, and, in any case, why would I want to consider joining a company with such a negative reputation, largely because of a drinking water contamination scare in Camelford, Cornwall in 1988?

End of story. And yet…the magazine was still lying on my desk after several days of honest endeavour. Each night I went to throw it in the bin but didn't. Was there more for me at Severn Trent? Was it time? After all, Jim, my boss, was still a young whip of a thing, so no upward movement possible. I had a lot of Severn Trent mileage on the clock…Been there, done that, got the T shirt…Devon would be a great environment to bring the kids up…time to talk to mentor; Brian, who would go on to be Managing Director of Severn Trent Water.

I told him of my latest thinking and the South West Water (SWW) possibility. He remarked that Severn Trent wouldn't want to lose you. "But, if you are looking at your future career and more experience it could well be a good move. You would be moving to one of the smallest UK water companies from one of the largest.

That creates opportunities. Sharing what you have learned here will benefit you and them. And as for their reputation, what a fantastic

Brian Duckworth Managing Director
Severn Trent Water 1994 – 2004

challenge for a simple Derbyshire lad! But first you've got to get the job!"

We talked as a family about yet another potential move and understandably some concerns but no outright demonstrations. Anyway early in the process. So I submitted my application and waited. Within a couple of weeks I was invited for an interview and sat facing two senior SWW people. They noticed the large expanse of plain white paper under qualifications, and I freely admitted that I did not expect them to appoint me if academic prowess was the criteria. Also they noted that I had recently undertaken psychometric tests with Severn

Trent, and would I mind if they could obtain a copy? Not a bit, I confirmed, but advised that they were not good, and I had got the previous role on reputation and delivery, not ticking boxes.

Psychometric box ticking seemed to me a management cop out. Silence.

I was asked for second interview the following week. It was to be with my potential future boss, Bill Fraser, Managing Director of South West Water. I learned later that it was now a choice between me and a PR Manager from British Airways.

I set off from my Birmingham home early on the morning of the interview but within a mile had a road to Damascus moment and decided to return home. I drove on to the drive, rang the doorbell, and greeted by a puzzled wife.

"Have you forgotten something?" she said.

"No, I said. "Do we really want this job?"

She paused, eyes in the air for a moment, and then said, "Yes, let's go for it!" I then got back in the car and made my way to Exeter. Sounds a bizarre thing to have done but post the privatisation adrenaline, the motivation of wanting to challenge myself again, and the competition of wanting to be offered the role, I had never seriously got my finger out to ask the question, "do I really want it?"

The door step conversation was brief, but the answer cleared the fog. We did want this job. Just after Bristol on the M5 I decided to have a Reginald Perrin moment. No, I wasn't losing the plot, just following an idiosyncratic formula to prepare myself in the best way I knew for the upcoming interview.

I drove off the M5 to Weston-super-Mare, a nearby seaside resort. You can drive straight on the beach there. I parked the car on the sand and, dressed to kill in my navy pin stripe suit, proceeded to stroll on the tidal water's edge of the Bristol Channel and contemplate.

The bucket and spade families were watching, with understandable curiosity at this overdressed, business-attired mans' odd behaviour. Surely business was not that bad. Is he going to do a Reginald Perrin?

Meanwhile I tried to think about all the obvious, awkward, unreasonable, practical, theoretical, questions that could be thrown, and after about 30 minutes got back in the car, all the better for a fresh sea air clearing of the mind. On to Exeter.

With 10 miles to go, the final Smith pre-interview motivational preparation. Loud volume on car sound entertainment system of Elmer

Bernstein's 'Magnificent Seven' film score. Whenever I had a public meeting, difficult media interview, or high-level one-to-one, I always had a fix of the rousing Western theme music to get the adrenaline flowing.

After that I felt I could walk on water, as well as talk about it. Bill Fraser, Managing Director, and my interviewer, was a straight-talking Glaswegian, who had made a name for himself in the Middle East oil and gas industry, and had been hired by SWW, in part because of his reputation for delivering large scale capital programmes on time and cost.

We had a long conversation and I thought it went well. I thought I could work with him, and I sensed he was OK with me. A few days later I was offered the job and I accepted it. Jim the ST boss was disappointed but understood.

I had 3 months' notice to serve and in that time he wanted me to go offline and produce and deliver a 100K budget film for the upcoming first Severn Trent AGM in July 1990.

I showed him the finished article 'We make it work' in a London edit suite on the last day of my employ. He liked it and we went for dinner, him departing north, and me south, and that was the last I was to see of him. Another great water industry guy.

Severn Trent leaving card – so sorry to see me go!

Getting off on the right foot?

I thought the last few years had been challenging, but they were a cakewalk compared to the next five years. OK so I was leaving Severn Trent, the only land-locked water company in the UK and joining South West the water company with the longest coastline, which included Devon, Cornwall, and parts of Somerset and Dorset, with all the regional, national, and international environmental issues and profile that came with it.

A region with the highest concentration of popular UK seaside resorts, beaches, and 83 EU designated bathing waters, with virtually no coastal sewage treatment; 227 crude sewage outfalls scattered across the peninsula spewing human sewage and more into the sea.

Add to that the common issues of every other UK water company; old, leaky, Victorian water mains causing discoloured drinking water, sewerage systems overloaded, and inland sewage treatment works not meeting latest discharge standards.

And if that wasn't enough, a drinking water contamination scare two years before (1988) in Camelford, Cornwall, that had justifiably attracted massive press and media coverage, as well as condemnation from local and national politicians and commentators.

Small wonder that the Editor of the region's most popular daily newspaper, the Western Morning News, likened my appointment to that of the 'Entertainments Officer on the Titanic.' Realistically, we did have a good tale to tell post privatisation. A massive £4 million per week capital investment in water and wastewater services across the South West, including the elimination of unacceptable raw sewage coastal outfalls.

However, the pace of improvements versus cost was to be the big issue, both practically and politically. Trying to put right over a century of neglect and under investment in water infrastructure and all its facets over such a short time period was a herculean task. But cost was the over-riding customer and political issue.

Water bills were set to soar. Dropping on the door mats of one of the smaller water company populations, many retired, and also on fixed incomes. Improvements versus cost was to dominate the South West agenda, and my time, over the next 5 years.

Monday, 16th July 1990.

The start date of my 5-year roller coaster at SWW. [Ominous foreboding? 'Sacrifice' by Elton John was No 1 in the UK pop charts].

Usual time spent meeting the great and the good, particularly my mini team of press support. One experienced press officer and one junior. I needed to talk to the MD about resources going forward if we were going to achieve anything. I had already suggested at a pre start meeting, that we needed more press and media resource support in the team; for which the terse response came, "prove yourself first." Fair enough.

My first day included a 'get to know you' with Bob Baty, Engineering Director, an excellent water industry professional who had joined from North West Water and a really likeable man. We went on to have a great relationship and Bob progressed to be Managing Director and CEO some years later.

Our conversation that morning was very instructive. Bob talked about the massive task of designing and delivering engineering solutions for the coastal clean-up scheme. A two £ billion region wide programme; a critical part of which was communications at the local level. Everyone wanted clean beaches and bathing waters, but no one wanted to live near sewage treatment works and pumping stations, albeit new ones.

So seeking views, understanding concerns, addressing planning issues, and getting permissions, were essential precursors before construction could begin. I had already talked about this with Bill Fraser, MD, at the previous interview session.

As the meeting with Bob was drawing to a close, I asked what the programme was called? He said phlegmatically with classic engineering overtones, "it's called the European Community Designated Bathing Water Marine Compliance Programme." As I was leaving the room I turned and said, " I think we need to work on that Bob."

Two weeks later and following a number of sessions with a design agency in Exeter, the coastal branding was born.

SOUTH WEST WATER

THE CLEAN SWEEP

...lean Sweep is he...

...S AND BATHING WATERS FOR THE SO...

...EWAGE TREATM...

...OVEMENT SCH...

The legalese gone, we now had to make sure that every other aspect of our communications was easy to read and understand, available to all, and importantly targeted at our key audiences, customers, employees, planners, politicians, pressure groups, and owners.

Ironically, two weeks after starting at SWW, and at a high-profile event, I was to come face to face with one loud and effective member of that key audience, 'Surfers against Sewage.' This was a St Agnes, Cornwall based environmental pressure group who had been set up in May 1990 by local surfers, fed up with coastal sewage pollution. They were seen internally as a bit of a rabble-rousing entity who pitched up to cause maximum embarrassment at SWW events but little else. In my early internal briefings I had been made aware of them.

The high-profile event was SWW's first AGM as a private company in Torquay. As at all these type of events there is a sterile and proper atmosphere, exuding a determination to perform to your new owners with high levels of organization, pomp, and confident corporate words. The Board is committed…our strategy going forward…solid base for further growth…in the medium and longer term… etc. So in this scrubbed clean and well-rehearsed atmosphere, the communications team was an essential part. Greeting journalists, ensuring protocol was maintained, arranging media one-to-one interviews with Chairman, MD, Group FD and so on. Meanwhile, in the middle of this polished atmosphere, arrival in the car park of surfers bedecked in wetsuits and surf boards and with an obvious agenda. This was to be my introduction to Surfers Against Sewage. At the time I was a 'suit' talking to a group of shareholders inside the auditorium when the SWW Security Manager tapped me on the shoulder and asked for a couple of minutes.

He spoke in whispered and rather nervous tone of this circus that had just arrived outside the main AGM building, flanked by journalists and TV cameras. They were asking for a SWW representative to talk to before entering the building as bona fide shareholders. I reflected that less than 30 days ago I was 'at the heart of the nation.' Now I was at the heart of swash buckling, wet suited agitators with surf boards. I had a quick decision to make. Do I ignore the outside demonstration, and not give them their well-planned oxygen of publicity, or by doing so, do I create a potential unsavoury AGM mid-meeting outburst with all the embarrassment that would bring?

Decision made. Facing the outside music was preferable to the potential louder and higher profile rendition inside. I stepped outside and with some jostling, was introduced to Chris Hines and Mike Hendy of Surfers against Sewage. Wet suit meets pin-stripe suit. Mike, articulate, and playing to the cameras began the conversation by opening a bulging plastic bag, full of detritus including amongst other things, condoms, sanitary towels, and panty liners. He said it had been collected from local Cornish beaches that morning. I responded and said it was totally unacceptable, but that he could have carried out that same exercise any time over the past 100 years with similar results.

I went on to say that the good news was that we (SWW) were now going to do something about it, as part of the Clean Sweep programme. But it was going to take time. 100 years of shameful neglect was not going to be resolved overnight.

Needless to say Mike and Chris were not impressed, and with irritated shouts of rubbish, they made their way into the AGM auditorium. All this episode filmed By BBC TV Spotlight (South West) News programme and aired later. Had I played it right? Was I pleased with the outcome? Not pleased but satisfied. The confrontation achieved two key things. Firstly, it diffused any potential higher profile confrontation in the AGM auditorium meeting and secondly, I had met

Surfers against Sewage and that gave me an opening to follow up with more serious dialogue about the aims and aspirations of both organizations.

Not so pleased was Chairman, Keith Court. He called me in the following day and said that it was unfortunate that I had chosen to have a spat with SAS particularly in the glare of the TV cameras. I explained the rationale and the potential of condoms, sanitary towels, and panty liners littering the AGM stage during the meeting. He understood but I could tell was a little uncomfortable. Internal stirring maybe.

In the early days of settling in at SWW, one of the high profile and obvious issues was the lasting impact that the Camelford drinking water pollution had on some employees who were part of the workforce at the time.

Two years before, in July 1988, a relief delivery tanker driver had mistakenly tipped 20 tonnes of aluminium sulphate, used in the treatment process at the local treatment works, into the wrong tank, which ultimately went direct into the town's drinking water supply. Local people reported suffering from a range of health side effects and the incident attracted widespread, national, and international press coverage and condemnation.

The customer and political fall-out was understandably volatile and intense. To this day there is controversy over impact and long-term effects. It was something that was for eminent scientists and qualified regulators and health specialists to judge - not for me, although I understood and respected the public reaction.

It happened during my last two years at Severn Trent and the lessons learned not only rippled through the company, but also UK water industry wide. I remembered reading at the time that that there were local and national calls for the Chairman, Keith Court to resign, and a particularly hostile local political, as well as press and media, for him to go. Although the MD, Operations, and Engineering Directors had arrived, like me, after the event, I quickly picked up the internal mistrust of the press and media from some quarters, including the Chairman.

That mistrust spilled over in terms of trying to influence me and who I should watch out for in terms of South West editors and other journalists. Cards were supposedly being marked. Naturally I was having none of it.

If I was going to have a positive working relationship and gain the trust and respect of the regional press and media, I also had to trust them. A fundamental job commitment.

However the internal tension was soon to surface. I needed a quick win to establish my credentials and convince an internal audience that their appointment was right. I got in touch with Derek Lean, experienced local environmental reporter with the Western Morning News, and suggested we meet over a pie and a pint to get to know one another. He readily agreed and I also asked if he had seen the relatively, newly opened Roadford Reservoir in West Devon.

A spectacular and much needed resource that doubled the regions water storage capacity. Amazingly he hadn't. So a couple of days later with Bob Baty, Engineering Director, we gave him a conducted tour. Triple benefit in that Derek got to see the new and impressive water resource and meet Bob Baty, and yours truly. Added value was the promise of a major feature article on Roadford and its regional benefit.

Later that day I arrived back in the office, pleased with how the day had gone. However, in my absence a copy of an email had arrived on my system from the Head of Corporate Affairs to Bill Fraser, my boss. He was complaining that he had gone into the SWW press office earlier that day to find that only the junior was present and that in future we should ensure adequate coverage – in case of an emergency.
School playground stuff but I was livid.

Both myself and the other senior press officer were contactable in an emergency by mobile phone. Bill was underwhelmed. He understood the rationale and my annoyance. If we were going to turn around a lousy reputation it wasn't by sitting on our arses in the Exeter office. I let the Head of Corporate Affairs know my view.

He was the Chairman's man. He had been with SWW for some time and I was told managed most aspects of the aftermath of the Camelford incident and recovery programme. A tall order. He had also closely supported the Chairman through the press and political turmoil and the cries for the Chairman's resignation during this time. It was clear to me that he didn't trust the media.

He let me know early on that he recorded all press calls and that the Western Morning News was not at the top of his popular go-to list. Anyway an individual with an agenda I did not recognise.

My focus was on the task in hand. As if to underline the insignificance of the small-minded episode, a few days later the Western Morning News, then a broadsheet, carried a superb headline, inner-page major story on Roadford Reservoir entitled, 'Jewel in the Crown.'

SWW management team was delighted, and the mark was made. More importantly it was a fitting tribute for all of the engineers and many more who had played their part in its planning and construction.

Today Roadford Reservoir is one of the most popular visitor sites in the South West.

Close to Dartmoor and set in one of the most beautiful areas of the UK, Roadford Reservoir covers almost two square miles and provides vital water supplies to North Devon, and also through releases into the River Tamar system, supplies to Plymouth and parts of South West Devon.

Leisure activities include kayaking, canoeing, paddleboarding and sailing, to archery, climbing, fishing, walking, and cycling. Stephen Spielberg, Hollywood film maker, said of the area, "I have never before, in my long and eclectic career, been gifted with such an abundance of natural beauty as I experienced whilst filming on Dartmoor."

Chapter 11. Clean Sweep is coming...

Following the early settling in session of meeting people, AGM, and press contacts, I began looking seriously at how we were going to approach the huge communications exercise of talking to customers and other key audiences in each of the local areas where the 33 Clean Sweep schemes were planned.

No time for drawn out internal dialogue or prevarication. Instead the creation and implementation of a master plan that could be used to deliver a simple but comprehensive set of honest and clear messages of consultation on what we planned to do and why. No PR – just effective communications. The local problem, the solution, the benefits.

All of this in close cooperation with the project engineers in Bob Baty's team who were responsible for the specific scheme construction and delivery. I needed additional support – and quickly. I went to see the MD, showed him the plan and justification for the appointment of another experienced Press Officer.

He quickly agreed and I contacted Stephen Swain, who worked for me at Severn Trent. He was waiting for a promised call made months earlier when I left Severn Trent. Still interested Steve? Yes. Good. Can you come and meet the MD for dinner next week in Exeter? Yes. Dinner came and went. Stephen appointed.

I remember Bill Fraser quizzing me following the dinner saying he is not an Alan Smith is he? I told him you don't need an Alan Smith; you've already got one. He brings skills that I don't have to the team, that's why we need him. Steve was a fantastic professional who was delighted to be moving his young family from the Birmingham smoke to the idyllic South West.

Over the next 5 years he was to be a key trusted figure in making sure we delivered internally and supported the under-pressure Clean Sweep engineers and the many journalists who were fundamental to us in getting the message out.

Not only talking about the benefits of a Clean Sweep scheme for the local community; the local beaches and bathing waters, impact on the local economy, but also feedback and reaction to potential and often controversial, local sewage treatment sites, and liaison on construction activity.

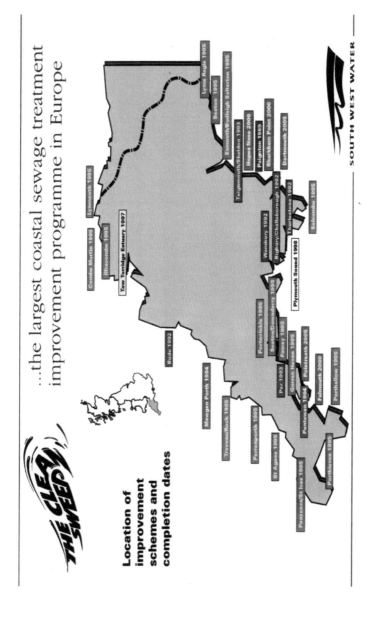

...the largest coastal sewage treatment improvement programme in Europe

Location of improvement schemes and completion dates

THE CLEAN SWEEP

SOUTH WEST WATER

Combe Martin 1995
Ilfracombe 1995
Lynmouth 1995
Taw Torridge Estuary 1997
Bude 1992
Mawgan Porth 1994
Trevone/Rock 1995
Perranporth 1995
St Agnes 1995
Penzance/St Ives 1995
Porthleven 1995
Porthallow 1995
Falmouth 2000
Polstreath 2005
Pentewan 1994
Gorran Haven 1995
Fowey 1993
Par 1993
Seaton/Downderry 1995
Portwrinkle 1995
Plymouth Sound 1998
Bigbury/Challaborough 1992
Thurlestone 1992
Salcombe 1995
Wembury 1992
Teignmouth/Shaldon 1993
Exmouth/Budleigh Salterton 1995
Seaton 1995
Lyme Regis 1995
Kings Nose 2000
Paignton 1989
Shaldon Point 2000
Dartmouth 2005

Surfers against Sewage

In the meantime I had not forgotten the high-profile encounter with Surfers against Sewage (SAS) at the AGM. We needed to talk, and Chris Hines of SAS readily agreed.

We had a great one-to-one conversation in St Agnes away from the cameras and the demonstrations. I said we were singing from the same hymn-sheet. We wanted the improvements just as much as SAS but it couldn't be done overnight.

Going forward we agreed that SAS would meet with SWW directors on regular agreed dates and likewise SAS would extend an invitation to meet with their key people at St Agnes. We could learn from them, and they would be kept up to date with Clean Sweep plans and progress. We both knew that we would not agree all of the time, but better than no understanding.

A positive relationship quickly developed. We talked about what we could do to deter the public from flushing condoms, sanitary towels, panty liners, nappies, baby wipes, down the toilet. The existing 227 crude sewage outfalls spewing poo, pee, and paper on to beaches and bathing waters was disgusting enough, but the other equally unacceptable stuff only exacerbated the problem.

Very soon afterwards a joint SAS/SWW regional "Bag it, Bin it, please don't flush it" campaign was launched, with Seb Coe (now Lord Coe), then a Cambourne MP, Chris Cook SWW, and Chris Hines, fronting the press launch. Following the South West example, many similar initiatives followed across the UK, including a national campaign in 1999. I was pleased with the outcome and new relationship with SAS, particularly the regular dialogue which was to benefit both parties.

After 12 months plus at SWW, we were starting to see the wood from the trees. Our reputation was still grounded in past deeds, but I felt the tide beginning to turn, so to speak. Clean Sweep communications was having a positive local impact with the many interested and diverse stakeholders across the region.

In many respects it was the perfect vehicle for show casing SWW's local, committed, and dedicated water industry operational and engineering people, as opposed to corporate and distant animals at Exeter HQ. Much the same as the SAS dialogue, we needed the community trust and support, as much as they wanted the local improvements.

We were tasked with delivering a massive engineering and environmental programme but equally that could not be done without the participation and endorsement of local people and their planning representatives. That is why I was paranoid about the need to deliver honest and effective communications, as opposed to PR jargon. I hated my job title.

Increases in water bills

The momentum of Clean Sweep in the early 1990's and the coastal improvements being delivered, plus inland treatment, mains and sewer improvements, all part of a £4 million per week investment, led to big increases in customers' bills.

Hikes of 16.2%, 15.8%, and 14% in the three years following privatisation in 1989.

Increases falling on many of the lowest paid in the UK, including pensioners, and others on fixed incomes. The political dimension increased. Privatisation was universally unpopular and linked to the rising bills and board room payouts. Local South West MP's had campaigned for some years on the need for coastal sewage and bathing water improvements but, like all politicians, did not take kindly to the rises in constituency water bills to pay for it.

On one evening I was part of a very lively public meeting in North Devon at which Nick Harvey, the sitting MP attended [he went on to be Minister of State for the Armed Forces]. Following a number of local customer questions, Nick stood up to support the generally hostile atmosphere, with a classic diatribe of political grandstanding, much to the delight of the gathered.

I had to take exception however to his well-received rhetoric on Margaret Thatcher, water privatisation, and an exercise in "selling the family silver." I responded by inviting Nick on a tour of the family silver, which would include sites of old, rusting, Victorian water mains, delivering discoloured tap water, overloaded sewage treatment works, leaking pipes and sewers, and raw coastal sewage outfalls; all in his North Devon constituency. Nick's interpretation of decaying infrastructure as 'family silver' was interesting, I said. There was no response or acceptance of the invite.

Despite the altercation, Nick and I continued to have a very positive relationship during my time with SWW and when I left he was one of a number of MP's who wrote to wish me well in my new venture.

However, this parochial snapshot of political intervention was soon to escalate to a regional and national momentum and profile; the growing and highly charged debate of 'standards versus costs' and who pays?

Local and national media relations

We were now getting to know many of the key editors and journalists in the region, as well as some further afield. The heightened profile of the South West's 'standards versus costs 'debate was catching fire in many different guises. As was always the case, the media fed off the politicians and vice versa.

A number of good journalists stood out in the region. Colin Davison, Editor, George Parker, Political Correspondent, Phil Bowden, reporter, all with the Western Morning News, (George is now Political Editor, Financial Times), Rachael Campey, Editor, Express and Echo, John Ray, Reporter, Radio Devon, (now ITV News Correspondent) and there were more. I talked most frequently to George Parker and John Ray and got to know both of them well. It didn't mean that they were any less professional, and would hit us hard when we deserved it, but they understood the issues, particularly around funding. They knew there was something wrong with 3% of the population paying for the clean-up of 30% of the nation's bathing waters.

John Ray

I first bumped into John when he was a harassed and overworked, relatively junior reporter with Radio Devon. When we first met it was with a degree of formality and protocol, simply because both of our desires was to get rid of each other asap because we had other things to do. So the face-to-face meetings and interviews were hectic and quick-fire, but really enjoyable. He would bustle into my office in Exeter, tie askew, tape machine slung on his half-off jacket shoulder, throw a scruffy press release my way, and ask what the f**k was this all about. Whilst telling him he would be setting up tape to record. I would explain background. Both our view, and other view if appropriate. Press record. Tape our view – then exit office to track down other view. Life on local radio was like that. Too many stories, not enough reporters. John's output was prodigious. I knew he would get on – and he did. He went on to be Political Editor, Westcountry TV, Senior Political Editor, Sky News, and is now ITV News International Correspondent having collected many awards and worked in many countries.

George Parker

A reporter I was told to 'look out for' when joining SWW. George was a sniffer of news stories. When I met him he was Political Correspondent with the Western Morning News. Based in London and often ahead of others in suspecting a story or teasing one out of you if you were not discreet. Like John Ray, I trusted George and liked him and his style. We would often meet in London for dinner and share off-the-record briefings of where we were, and where the political chattering classes were in Westminster. George went on to work for the Financial Times as political correspondent before his latest role as Political Editor. He also presents Radio 4's 'Week in Westminster' and 'What the Papers Say'. More about George later.

As well as local media focus there were often national annual events that would raise the spectre of the state of our beaches and bathing waters – events that would attract national media attention.

One such event was the Marine Conservation Society's (MCS) annual publication on the state of the UK's beaches and bathing waters. The MCS is a fantastic charity that campaigns for a cleaner, better protected, healthier ocean. It did, and still does, great work in highlighting the issues and motivating society to monitor and improve our coastal environment.

However, at the time, it was difficult to get a profile or acknowledgement in their publication of what we were doing, as part of the £1 billion Clean Sweep programme, to significantly improve the regions bathing waters.

I thought it was important that we put that right. And so, on the next annual publication launch, I went to London to attend the MCS press conference. I had no idea when I was stopped at the door that it was by invitation only. I indicated that I was from South West Water, representing Water UK, the trade organization, which was almost true, and I was given a name badge and entrance documents. There were about 50 journalists in the room including the Times, Telegraph, and Independent.

Jonathan Porritt was the consummate guest launcher/presenter, talking through the years findings. Understandably, being in the early 1990's, it was pretty grim with examples of bathing water failures and the unacceptable quality of both ocean and beaches. And yet still no mention of the up-and-coming planned Clean Sweep programme. I judged that he was coming to the end of his presentation, and all journalists were still in attendance and scribbling.

Now was the moment. I stood up, apologized for the interruption, and asked why there had been no mention of the good news that was coming soon in the South West? 33 Clean Sweep schemes, costing over £1 billion, eradicating 227 crude sewage outfalls, improving compliance at 83 designated bathing waters, benefitting the ocean and the local beaches.

There was much shuffling, head turning, and embarrassment at the top table, and some hesitation of how to respond. Jonathan Porritt to the rescue, and graciously confirmed that, thanks to my intervention, it had now been mentioned. The press conference ended, and a gaggle of journalists approached me, asking questions, wanting further information and detail on Clean Sweep and other south west issues.

I was also aware of an MCS representative, from the top table, approaching. A little bruised but very polite he quietly enquired as to how I had got in. Representing Water UK indirectly, was that not OK? I responded. The silence of the response was deafening.

The next day's broadsheet press cuttings did acknowledge, amongst the negatives, that in the South West something of an improvement was planned and underway. Job done.

Chapter 12. Shooting oneself in the foot

West Country Television and SWW - Corporate versus core?
I have never been able to understand why we got involved in a joint bid with Brittany Ferries for the South West ITV franchise in 1991. It was a Group initiative and therefore not funded in any way by the core water business.

The obvious answer was shareholder investment and return. However, the initiative and then the ultimate bid success, stirred customer and political emotions, and not in a helpful way, for the regulated business.

We were trying hard to turn around a negative regional view, based on recent incidents, including Camelford, environmental legacy, and rising customer bills. The news of the of the franchise bid, and the go ahead in 1993, created a welter of negative criticism. It was not difficult to understand why. The obvious perception being that we could buy influence on news output, and as joint owners, look for more favourable coverage. Indeed the Chairman came into my office soon after the bid award and indicated that this relationship would certainly not harm the press office work and activities.

Life might get a little easier. I did not agree and subsequently was to be proved right. The reality was that, in order to be seen to be squeaky clean on impartial SWW news coverage, the Westcountry TV news desk would, if anything, take a harder line.

Integrity and journalistic professionalism demanded nothing less. I am sure on the franchise sale in 1996 the shareholder benefit was realised, but for me in the early 1990's and the hard graft we were doing to reposition the company's reputation, it was a case of shooting oneself in the foot.

From managing - to being the news – a home grown pollution story
The incident was bizarre but, as they say, if you step into the ring, don't be surprised if you get caught with a sucker punch. I didn't see this one coming. We lived in a very rural neck of the woods in a small hamlet just outside Honiton, Devon. A perfect bolthole to retreat to after frenetic days of holding back the media tide and political to-and-fro.

Like many, our recently renovated house, was served by a newly installed septic tank and drainage system. One weekend we were visited by a gentleman who introduced himself as a 'new neighbour' and had I got 5 minutes to look at something.

Apparently he had bought an old barn for conversion below our hillside property and was in the process of building and renovation work, being a builder himself. He took me to the large five metre old stone wall that formed the boundary of our respective properties, located at the bottom of our sloping garden. Oozing out of the wall was a trickle of foul water seepage and I didn't have to get too close to know it must be coming from our septic tank. I apologised and promised I would get it sorted as quickly as possible. He appeared reasonable and content with the undertaking. He was not yet in occupation and still carrying out building works and renovation.

We contacted a specialist local drainage contractor who would visit, investigate, and carry out remedial work. A few days later I got a call from a creepy Exeter Express & Echo local journalist who had been led to believe that I was polluting a neighbour's property. I was taken aback but, for obvious reasons, carefully explained the situation, and that it was being sorted over the next couple of days, and as far as I knew the soon-to-be neighbour was OK with that. The reporter, whose local operating territory was tiny, seemed almost disinterested, and said that he understood, but "as I would appreciate", he had a duty to follow up. I thought that was the end of the matter.

On the Saturday morning I took the kids into Honiton and whilst on a high street stroll towards the local newsagents, I was gobsmacked to see the news-stand outside, sporting, "Water Boss's Home In Pollution Row". Hurried purchase of Express and Echo later, there it was on page three, inside lead story. Never thought I would make page three. Picture of me, taken on my appointment day two years previously, and smiling. Perception of smug polluter. Not helpful. A polluter? Technically Yes. Unknowingly? Yes. Doing something about it? Yes. Big storm in small

84

tea cup? Yes. It's Devon. Not amused but bemused. Classic case of don't let the facts get in the way of a good story.

I went to see Bill Fraser on the Monday morning and briefed him on the story versus the reality. He would see the story in the press cuttings, but I wanted to assure him beforehand that it was one lazy local journalist taking an opportunity.

He was underwhelmed but sharply said that I had better get whatever was the cause fixed right away. It was. No other regional press or media outlet picked up the story or decided to run with it. And the moral of the story for the local journalist? Decide what is and is not the reality versus a good story. And of course is in your best interests or not.

Otherwise you may find that interesting press releases relating to your local territory, suddenly slip down the fax machine order, or don't appear at all. Unreliable fax machine and an unreliable reporter.

As an afterthought, I often wonder if that neighbour was trying to settle a score because I had objected to an unrealistic planning application a few weeks before? But now I'm getting small minded…

Chapter 13. Clean Sweep delivering…

By 1993 Clean Sweep schemes benefitting local beaches and bathing waters had been delivered in Thurlestone, Bude, Seaton, Bigbury, including Challaborough, and the Teign Estuary, with many more to come. Interestingly the first, and one of the smallest, Thurlestone, at £1.5 million, and the latter, Teign Estuary at £50 million and one of the largest, highlighted the Clean Sweep story and its diverse regional impact and benefit.

Thurlestone was one of the first and smallest local populations to benefit. So why first? Because it had a fantastic reputation for bringing their unsatisfactory and long-standing sewage pollution problem to national prominence and profile. A courageous pain in the backside to everyone and anyone who could possibly support and help to remedy the village's environmental plight.

Like most of the coastal settlements it enjoyed many seasonal visitors to its picturesque, but polluted, local beaches in Thurlestone and nearby South Milton.

The source of pollution was raw sewage spewing from a cliff face drain installed over 60 years ago. One of 227 raw sewage outfalls in the region. In the 1980's, the local parish council, under the stewardship of clerk, Bill Ladd, demanded improvements, holding high profile public meetings, petitions, and erection of unpopular local beach warning signs, attracting national media attention.

'Warning – Raw sewage outfall – Swimming from this beach may damage your health!'

The protests worked and in 1990, soon after privatisation and a Thurlestone visit, Chairman Keith Court set in train the new improvement scheme.

Once completed Thurlestone and South Milton, could now add clean and safe bathing waters to the already picturesque and beautiful local coastal landscape.

Teign Estuary received unacceptable raw sewage discharges at various locations for many years, including Teignmouth, a seaside resort

Teign Estuary sewage treatment scheme

SOUTH WEST WATER

at its mouth. The local population benefitting from the £50 million Clean Sweep scheme totalled around 100,000. The scenic estuary had a colourful history of fishing, including an EC designated shell fishery, beaches and bathing waters, SSSI's, and a local port. Add to that treated wastewater from Newton Abbott discharging into the estuary, it presented both environmental and engineering challenges. With such a large population, the SWW communications had to be thorough and reach many different stakeholders.

Local liaison committees were quickly formed, and we also published regular 'Teign-Scene' update magazines, talked to schools, and other interested groups, boat owners, fishermen, local politicians; in fact everyone who had either a vested or casual interest.

Generally we were well received, and my sense was that we surprised a few who had previously been critical and maybe cynical about our local commitment. Bad reputations were easily made, good had to be earned.

In the autumn of 1993, the scheme was officially opened by TV botanist and environmental campaigner, Dr David Bellamy. Over 33,000 invitations were sent to local residents and schools for the opening events. Talking was one thing, the satisfaction of delivering was another.

Chapter 14. Jamaica

In the meantime…talking of relationships…around that time I got a visit from a senior SWW manager who asked if I had been contacted by a chap called Andrew Joss?

Apparently Andrew had recently been appointed as Business Development Manager with Pell Frischmann Water, at the time a joint venture with Pell Frischmann, engineering consultants, and SWW plc. "He is a newcomer and will try to pick your brains about what we do and how we do it. I should tell him to go forth and multiply if I was you." Thankfully he wasn't me.

Cor Jelier DHV

A couple of days later a polite bespectacled Andrew Joss knocked on my office door. He explained his newly created role. It was to promote and market our expertise in water and waste water services, both nationally and overseas, outside of the regional regulated business, and through the joint venture partnership. I gave him an overview of my views and the way we operated, and he left thanking me for my time. The following week he asked if I would meet Cor Jelier, a Dutch Engineering Director from DHV International, who was located in Devon, and had seen the Clean Sweep communications which struck a chord in relation to what DHV was currently planning for the Caribbean.

I met Cor and showed him more of the strategy behind our communications and he explained the rationale for his interest. The National Water Commission of Jamaica (NWC) had obtained Japanese funding for the construction of a much-needed new sewage treatment and upgraded sewerage scheme for Montego Bay, the fastest growing urban centre in Jamaica. Significant local flooding and pollution of the environment, including precious coral reefs, had led to new and urgent proposals.

DHV was bidding for the design consultancy role. Eager to be different and to provide added value in their international bid, Cor was interested in SWW becoming a sub-contractor and providing a proposal for a communications strategy for the planned scheme, should the DHV bid be successful. Bill Fraser MD and Andrew were keen to go ahead, and Bill called me in. He asked me to support Andrew in drawing up a communications proposal to be included in the DHV bid.

Also if the Bid was successful would I be prepared to go to Jamaica to carry out a fact-finding study and subsequently deliver a recommended communications strategy for the National Water Commission of Jamaica? It took me two seconds to say Yes. And shortly after, began an experience of my life I would never forget.

Jamaica – for real mon!

Amidst all of the regional scramble and activity at Exeter HQ came news that DHV International had won the bid for design and delivery of a new and major wastewater treatment scheme for Montego Bay, Jamaica.

Two weeks later I was on a flight with Andrew Joss to Norman Manley Airport, Kingston, the islands capital, to meet up with Cor Jelier.

We met briefly with Claude Stewart, President of the National Water Commission (NWC), before making the bumpy 100 miles road journey across the island from the Kingston capital in the South East to Montego Bay in the North West. Cor had worked for some time on the island so was a mine of information.

Pulling together a communications strategy for a culture totally foreign to me was to be one of the biggest challenges of my career, and I had little or no time to display 'L' plates.

During a hectic week I spoke with anyone and everyone who could give me an insight into the island and its people. Government officials, local community, local press, hoteliers, NWC employees, both engineering and operational professionals at the sharp end. And of course those who opposed the proposed scheme. The local people were fantastic, welcoming, and friendly; the island's infrastructure was appalling.

Montego Bay sewage treatment works had not been fit for purpose for some time, overrun, and not designed to cope with the flows generated from rapid and further planned growth. Local sewers were overloaded causing flooding and ocean pollution, a real threat to the sensitive coral reefs and the marine life.

However, locally, the planned preferred solution was almost as controversial as the flooding and pollution. I had already picked up the tension between the capital, Kingston, and its noisy, independently minded, North-West neighbour. If approved, it would mean the creation and implementation of stabilization ponds over a vast 60 plus acres of existing prime sugar cane production fields. The fields would be compulsory purchased by the NWC if negotiations for sale could not be agreed.

Stabilization ponds were used world-wide in hot climates and were low energy and environmentally very effective, in producing high quality treated water – so essential for the local marine environment and coral reefs. The process includes passing crude untreated sewage slowly through several man-made large pond stages, during which with the sun provides a natural ultra violet disinfection before safely discharging to the environment.

The alternative option of a traditional European type of mechanical plant, albeit on a much smaller footprint, brought with it much higher maintenance and energy costs, as well as heavy reliance on overseas imported mechanical and electrical equipment. Not the best use of the islands hard earned foreign exchange.

So in a nutshell there was the challenge. To create an effective and open communication strategy that would not only talk to all interested parties about the improvements that were coming, but to persuade a doubting local community of the NWC's best intentions and preferred option for Montego Bay and its sensitive and precious environment.

Negril - going Jamaican – and lingering longer

In our early fact-finding journey we stayed overnight in Negril, probably as close to heaven as you are going to get. 50 miles south west of Montego Bay, it has the most glorious seven-mile stretch of golden sand and crystal-clear Caribbean Sea. To say nothing of the marine blue skies and the ever-present golden sunshine. Paradise. Aptly named Foote Prints, the small hotel where we were staying was literally right on the beach.

Very early the following morning I decided to take full advantage and stroll along the deserted beach before breakfast and onward journey. Ambling slowly along, kicking the sand, and thinking about the communication practicalities, I was aware that someone was following me, hidden in the ferns and palm trees that skirt the beach. I stopped and so did the rustling. I continued and there it was again. After a few moments there was also a psst…psst…psst…I was thinking of communications and bizarrely so was someone else.

Stiff upper lip, and all that, I stopped and shouted 'hello?' The ferns parted and an individual with large brown eyes encircled by Rastafarian dreadlocks, asked in a hushed voice, 'do you want any shit mon?' To which I replied, 'thanks, but at the moment I'm up to the neck in it' "Where did you get it?" said my fellow early morning stroller. "Montego Bay," I said, and with that both me and the would-be therapeutic retailer went our different ways. On the way back to the hotel I mused that any attentive passer-by might have thought we were in the same business.

We returned to the UK, and I wrote up my findings and recommendations. Two weeks later I was back in Jamaica presenting the proposed communications strategy to the National Water Commission Board in Kingston.

The proposed corporate branding for the islands long term coastal sewage treatment improvement programme would be 'Clean Sweep for Jamaica;' the first of which being 'Clean Sweep for Montego Bay.' Further similar schemes were planned for Ocho Rios and Negril.

The recommendations included a comprehensive and detailed programme of specific events and communication activities to be carried out in the Montego Bay community prior to planning go-ahead, and during the construction phase. Also training for NWC PR employees in the UK.

The NWC Board agreed the approach, strategy, and plans. A date was set for the launch in Montego Bay a month later, followed by UK training for the NWC PR Manager. I returned to the UK. Job done.

Back in a busy Exeter press office on the following Monday morning, I was called in by Bill Fraser. He said he had just had a telephone call from Claude Stewart, President of the National Water Commission, Jamaica. Bill said that Claude was really pleased with the presentation and approach the previous week.

I said that I had got the same impression. I was about to walk out when Bill added, "He wants to know if I would approve you going out there for the next three or four weeks to project manage implementation and delivery of your proposals. He is not confident that the current NWC PR team will be able to manage it."

The next day I was back on a plane bound for the island again. Ably supported by Cor Jelier with all of the technical information input, I worked with the willing Kingston HQ PR team to deliver the many facets of the strategy. To guarantee delivery on time, some of the material, exhibition boards, information leaflets, had to be produced by local Exeter design house, AB Graphics and shipped to Jamaica. The 4500 miles delivery from Exeter to Norman Manley Airport was not a problem. The 10 miles journey to collect from the Airport was.

'Soon come' was a delightful if not at times frustrating Jamaican expression which meant, 'No I haven't done it yet.' Muggins would do it.

The launch date in Montego Bay was fast arriving. I was also asked to put together the press launch and public meeting presentations for the NWC Chairman, Dr Wayne Reid, and President, Claude Stewart, and coach both men through slide presentations and delivery rehearsals.

Invitations to the public meetings, press advertisements, releases, employees magazines, leaflets, and more were all in production. Claude Stewart, President, was always anxious to be kept up to date.

I would get a message from his secretary to say that 'Mr Stewart would like an outdoor conference update later today', which meant meet him at the Half Moon Golf Club in Montego Bay and brief him over a round of golf at the Bond film location of 'Live and Let Die' – tough but somebody had to do it.

By now I was becoming Jamaican. I got on famously with the NWC team and we worked well together. They were the most engaging people, from the Board room to the sharp end operatives at remote treatment works.

But inevitably, as in any country, there was a dark side. By this time, thanks to Cor's guidance, I was finding my own way around the island. I was warned that there were places not to go alone and what to do in certain situations. Whilst I was on the island a visiting European Community official had, by accident, driven into and damaged, a rural roadside jerk chicken stand. He was killed (or slain as the Kingston daily newspaper put it) by an angry crowd after making the mistake of stopping.

On an earlier visit I had also been in Jamaica at General Election time – always a charged and tense atmosphere in terms of law and order and unsavoury incidents.

Occasionally, walking from the Kingston HQ offices of the NWC back to my nearby Hotel late in the day and about ½ a mile away, I would be approached by an individual who would say he would walk with me make sure that I got back to my hotel safely.

To refuse was a dangerous option. You were expected to pay him for the uninvited security. I always had money, about 200 Jamaican dollar notes (about £1) rolled in my pocket and ready to hand over after arriving at hotel security. You didn't argue or try to barter. You might see him the next day. And it might not be pleasant.

Smith and the spliff…

On a lighter note, at the end of a working week, Cor would often suggest that we spend the weekend in Negril at the famous Foote Prints, scene of the therapeutic retailer. On this particular day Cor also wanted to show me the Negril sewage treatment works which was badly in need of a Clean Sweep renovation upgrade.

Located about 1 mile inland we drove down a dusty, unmade, crater ridden, track and called in to see the local NWC treatment works superintendent who appeared from his works shack.

He complained about lack of replacement pumps and other spares. Because of this he said, raw sewage arriving at the works inlet was by-passing essential treatment processes before discharging, untreated, into the local river and ultimately polluting pristine local bathing waters.

Another practical example, Cor remarked, of why the Montego Bay proposals of stabilization ponds, versus mechanical plant, was the best option.

At the works it was hot, humid and very dry. I was distracted from the conversation by the roar of a tanker lorry coming from the direction of the track we had just negotiated.

In an almighty cloud of dust and sand resembling a Laurence of Arabia scene, the diesel beast bumped its way towards the works inlet, before juddering to a hand brake halt a couple of metres away from me.

It was Leroy. He told me he was responsible for emptying private sewage tanks from local hotels and restaurants in Negril and bringing the spoils to the works for treatment and safe disposal. As he dropped the lorry's discharge hose into the inlet works I did mention that I thought the pump that lifted the raw sewage to the treatment stages was not working.

Leroy said he knew that but carried on anyway. An irony in that he had worked hard that morning taking sewage away from posh ocean side resorts, only for that same sewage to find its way via the river, flowing into the ocean, close to where he had collected it from.

Cor was still engaged in technical talk with the superintendent. Meanwhile Leroy had clambered back into his lorry cab and, as I looked up to continue our casual conversation, I couldn't help noticing that he had just set fire to what appeared to be a tightly rolled up white handkerchief and was smoking it.

I was later told by Cor this was in fact a spliff. Which explained why I was beginning to feel very relaxed as I chatted to Leroy amidst the pall of white smoke emitting from his cab.

I pondered later that not many spliff smokers would choose to hallucinate at a sewage treatment works, whilst on a lunch time break emptying sewage tanks.

Leroy and me…

……discharging sewage before discharging spliff….

Clean Sweep Launch in Montego Bay

The big day arrived. Early morning presentation rehearsals with the Chairman and President, followed by the actual press launch, and later the packed public meeting.

I witnessed at first hand the local and national level of interest. The events were standing room only and from my, and more importantly the NWC's perspective, they went well. Employees and other groups were briefed on the same day.

From understanding and communicating local plans and issues, to seeing them successfully carried out 4500 miles away from my Exeter base, was really satisfying. A later message from the President sent to Exeter HQ confirmed the NWC's view.

Dear Alan all factors considered I have to agree that the Forum (launch) went quite well. This, however, was due (in no small way) to your assistance and on behalf of the Chairman and the Management and Staff of the National Water Commission, I would like to offer our sincere thanks for your support.

Overall there is now a better acceptance of the (stabilisation) 'Ponds' from the citizens of Montego Bay and certainly a lot of the controversy and misunderstanding has been cleared up. I graciously give you an opportunity to even the score by inviting you to participate in an 'outdoor conference' scheduled for December in Montego Bay. Once again our sincere thanks to South West Water for their assistance in our Clean Sweep campaign,

Yours sincerely,

Claude B Stewart

President, National Water Commission Jamaica

My last day on the Jamaica project, before flying home, was memorable. Cor said he knew of a little-known beach near Kingston which was predominantly used by the local community, and far from the popular tourist trail. True enough it was idyllic. A natural sun-kissed sandy cove with a few Jamaican families enjoying the day.

After a stroll taking in the environmental sights and sounds, and reflecting on the previous day's events, Cor said this is where we have lunch. There was nothing there. No cafeteria, beach restaurant, or jerk chicken stand.

Nothing.

"Where?" I said.

Here look, on the beach," Cor said. "This is the restaurant."

The only semblance of anything in sight was a rusted set of corrugated roofing sheets. This was the restaurant. Really? We approached the makeshift shack, to be greeted by a beaming, diminutive, Jamaican who obviously knew Cor and gave him the traditional lung squeezer and slap on the back.

He invited us into the corrugated café. Below was the beach floor, above blue sky, charred cooking pot on a driftwood burning grill, and an unstable table and bench, half buried in sand. I tried hard to keep up with the conversation, struggling with patois phrases and humorous exchanges.

A boy entered with freshly caught fish still showing signs of life and caught from his nearby rocky outcrop perch overlooking the ultramarine ocean.

The supply chain was more efficient than a Michelin 5 star. Sky was the only overhead. 15 minutes later we were eating. 30 minutes later I had enjoyed one of the most delicious, natural meals ever.

The ingredients? Take 4 sheets of corrugated roofing, add locally grown bench and table, insert cooking pot, driftwood and grill, spear fresh fish, cook gently by smiling Jamaican host, under a cloudless blue sky.

Simple.

Chapter 15. Rising bills – rising tide of anger

Back in the UK the level of hostility was growing in the face of steep SWW billing increases. It was now being talked about at national as well as regional level. I was uneasy. Over simplistically, I was always told that the water sector model following privatisation was that legislators and regulators set the rules and standards, we delivered them, and the customer paid.

If you like, a regulated contractor delivering on behalf of the client/ customer. Never mind about the politics, I was never comfortable with the rationale. The customer had not been asked about the level or pace of improvements, nor the affordability.

After all Government had clearly said they could not afford it, hence privatisation. Not for the first or last time, politicians of all colours and persuasions had got themselves into the most almighty fix. Talking to many of them in the South West, either directly or through the press and media, they all agreed that the improvement programme, particularly on the coast, was both necessary and long overdue.

They also agreed that the level of the billing increases was too much to bear for many of the hard-pressed low-income families. None of them agreed on a practical solution. It was a buggers muddle.

We met and briefed MP groups and individual MP's on a regular basis. Perhaps the most bizarre was the regular gathering of West Country Conservative MP's in the House of Commons, the largest political party representation in the South West. Bear in mind that we had been invited, and supposedly they were keen to learn of the latest plans and progress, and how they would be affecting local constituencies.

It was an utter shambles. MP's would arrive late, go early, continuously pass paper notes to each other, whisper behind cupped hands. It was like making a presentation in Tesco's. I recalled I had more attention and good manners whilst talking to 5-year-olds about Willie the Waterman, Ronnie the Riverman, and Sam the Sewageman. In fact if I had digressed into the Watermen adventures, few of the MP's would have noticed.

I knew the game. The reality was that the majority were there, for whatever period of time, to say to constituents that they had attended, and therefore justified subsequent press releases like "MP demands answers from SWW." These political charades were easy meat for electioneering but gave no comfort to locals looking for real answers.

I recall, in particular, Simon Hughes, London Liberal Democrat MP, who was electioneering in the South West on behalf of local Party MP's, calling at various coastal resorts and attracting cheap press and media coverage with anti SWW rhetoric. Need for targeted response. I quickly found out his next port of call and ahead of his visit, issued a proactive press release calling him out, and talking about positive Clean Sweep improvements and criticizing unhelpful statements.

On arrival at the next constituency stop, he was on the back foot and faced a forewarned media asking legitimate questions raised from my release. Realising the ambush, he contacted our Chairman, demanding that I be immediately dismissed. Following our next day morning meeting, Bill Fraser said "Oh by the way, Simon Hughes wants you fired" as I was walking out of his room, but obviously not for the last time. I think the expression I used at the time was "like being savaged by a dead sheep."

Meanwhile, with no real sign of tangible help from the political fraternity in the South West or Westminster into cushioning the blow of significant local billing increases; Bill Fraser once described their efforts as 'sympathy and support but no success,' we ventured to Brussels to meet a delegation of senior EC officials.

Our approach was to focus on European financial support from something called the EC Cohesion funds. This was a pot of potential financial support used to help poorer regional economic areas of the Community. Spain, Portugal, Greece, and Southern Ireland had already successfully applied and benefitted.

We cited Cornwall's economy as comparable to those previously benefitting. Economically the poorest county in the UK, high unemployment, low wages, many fixed income families, including pensioners and the seasonal self-employed. Again our journey was tea and sympathy.

Brussels bureaucrats listened but offered little else. It was emphasized that the EC Cohesion Funds were not available to private companies, even with our guarantees of transparency and openness as to where any potential support funding could and should be directly targeted.

Hot air and inertia continued to dominate the debate in the region and nationally. No apparent Governmental appetite to lobby either our EC friends in Brussels or press the Treasury for priority additional funding. I respected the Liberal Democrats who punched above their representative weight in campaigning for regional financial help.

However the likes of Paul Tyler, Matthew Taylor, Nick Harvey and others were in the enviable political position of banging the drum for both improvements and billing restraint at the same time. The noise was appreciated, but the net result in terms of a solution was nil.

The Tory wing became unusually becalmed on the 'standards v costs' matter, and there were briefings from Ministers to local Tory MPs to tone down the additional funding clamour, arguing that the rest of the country should not subsidise the South West. Their counter argument being what about nitrate elimination in the East, or collapsing industrial sewers in the North West? Are they not a special case for subsidy or additional funding? An unsympathetic and unbalanced economic argument against special South West treatment but it had legs for the Government in the debate.

In all of the political fog Keith Court, Chairman, was summoned by Michael Howard, then Secretary of State for the Environment, to a meeting in London. It was relatively short, and sharp. In summary the message was, "we will look after the politics; you get on with delivering what you're supposed to deliver." Close to, but perhaps not altogether, 'of the night', but an unmistakeable and unambiguous warning to keep out of the political fray. I was getting increasingly frustrated and annoyed with the political noise and posturing and lack of any solution.

So was another SWW Director. We decided to further investigate the possibility of lobbying the Government, despite Michael Howard. This is where the relationship with George Parker and John Ray proved helpful. We could not help but notice the success of another key regional player, Plymouth based Royal Devonport Dockyard, owned by DML, in securing the Government's lucrative contract to refit the Trident Royal Navy nuclear submarines.

They had carried out a long and successful political campaign, despite strong competition and political opposition from Scottish arch rivals Rosyth Dockyard. We needed the same tenacity. Following enquiries, we were told that the Plymouth Dockyard had received excellent and critically important campaign support from a London based lobbying organization, Rowland Sallingbury Casey (part of Saatchi & Saatchi).

We met them for dinner in London. John Maples, former Economic Secretary to the Treasury, and Chairman of Saatchi and Saatchi, and John Bercow, Director of RSC, and future House of Commons Speaker, were in attendance.

Following considerable briefing on South West's 'standards versus costs' dilemma and the impact on water bills, they believed we had a strong case for further Government funding. A couple of days later I met with John Ray, now with Westcountry Television. He told me that the additional Government funding potential was actively being discussed at ministerial level but that Michael Portillo (then Chief Secretary to the Treasury) was not in favour of making the South West a special case. An irony here in that fancy pants went on to meet local people in a TV walking 'pilgrimage' across Devon and Cornwall, lauding its beauty and landscape. The same special appreciation failed to show from his Treasury wallet.

All of the discussions that we had remained discreet, bearing in mind the feeble SWW Board neutrality position, reinforced by the Howard intervention. However the lid really did blow following a London meeting I had with George Parker.

We chewed the fat and I told him where we had got to in terms of current Government funding exploration. He could tell that I was not feeling optimistic. He still believed there was a case. Little did I know what was to follow. After the meeting with George, I stayed overnight in London, for lunch and catch up meeting the next day with Charles Clover, Environmental Editor, Daily Telegraph.

The following morning I was about to exit the hotel room for breakfast when the phone rang. It was Bill Fraser.

"Have you seen the f*****g Western Morning News this morning?" Holding the phone a little further from my ear I said no, I was still in London and due to meet Charles Clover.

"Well, the front-page headline reads, *You've got to help us Mr Major,* and I've got a ******* Board meeting today."

"Who's done the story?" I said. I had an inkling.

"George Parker, have you seen him recently?" asked Bill.

"Yes," I said, "in fact yesterday. Just briefed George on the Clean Sweep scheme programme and where we were."

I used to be a chorister and that experience helped wonderfully well with my tone, bordering on self-righteous unawareness and innocence of 'surely not me Gov.'

Bill faced the Board later that day and I understand the article was discussed. Meanwhile, I rang George to thank him for the support. He was as phlegmatic as ever.

"I write the story and as you know, it's up to others how they headline it, and where they put it." A short time later George was to write another water piece. This one I could have done without.

We agreed to meet and brief the South West's Liberal Democrat MP's in London. Included from SWW was Keith Court, Chairman, Bob Baty, Engineering Director, and myself. As you would expect the Lib Dem's tipped off the press about the briefing. We were relaxed about it and agreed to do a press update after the meeting.

It was very informal and attended by a small number of London based journalists from South West TV and press. When it broke up, two of the journalists wanted a further one-to-one interview with Bob Baty.

George Parker was one, and BBC TV (Spotlight) the other. Spotlight had a lunch deadline, so TV went first. I apologized to George but said I would firstly go with Bob to "mind" the BBC TV interview on nearby College Green, close to the Houses of Parliament and get back straight after. George was relaxed and said he would wait.

As I was apologizing, Keith Court appeared from the meeting room and said that he would "look after" George and answer any queries.

I knew that of all the senior SWW guys, Keith would be the last I would want left alone with a press scribe, especially as experienced and canny an operator as George. I was between a rock and a hard place and had no choice. Or say something that might humiliate the Chairman.

I hurriedly returned from the 'Spotlight' interview just as they were wrapping up and shaking hands. George had got his exclusive.

The following morning Western Morning News was running with a story that quoted the Chairman as saying despite billing increases, the South West was generally affluent, and affordability was not a key issue.

What a pain in the arse. Reputations are built over a long time but ruined over a short time - in this case 20 minutes.

Meanwhile, the final, if unsatisfactory answer to the seemingly intractable standards versus costs dilemma was about to happen. But first...

Chapter 16. A Jamaican visitor

Part of the contract with the NWC of Jamaica was UK training for members of the PR team. Their senior PR Manager arrived in Exeter following the Clean Sweep launch in Montego Bay several weeks before. She was, like most Jamaicans, a larger-than-life character, exuded confidence, and was excited by a first time UK visit. Midway through her training programme, I arranged to take her to London for a one-day seminar at BAFTA, Piccadilly on 'Effective Promotions and Publicity,' followed by a visit to the House of Commons, and then to a West End show in the evening. Her enthusiasm shone through on the first morning of our London visit.

We arrived at the BAFTA seminar, and, as usual with these things, coffee was provided at registration before an early morning start. True to UK form the clanking of coffee cups at reception was louder than early morning small talk, with blank pasty faces and un-Jamaican lack of conversation. I could tell my visitor was buzzing and keen to get into the auditorium to hear the first speaker. We duly filed in with the squeaking of tipping seats and a funereal atmosphere.

The first speaker was announced with brief bio introduction. Two or three hollow claps from the 150 gathered delegates as he came to the lectern. He mumbled a monosyllabic 'Good morning' whilst arranging his lecture papers.

From towards the rear of the auditorium someone sitting next to me bellowed a hearty retort. 'GOOD MORNING AND WELCOME MR BROWN!' My Jamaican friend was determined that she, if no others, was going to show her enthusiasm for 'effective promotions.' I pondered later that she was in the UK to learn, although many of the head-turning gathered could have taken a leaf from her resounding and impactful, participative playbook.

Seminar over and, following a brief visit to the House of Commons, we looked forward to attending Rogers and Hammerstein's, 'Carousel' in front of a sell-out 1400 plus audience at the Shaftesbury Theatre in the West End. Briefly the musical follows the raucous, haphazard life of fairground worker Billy and his romance and love for pretty millworker, Julie.

Tragically an unlawful exploit leads to his demise. However he is given a one-chance return to earth opportunity to see his beloved Julie for the last time. Captured in a ghostly hologram light, Billy is pleading with Julie, who is reminiscing in her porch rocking chair, for forgiveness and pledging undying love…a hushed capacity audience.. you could hear a pin drop…until, that is, a young Jamaican lady from the dress circle offered advice to Billy in authoritative and firm tone.…

'TOO LATE NOW…IT'S TOO LATE NOW…'

The swivel of heads sideways and backwards to the seat occupied by my very good friend was instant. I melted further down into my comfortable circle seat, feeling distinctly uncomfortable.

It was not the right moment to explain to the 1400 head turners that if you have not seen a theatre production in Jamaica, which I had, you will not know that often there is more participation and dialogue off the stage, than on it.

Living the production, and articulating that living, is part and parcel of Jamaican theatrical culture and tradition. Not sure it would gain traction in the less participative West End.

Swan song to Jamaica

In between Clean Sweep, standards versus costs, Government funding, political posturing, the work that I had been involved with and the people I had met in Jamaica was so refreshing and motivating.

It might have continued but ended abruptly. We had been invited to bid for a major European Community-funded institutional strengthening contract, which would benefit the National Water Commission of Jamaica, its people, policies, and working practices.

A 3-year contract which would involve the transfer of UK knowledge and expertise in the running of a water utility from the sharp end to Board level, and involve engineering, operations, science, finance and regulatory input.

If we were successful in the contract bid, SWW had asked me to be project manager and to live on the island for the duration of the contract.

Relocation for the family and Jamaica beckoned. Essentially managing the programme of individual professional input and delivery sourced from the UK, and the contract progress and impact within the NWC.

After a lot of family deliberation, we agreed to put my name forward. SWW had to be in a strong position to win the contract. Our work on the island had not gone unnoticed by the European Community boffins and we had very positive professional and personal relationships with the NWC management team and staff. There were rival bids by Thames Water International, Severn Trent International, South Staffordshire Water, and two other European utilities.

SWW was unsuccessful. Thames Water International (TWI) won the tender bid with a seemingly below cost number.

We knew they were keen to establish a base in the Caribbean and so this particular vehicle provided that opportunity. Were they ultimately successful in moving the NWC forward? All I can say is that within a few years of their involvement, a further institutional strengthening contract was up for grabs on the island. Say no more.

And so my potential elevation to Jamaican citizenship and being a permanent islander was not to be. I knew that the NWC was looking forward to continuing the established positive working relationships and really disappointed that we had not won.

However the financials were obviously key. He who pays the piper, and the EU funding rules were rightly followed and executed. So no more 'outdoor conferences'….no more banquets on the beach, served in a corrugated cornucopia….no loaves but two fishes…no spliffs at sewage works…

Making a late bid…

One final humorous anecdote relating to the normally boring and tedious bidding process for the 3-year contract. Humorous that is if you didn't work for Seven Trent Water International.

After months of hard work putting the tender bid together…
...nominating key personnel who would input into the programme ..training capabilities…actual courses devised, planned, explained, drafting…all aided and abetted by supporting operational, scientific, engineering, regulatory colleague input…and finally costing…there is one further drop dead, no-brainer question.

Q. How do we get the very professional and detailed comprehensive tender document to Kingston, Jamaica.

A. I know, send it by courier. What about DHL, absolutely fine.

Q. When is it due in?

A. Deadline is 12 noon on Monday so let's send the previous week. Mission complete. DHL handed package, then package flown 4604 miles. Arrives several days before 12 noon deadline at….wait for it…Norman Manley International Airport, Kingston. The respite location of my exhibition boards and many a parcel flown in from overseas. After such a strenuous journey the package rests…and rests…and rests…and rests…and rests…and rests…get the picture?...

Meanwhile the ultra-sensible and goody-two shoes Andrew Joss and Alan Smith deliver SWW tender document by hand to NWC HQ two hours before 12 noon tender submission deadline, having flown in the night before to speak at the Annual Caribbean CWWA Conference in Kingston that week.

Joss and Smith attend the NWC tender opening ceremony at 12.00 noon. All bids from companies expressing interest received and formally confirmed by NWC……except Severn Trent Water…..?

Look of surprise on all attendees faces at the tender opening ceremony except A Smith who knew exactly where it was. "Soon come," I whispered to Andrew. Sure enough the Severn Trent package arrived 45 minutes after the tender deadline, delivered by sweating DHL airport-based courier.

Bid not allowed. Moral of the story, there is airmail, 1st class, 2nd class, and 'soon come.'

Finally I recollected the pearls of wisdom from my Jamaican guest to Billy in London…**"too late now…it's too late now."**

Chapter 17. Standards versus costs – political deadlock - and the Del Boy fix

In the midst of the political fog SWW carried out a comprehensive 'Water-Your Views?' customer consultation which included MORI market research, 60,000 leaflet/questionnaires distributed, region-wide public meetings, schools participation packs, and more.

Customer views were captured in a Market Plan which was submitted, along with our detailed long-term plans, to the Director General of Water Services (Ofwat) in the Spring of 1994 for his deliberation.

This exercise was known as the 'Periodic Review' of the England and Wales water companies, including performance, obligations, and importantly the setting of customer charges for the next 5 years (1995-2000). It didn't take Einstein to work out the findings from our customers.

Yes, customers wanted an end to untreated coastal discharges, but the pace and cost was a real issue; water resources security and treatment was also a priority, and old water mains renewal and the elimination of lead service pipes was considered important.

Concern was expressed on river water quality and the need for improvement, along with reduction in flooding, including storm and sewer overflows.

In summary, overwhelming support for improvement programmes across all water and wastewater services, an acknowledgement that the '100 years of neglect' was a driver in the changes that had to happen, but pace and billing affordability was key to many customers.

They also felt it unfair that the costs of the massive Clean Sweep improvement programme was falling on a tiny population of bill payers, compared to the many more millions who enjoyed South West beaches and bathing waters from across the UK and beyond.

How to square the circle? A long overdue £2 billion capital investment programme improving the regions water and wastewater services but falling on a population struggling to afford it. Particularly the £1 billion Clean Sweep improvements, accelerated by a Government not paying for it.

Time for basic 'standards v costs' facts:

FACT: **1985** - 133 European Community (EC) Designated Bathing Waters identified by the Government in the South West.
- almost $1/3^{rd}$ of the overall total in England & Wales.
- no Government commitment to invest to comply with the EC Bathing Water quality standards

FACT 1985 – 227 crude outfalls daily spewing raw sewage, condoms, panty liners, sanitary towels, into local bathing waters.

FACT 1989 – Clean Sweep programme devised to improve or eliminate those outfalls contributing to EC Bathing Water Quality failure. Completion date 1999.

FACT 1990 - EC threaten legal action if completion is delayed by the UK to 1999.

FACT 1990 – hasty Government rethink. In March 1990:
(surprise, surprise, weeks after privatisation)

   1. agreed to meet EC Bathing Water Quality compliance standards by 1995 not 1999.

   2. agreed to meet EC Urban Wastewater Treatment Directive meaning enhanced biological treatment for larger Clean Sweep projects.

   3. agreed to stop sewage sludge disposal to sea.

COSTS

FACT 1990 - none of the major changes in 1,2,3, above, had been included or costed by Government in SWW's investment programme at privatisation in December 1989.

FACT 1990 - This meant that overnight the 'Clean Sweep' programme costs rocketed to almost £1 billion from the original £435 million - more than double the original estimate.

FACT 1990 – Despite its expedient and costly rethink, Government refused many appeals to provide additional funding to cushion the impact on customer bills in the South West. Go to the economic regulator (Ofwat) they said.

FACT 1991 - In December Ofwat reluctantly agrees to a huge hike in South West customer bills for a 3-year period commencing April 1992 – to pay for the Government's decision to accelerate coastal environmental improvements and meet EC standards. The increase per year was RPI + 11.5% (actual 16.2%, 15.8%, and 14%)

FACT 1993 – Government Environment Minister disowns all financial implications. "Responsibility for water charges rests with the Director General of Water Services (Ofwat)." April 1993. Classic Sir Humphrey.

FACT 1993 - Director General (Ofwat), faced with angry and mounting customer criticism, responds with the classic hot potato routine. His quote in May 1993;

" the Government can stop South West Water bills spiralling ... price limits are based on environmental obligations laid down by the Government," adding that "he had little room for manoeuvre."

FACT 1994 – Deadlock! primary school playground politics "it wasn't me sir, it was him."

The Del Boy Political Fix

The regional impact and anger of billing increases had reached a crescendo. Bills had doubled in five years since privatisation in 1989. Try telling bill payers that it was not privatisation, but a massive £2 billion improvement programme that had caused the increases.

With water privatisation so deeply unpopular, it was inevitable that fingers were pointed at the big P. Remarkably the same duplicitous Government that was now denying responsibility for the five-year billing increases, e.g. "go and talk to the regulator," had in 1989 publicly stated that water bills in the South West were likely to rise by RPI plus 5.5% in the second five-year period between 1995 and 2000.

Simply because of the sheer size, scale, and timing of quality and environmental obligations. However with a General Election only two years away, a Governmental political fix to a botch of their own making was inevitable.

A Del Boy fix was on the way that Derek Trotter would have been proud of. Here's how it went.

In Spring 1994 we (SWW) submitted our five-year Periodic Review Business Plan (1995-2000) to the Director General of Water Services (Ofwat), based on our legal obligations set and audited by the National Rivers Authority (NRA), Drinking Water Inspectorate, and others.

Around the same time the Government had urgently put in train an NRA study to look at Clean Sweep and other environmental schemes that could be delayed or slowed. The same Government (now feeling the political heat) that accelerated them in 1990!

By July 1994 the political Del Boy fix and bear trap was complete. Ofwat announced in its 'Periodic Review' conclusions that it was slashing the previous Government predicted five-year charges increases to an average RPI + 1.1% per year.

A far cry from the Governments (RPI +5.5%) 1989 forecast. Also a slow down or halt to numerous local coastal bathing water improvement schemes and other planned inland water and wastewater infrastructure upgrades. At the time Ian Byatt, Director General of Water Services, Ofwat said,

" In the South West, where customers have experienced disproportionately large increases in the last 3 years, future increases have been contained by using scope within legal requirements to defer some environmental schemes."

Bear in mind that the "disproportionately large increases" were approved by, guess who, Ian Byatt. Sir Humphrey speak was becoming as common as Cornish cream and Devon scrumpy in these 'ere parts. No doubt his regulatory cage had been rattled and collar felt by Whitehall 'Trotter' heavyweights, and, surprise, surprise, the Del boy fix was now complete – but not quite.

Ian Byatt duly went on to be knighted in the 2000 Birthday Honour List. Well, there's a real surprise.

An MMC appeal and the tie

SWW decided to take its case to the Monopolies and Mergers Commission (MMC) and appeal the Ofwat decision.

When we announced our MMC referral intention I was interviewed by BBC Television and ITV, both outlets featuring the piece across national networks. Later that evening my mother rang from her Derbyshire home.

"You'll never guess what," she said, "Your Dad and I were having a sandwich and watching lunch time news when you came on…and then at teatime we were just doing the dogs dinner, and you were on again on the other side!"

"What did you think of it?" I asked,

110

"Can't remember what you said, but you looked smart, and we really liked your tie," she said. At least, two sartorial-supportive viewers.

Twelve months of hard work from regulatory teams on both sides of the fence later and the MMC appeal decision was announced.

In July 1995, we were informed by the MMC that a similar level of charging increases should be applied to those stipulated by the Ofwat Review one year earlier. The marginal change was a reduction of 0.5% in the 1995-96 year.

Despite the disappointment, the failed appeals for Government funding, the nasty taste of political expediency, and the two-faced duplicity of the 'Del Boy' fix , I always thought it was inevitable.

However, in the twelve months appeal process, we did something that Government could not do in five years of political vacillation. We cracked the five-year unsolved debate into standards versus costs. Costs, in the shape of lesser customer billing increases, and longer periods of delivering improvement programmes, had won the day.

No Conservative Prime Minister, Minister, or MP had the balls or had come close to unlocking the muddle that they had themselves originally created. By taking it all the way to the MMC, we had. We did Governments work for them. They should have picked up the tab for the MMC referral costs.

So what was the message and how did we manage it? Clarity was the key message. Shining a light through the politically induced fog.

Clearer understanding of priorities in future investment, and that charges were of paramount importance. I felt sad for customers who had to wait longer for replacement water mains to eliminate discoloured tap water, or for greater reassurance on sewer flooding, or for a delayed Clean Sweep scheme to replace an antiquated local Victorian sewage outfall, but the dye was now cast, and clarity was the winner.

As for the wide-spread national news reporting and Regulator comments on the MMC conclusions, it was predictable. We were always going to be painted as the bad boys by the superficial scribes. "Severe blow to SWW"... "SWW has been stuffed".. .."whole episode has been bad for South West Water"...

As he romped excitedly to an anticipated knighthood, Ian Byatt, Director General of Ofwat, commented,

"This is excellent news for customers in the South West. The company's decision to appeal against the price limits I set caused considerable

anxiety for customers who feared their bills might continue to rise well above inflation. I am now completely vindicated in my decision made last July."

Such a modest chap and from a customer champion who "had little room for manoeuvre" barely two years before. Sufficient however to doff the glasses, don the cloak, and morph from Clark Kent to (Sir) Superman.

The MMC report noted "serious concerns among South West's 1.5 million customers that their bills - on average £300 a year - were about 50 per cent higher than average," and went on to say, "there was a high level of unwillingness and in some cases inability to pay - even to secure environmental improvements."

Moral of the story? Two-fold: Never trust a politician unless he is out of office – perhaps on a well-paid coastal walk or watching cricket at Lords and never trust an 'independent' regulator appointed by the Government – unless you are a Minister.

Managing the message – but which one?

As you can imagine there was a frenzied interest from the press and media to seek our views on the "humiliation" of the MMC announcement. Local, regional, and national journalists were in touch and a press conference arranged at SWW HQ, Peninsula House, Exeter in the last week of July 1995.

The previous day we went through the usual routine preparation for any major announcement, preparing the MD's presentation, press release, Q/A's, and rehearsing with Bill Fraser. Bob Baty, Engineering Director, was also going to be on the top table with Bill and myself. The buzz of the day arrived, and I was expecting around 30 journalists, with BBC Television, ITV, Channel 4, amongst other local press and media to confirm attendance.

I was in my office early, going through various likely questions and answers, when my phone rang. MD's secretary letting me know that a journalist was asking for Bill, and only Bill, at reception, and could I go and sort.

At reception I introduced myself to a tall, greasy haired individual in a crumpled suit who was asking for the MD. He seemed nervous, but to the point. I explained that the MD had a very busy day ahead and could I help him with anything?

" I am keen to talk to him direct," he said. I reiterated that would not be possible today.

"He will want to talk to me when he sees these," he said, reaching into his brief case for an open-ended brown envelope containing photos, and handing them nervously to me. I quickly fanned through the photos which appeared to show Bill, at various locations, with a female companion.

I asked the individual where he was from and who did he represent. He explained that he was a stringer (free-lance journalist) from the Bristol area and representing 'The Sun' newspaper.

"Now, can I see Bill?" he added, rather impatiently.

I told him to wait in reception, and I would give him the courtesy of asking Bill if he might want to spare a few minutes but doubted it because of the busy schedule of the day. As I made my way to Bill's office, I thought this was not a good day for odd individuals brandishing supposedly interesting photographs.

I briefed Bill about the journalist, his photographs, alleged newspaper connection, and insistence on wanting to see him. Bill opened the envelope and glanced through the photographs. After a few moments silence he said they were pictures of himself and a professional who was helping him write a book. I could see he was thinking and purposely kept quiet.

His reaction was unusually detached, although little had been said, and I sensed he had not liked what he saw.

I broke the silence. " I will tell him that you are too busy to see him, return his photos, and we have nothing to say. OK"?

"Alright," he said quietly. With that I went downstairs and saw the crumpled suit off the premises but not before he said, "any comment?" to which I confirmed No, and he was gone.

I then walked slowly back to Bill's office, knowing what to say, but thinking of how to say it.

"I don't think you should do the press conference," I said. I got an immediate reaction.

"Why not? Bill replied, "of course I am going to do it. Why the hell shouldn't I?"

It was time for straight talking.

"Look Bill, I have no idea why they have the photos, or why they have been taken. That's your business not mine." I paused and went on,

"I can ban the journalist from coming into the press conference if he tries. What I can't do is stop him from briefing others and for you to be asked potentially embarrassing questions in front of three national network television cameras recording the whole shebang."

Bill sat behind his desk, swivelling his black leather chair away from me, constantly drawing on a large Cuban cigar, and gazing at the distant moorland hills. Nothing was said for at least a couple of minutes. He then swivelled back.

"You're right, better get Bob involved," he said in a low monotone. I knew I was right and with that I beat a hasty retreat.

"Bob, you're on," I said, gate crashing his room with a set of slides and Q/A's.

"What's gone on?" said Bob, in his Wirral way.

"Too complicated to explain now Bob," I said. "Tell you later. Need to get you up to speed with this presentation – we're live in 45 minutes!"

As predicted, it was a full house for the MMC press conference. I did get some journalists asking where the MD was on such an important day, but with 'other engagements' and contrite excuses, no-one pushed the issue or made it one.

In any case Bob Baty was generally well liked and most journalists present knew him and respected him from many previous interviews. So together we did what we could with a perceived poor hand of cards. It went as well as could be expected. We urged them to look at the clarity rather than the political aspect.

After years of political fudge, we now knew the answer. Costs and not pace had won the day. As it had over the previous 100 years. That's why Ofwat and the MMC were convenient vehicles to make pragmatic decisions that politicians couldn't.

Later that day BBC Spotlight, regional TV news programme for the South West, requested a live interview that would be at the top of the early evening programme.

Ken Hill, Group Finance Director, agreed to do it from the BBC Exeter satellite studio. After a frenetic day, I was beginning to wind things up in the press office when Ken phoned in to say that he could not make the BBC Spotlight interview because of train delays from London.

None of the Directors were now in the office and the programme was due to start in 45 minutes. There was only one sacrificial lamb available. Me. I hot footed to the Exeter studio whilst blasting out the

Magnificent Seven theme on the car radio, and arrived just after 6pm, wired up and ready to go.

Sitting in a darkened TV studio, awaiting the live broadcast to over 1 million viewers, as well as thinking of Yul Brynner and Steve McQueen, I decided that polite offence and not defence, was the order of the day. I knew what their approach would be.

'Live' light on and through to Plymouth BBC TV news desk. As anticipated all the usual superficial, easy questions, isn't this a humiliation?, shouldn't you take less profit? shareholders, greedy? etc. To which I responded that "if you (the interviewer) would like to go and ask local customers in Teignmouth, Bude, Penzance and St Ives, Thurlestone, Seaton, and other areas in the South West who have had brand new Clean Sweep schemes replacing old Victorian raw sewage outfalls, they are 'tickled pink' with the result of improvements. Yes, bills have had to rise but what the MMC and Ofwat has said was steady down on the pace of improvements and that will mean inevitable delays to some schemes, but also less impact on bills. And that is what we are going to do." Job done.

Just after I got a call from Neil Gallacher, BBC TV Business and Industry Correspondent, saying that he had seen the interview, congratulated me, and thought that it came over really well. A gamekeeper compliment to a grateful poacher. Much appreciated after a knackering day.

The other message – and the photos

On the Friday following the MMC announcement, and with no contact from 'The Sun' news-desk, and no publication of a story involving Bill and the photos, I was beginning to think that they were not running the story. I was right.

However, later that day, I knew why. The press office was contacted by the 'News of the World'. Obviously, the stringer had failed to sell to 'The Sun' but had done business with the 'News of the World.' Again we made no comment. I alerted our financial PR agency in London, who undertook to scour the early Sunday edition as soon as the newspaper hit the streets in the capital and send me any article copy. Forewarned was forearmed. Usually first issues came out just after midnight, early on Sunday morning.

There was a story. It was not good, either for Bill, or the company. Whether the content was true or not was of no concern for me, nor should it have been. It was a personal issue for Bill.

I had to protect the company and the anticipated follow-up in the coming week ahead. There was none. Not one. Not a single journalist call, either from any other national or more likely, regional press and media outlet.

Later that following week I had a working lunch with the BBC local TV news editor. Way down the list of topics discussed, and just before we concluded, I asked him if he had seen last Sunday's News of the World.

"Oh that," he said with a smile, not mentioning any names or any particular story. "We talked about it at the editorial meeting on Monday morning, grinned, and moved on."

They had considered that it was not in any way related to his SWW management role and a private not public matter. Honour amongst thieves, I pondered on the drive back to the office.

Chapter 18. Time to move on?

At the beginning of 1995, I had started to think about my future and whether it might be time for a change. I was still in a position of strength and enjoying the role but coming up to five years in the company, was it time for a fresh challenge?

I always remembered my mother's advice in the shape of a poem after the excitement of a promotion and higher profile in Severn Trent. "Keep your feet on the ground," she said and handed me a hand written note she had copied from one of her many reading books. Particularly apt for the water industry.

Sometime when you're feeling important
Sometime when your ego's in bloom,
Sometime when you take it for granted
You're the best qualified in the room,

Sometime when you feel that your going
Would leave an unfillable hole,
Just follow these simple instructions
And see how they humble your soul.

Take a bucket and fill it with water
Put your hand in it up to the wrist,
Pull it out and the hole that's remaining
Is a measure of how you'll be missed.

You can splash all you wish when you enter,
You may stir up the water galore,
But stop and you'll find that in no time
It looks quite the same as before.

The moral of this quaint example
Is do just the best that you can,
Be proud of yourself but remember,
There's no indispensable man.

[Saxon White Kessinger 1959]

I had always hankered after starting my own communications/PR business and at this stage in my career, having good relationships and contacts with many regional and some national journalists and news desks, this could be the right time.

A further attraction, in terms of timing, was the potential for a reasonable redundancy package which had recently been introduced and might be on offer.

I decided to approach Bill and talk it over with him. He understood the sentiments but did not want me to go. We came to a compromise. He said that if I stayed a further 6 months, until after the MMC appeal was concluded (which I did), he would let me go on a voluntary redundancy package. Date to go 31st August 1995.

In the final few weeks with SWW, I was busy letting a number of key South West and national contacts know what I was doing in the near future, including launching 'Alan Smith Communications' based in Exeter, when I had two unexpected approaches.

First, the News Editor of West Country Television invited me to lunch in Plymouth, and after pleasantries and general catching up, he asked what my future plans were. I explained and then later he asked if I might want to consider or think about the potential of joining West Country Television? As what?

Head of Public Relations came the response. He went on to say that the Chief Executive liked me. I had met him on a couple of Plymouth events and had decent, friendly conversations with him, but nothing serious.

"Think about it," he said.

On the drive back I knew I was not interested, however flattering. SWW had a 50% stake in the company, so it would have felt incestuous and not a clean break. I also knew the current incumbent and he was a good guy, and that too would have made me uncomfortable.

The other unexpected conversation was with SWW Chairman, Keith Court. He walked casually into my office about ten days before I was due to go. Informal small talk followed…what was happening at the sharp end etc.

All of that and then, out of the blue, he said, would I consider the role of Head of Customer Services? I think feather, and being knocked down by one, came to mind. Of course mentally I had already gone some weeks ago. What a bizarre suggestion at a bizarre time.

Think about it, he said. I gave him the respect of saying I would, but realistically it was of no interest whatsoever, even if he had proposed it six months before, I would have said no.

Keith was a complicated soul. I liked him but always thought he was an insecure individual, cast in a responsible position and very capable, but at his heart not really enjoying his lot or suited to his position. Always aware that the bomb could go off when there was no bomb there.

I often wondered if the dramatic and unfortunate implications and ramifications of Camelford had left an indelible mental scar. It takes fortitude to withstand the wholesale cries of resign from all quarters over such a long period of time and I think that might have taken its toll.

My own instinct was that he should have resigned, not because of the baying crowd, but simply for his own peace of mind and better enjoyment of life in the longer term. Often misunderstood but a kind man at heart.

On the other hand Bill Fraser was a Glaswegian street fighter, never a detail man, whether managing oil and gas projects in the Middle East or a historically difficult utility in the South West. You always knew where you were with him and he trusted me and others in terms of delegation and licence, just so long as you got it right.

Not the easiest in terms of press and media relations. I reckon he saw them as a necessary evil and went along with my thoughts most of the time, which is why he was happy for me to do so many media interviews. I liked that. I was confident enough to think I had the common sense and nous to get it right more times than not.

Public meetings wise, Bill had a relatively short fuse. I remember when we were promoting the contentious Clean Sweep Penzance & St Ives Scheme in a large and packed public gathering in Penzance, the natives were getting restless.

Bill suddenly banged the top table and bellowed, "you've have been talking about this issue for the best part of 20 years and got nowhere. No solutions, just talk. I'm going to deliver the solution in the next couple of years." Meeting ended. And he did.

In the last few days with SWW I received fantastic and emotional letters from Keith, Bill, and Ken Hill wishing me every success for the future. Also a very emotional heartfelt conversation with Bob Baty which brought tears to the eyes. And that was only Bob.

Clean Weep!…and time to move on.

Alan Smith Communications (ASC) – but not for long

Unemployed Friday 1st September 1995. Started ASC on Monday 4th September 1995 - Top of the UK Pop Charts? 'You are never alone', by Michael Jackson.

By an enormous stroke of luck and generosity I wasn't alone. I immediately had the offer of an office and secretarial support, rent free, from my very great friend Cor Jelier who I had worked with on the Clean Sweep Jamaica project.

The former Exeter city centre office of DHV Burrow Crocker had been vacated due to a company relocation, but the lease had not expired, and Cor had decided he was going to continue to operate from there, with one other member of staff, Sarah, his secretary. It was a huge and cavernous office floor space, previously accommodating around fifty design engineers, with redundant drawing boards still scattered around.

Cor knew of my plans and generously offered me a desk, and secretarial support. Unbelievable start. For the next couple of weeks I commuted into the Exeter office each day, spending time letting the world and his grandma know what I was doing. Phone calls, letters, meetings, and offers from very supportive local news editors, including the Western Morning News and Exeter Express and Echo, to put together feature articles on yours truly.

Within the first few weeks I had landed my first assignment with a locally based engineering design company. I had to write, edit, and produce their first company magazine, for internal and external audiences, including brand design artwork and recommendations. A £2000 assignment which was really timely. ASC was up and running.

By late October I had just completed and delivered the magazine assignment when I got a phone call at the Exeter office. It was from an individual called Margaret Stewart.

She explained that she had recently joined Yorkshire Water as Director of Corporate Affairs and they were experiencing critical operational water supply issues due to the ongoing drought impact in Yorkshire.

This had greatly increased the pressure on her communications team, and she was looking for temporary support to manage the burgeoning workload. A number of consultants were to be taken on. Was I interested and was I available quickly?

"How long for?" I asked

"Probably two weeks but let's see how it works out in the first week," she said.

We haggled over daily rate but came to an agreement. Start date Monday 6th November 1995 at the Bradford office. A combination of a further and longer conversation with Margaret, and calls to people I knew, made me aware of the seriousness of the Yorkshire drought situation.

The company was approximately 14 days away from introducing standpipes and rota cuts to approximately 600,000 people in West Yorkshire. This was obviously generating significant press interest from the UK and overseas. Hence the need for support.

The messaging had not been helped by two recent gaffes. The YW Media Relations Manager had recently been sacked following a remark made live on Radio Leeds. He was asked why he thought Yorkshire customers had not responded sufficiently to appeals for water savings? He replied that he thought it was because they were 'culturally ignorant.'

Also the Chief Executive, Trevor Newton, had apparently made claims that, thanks to altering his washing and cleanliness habits, which he demonstrated on local television, he had not had a bath or shower for 3 months. It was then revealed he was allegedly going to relatives outside of Yorkshire for his baths.

So began a second, albeit short contract for Alan Smith Communications and an early morning drive to Yorkshire on Monday 6th November 1995. UK Number 1 "I Believe" Robson & Jerome. I needed to.

Chapter 19. You can always tell a Yorkshireman ...but not very much

I had never been further north than Sheffield so expected a nose bleed at any time on the long drive to Bradford from Devon. What I didn't expect was to get mixed up with an almost continuous line of road tanker lorries as I drove west from the M1 on to the M62.

All ominously emblazoned with huge *' Tankering Water for Yorkshire'* signs. It didn't say, 'You are now entering a war zone', but it felt like that. I was met at the Yorkshire Water Services (YWS) Bradford office reception by a smiling Senior Press Officer and escorted into the makeshift, enlarged press office which was full of busy people, ringing phones, and desk-top computers.

It reminded me of a student classroom, with five long rows of bench/desks all facing one way, and all resonating to the clacking of keyboards.

My first problem. Back in drought free Devon, and even further back in Brummie-land, I was always afforded the luxury of a secretary. Following introductions, it became obvious, as I was shown to my 'workstation,' that I had lost a secretary but gained a screen and keyboard.

It was almost like showing Mr Bean the dashboard of a Jumbo Jet. I tried to remain calm, not to panic, to look self-assured, but the reality was my bowels were on the move. Mr Quartermain would have been delighted. Further humiliation as I tried unsuccessfully to switch the appliance on.

" Are you familiar with Lotus Notes?" came a voice.

It sounded to me like an expression from the 'Kama Sutra', but in reality only enhanced my increasing brain fog and lower region bowel movement. My current office dilemma was far more important than ancient Indian alternatives.

"No", I said. "In which case, I will talk you through it," said a very helpful assistant called Joanne.

At this point I should like to acknowledge that without Joanne's considerable support, patience, and friendly help, my stay in YWS would have been very short and not so sweet. I had to learn and fast. Time and again in the first days of my stay Joanne helped, tutored, educated, and dragged me through the finer points of using a computer including Lotus

Notes and all other techno knowledge and software packages necessary to look as if you knew what you were doing. Thank you Joanne for transforming an IT agnostic into a basic, but much more knowledgeable, keyboard plonker.

In those early hours and days, I got to know the other five or six temporary consultants who had been drafted in to help. A mixed bag from ex BBC journalist, ex NRA professional, to PR agency consultants, and me. They could all make a keyboard smoke, a million light years more proficient than me, but modestly he says, none could match my water industry knowledge and experience.

The hired hands supported permanent members of the press team, all of whom had been battling away for the best part of six months as the water crisis deepened, to satisfy the hunger and chaotic demands of a volatile press. I was now on board and helping with press enquiries as well as preparing company positions on imminent announcements.

Monday 6th November 1995. The water crisis in Yorkshire.

- Pennine reservoir levels serving thousands of homes in West Yorkshire at critically low levels of 10-15%
- 24 hour/7-day cycle of road tankering of water had begun from east and north Yorkshire to west Yorkshire.
- YWS was approximately 14 days away from an emergency plan to introduce water supply rota cuts (24 hours on/24 hours off) to approximately 600,000 people in West Yorkshire.
- Imminent erection of thousands of standpipes in West Yorkshire
- Imminent wide-spread distribution of rota cuts advice leaflet (ultimately not distributed).

'Too little, too late' in water crisis

by JON SHARPE
T&A Reporter

A Government report released today suggests Yorkshire Water did too little, too late to cope with the drought.

And it urges the company to do more to deal with leaking pipes.

YW under fire over 'failures'

WATER CRISIS: *Public health expert warns inquiry ...*

'Rationing could lead to deaths'

by HELEN MEAD
Environment Reporter

People could die as a result of water rationing, a top public health official has warned.

Dr Chris Worth, West Yorkshire's director of public health, told a public inquiry that under no circumstances should rota cuts go ahead.

Yorkshire Water is seeking the re...

M-way bid may g

A proposal to close off one lane of the busy M62 since tankers bringing supplies to West Yorkshire...

Yorkshire Water's production technical manager...

by JULIA HINDE and SHARON DALE
T&A Reporters
The National Rivers A...

around 25 per cent of Yorkshire Water's supplies were lost through leakage.

The NRA says Yorkshire W...

Yorkshire Water accused of 'failing people of county'

Hundreds fill hall to protest at YW move

Repeat of crisis would not be tolerated, says Minist...

MPs line up to pour torrent of criticism on Yorkshire Water

HULL DAILY MAIL FRIDAY NOVEMBER 24 1995

by HELEN MEAD
Environment Reporter

NIGHTMARE GOES ON!

Yorkshire Water 'made it worse'

Yorkshire Water under fire from Ofwat and others

THE day before it faces a public inquiry into rota cuts, YW stands accused of 'cheating' by Ofwat.

Ofwat alleges sub-standard services at Higher charges with the company more interested in...

A Government report released today suggests Yorkshire Water did too little, too late to cope with the drought.

And it urges the company to do more to... with leaking pipes.

The report to Environment Secretary J...

Tankers stop but lives left in tatters

Yorkshire Water 'has lost trust of customer'

ROTA CUTS

Advice to Customers

VERY IMPORTANT INFORMATION
Please read and keep for future reference

بہت ضروری معلومات
ترجمہ کی ہوئی کاپیاں دستیاب ہیں۔ تفصیلات کے لئے اس کے اندر دیکھیں۔

અતિ મહત્વની માહિતી
અનુવાદ કરેલી નકલો ઉપલબ્ધ છે. વધારે માહિતી માટે અંદર જુઓ.

बहुत जरूरी जानकारी
अनुवाद की हुई कापियाँ उपलब्ध है। विवरणों के लिये इसके अन्दर देखें।

অত্যন্ত গুরুত্বপূর্ণ তথ্য
অনুবাদ করা কপি পাওয়া যাবে। বিস্তারিত বিবরণের জন্য ভেতরের পৃষ্ঠা দেখুন।

ਬਹੁਤ ਜ਼ਰੂਰੀ ਜਾਣਕਾਰੀ
ਅਨੁਵਾਦ ਕੀਤੀਆਂ ਕਾਪੀਆਂ ਉਪਲਬਧ ਹਨ। ਵੇਰਵਿਆਂ ਦੇ ਲਈ ਇਸਦੇ ਅੰਦਰ ਵੇਖੋ।

 Yorkshire Water

**For further help or information call
FREEPHONE 0800 454608**

[Customer leaflet prepared but ultimately not distributed]

The Operations Director told me that YWS had never extracted reservoir water for treatment at such low levels and that water quality was being closely monitored for potential issues arising from sediment and turbidity problems.

To complicate matters further, John Gummer, the Secretary of State for the Environment, some weeks before, had summoned Sir Gordon Jones, Chairman of Yorkshire Water, to London for an update on the crisis. Gummer made it clear that "there would be no water rota cuts in Yorkshire" before tersely, and prematurely, closing the meeting.

As a result of this and other pressures, it was decided that road tankering of water would be massively ramped up. From a token start of 20 vehicles in the early Autumn, (I was later told by a senior YWS manager that this initial exercise was more for a public show of proactivity and effort than any realistic impact), there was a fundamental internal sea change, with significant financial and huge operational clout put behind the road tankering operation.

Filling up with River Tees water - the huge tankering gantry at Long Newton Reservoir site, Darlington

In the words of one national commercial vehicle magazine at the time...
"Yorkshire's desperate need for water has led to the biggest UK haulage operation in peacetime history, leading to employing 750 road tankers and more than 3,300 drivers, subcontracted and executed by Exel Logistics."

In a 24 hour/7-day continuous operation, around 60 million litres of water was transported every day from near Darlington (River Tees) and York, into Eccup Reservoir, near Leeds, and from Barmby and Halifax, across to Scammonden Reservoir. Each vehicle travelled approximately 600 miles per day with average earnings rumoured at £4000 per day (over £8500 in today's money).

My first week

Despite the lack-of-clack keyboard competence, I was now, along with others, in the thick of the action. Hostile and angry local customers, strident regional and national regulators, bandwagon politicians; all ensured a huge number of good, bad, and ugly press and media enquiries.

126

Being a South West Water veteran, that was nothing new to me, but the sheer volume was. Unremitting and unreal. But, as the Americans were saying, "no water in Yorkshire? You gotta' be kidding me."

And that was the story. The facts were incidental. Ironically that same week YWS had needed to put together a press briefing package on the soon-to-be published Ofwat annual levels of service standards, a sort of end of term annual report into how each water company in England and Wales was performing.

To add fuel to an already inflammatory fire, YWS results were very poor. The briefing statement therefore had to be crafted to make the best of a bad job. I was asked to put it together. Not difficult in process terms because I had done exactly the same in two previous water companies.

Late in my first week Margaret Stewart, Corporate Affairs Director, surfaced. The first time I had met her face-to-face. She too was up to the neck in it, but at a more strategic level. Just before we met she had obviously been briefed by the senior press officer as to who, amongst the band of temporary mercenaries, was doing what and how well.

Margaret asked how I thought the week had gone. I said OK, but added, not a time for the niceties, just a matter of getting stuck in and managing a difficult situation. She referred to the Ofwat response press package that I had put together and said that it had gone down well internally, and would I stay for another week?

I ended up staying a further three weeks, until shortly before Christmas 1995. By now the other mercenaries were slowly being stood down. The immediate crisis had not gone away but the frenetic earlier pace of press enquiries had steadied.

At the start of my last week in early December, Margaret asked me to pull together my thoughts and recommendations for a significant YWS gesture that would make a positive contribution to the Yorkshire community and slowly begin the long haul of clawing back a damaged reputation.

Her initial idea was to sponsor monument(s) and plaques in local town centres to commemorate worthy and well-known dignitaries who had made their mark to the benefit of local townsfolk.

"What do you think?" she asked.

"I don't. I will come back to you with my thoughts," I replied.

It was obvious that deep-seated damage to the YWS reputation through sometimes perceived, and sometimes real, poor management of the drought and supporting communications had been done.

And in December 1995 it still had not run its course. It could get worse. Not that 99% of the hard-working YWS people were to blame. I talk about my view of blame and how I saw it later. Meanwhile trust and reputation had to be won back by doing the right thing, as perceived by the customer.

It would also depend on inevitable changes at the top, alongside huge and urgent capital investment in water supply improvements. The latter already being planned and started. Changes that would signal it would never, as far as humanly possible, happen again.

All of that healing process would take time and no quick fixes. No PR stunts. But I did see an early opportunity to make a positive, reputation-building impact on another significant and challenging area of YWS responsibility and profile.

An initiative that would bring genuine benefit for local people and the coastal environment, as well as YWS being seen as the UK market leader on coastal wastewater (sewage) treatment strategy. Here was my rationale.

During my time with South West Water, I had worked with some of the brightest environmental scientists in the UK and learned a lot. I had listened intently to them about their knowledge of the ever-changing, and progressive European debate on higher standards of wastewater treatment, particularly coastal wastewater treatment, and the positive impact on the quality of popular beaches and bathing waters.

The UK Government had already signed up to EC legal requirements for secondary (biological) treatment in the early 1990's. Subsequently it became mandatory for all UK water companies to progressively introduce and achieve compliance.

The SWW guys had told me that it was inevitable that a further treatment process, ultra violet disinfection, the ultimate treatment and bug zapper, would follow and become EC Law and mandatory in the next couple of years.

So given that as a background, here was the proposal I gave to Margaret for her and the YWS Board to consider. On the east coast, Yorkshire had popular family seaside resorts at Whitby, Filey, Scarborough, Bridlington, amongst others.

All of them required major new treatment works to be built or extended so that treated discharges would comply with latest EC Bathing Water Directives. Why not get ahead of the game and announce that YWS was going to be the first UK water company, and one of the first in Europe, to include ultra violet disinfection, as well as secondary (biological) treatment, on the end of the coastal treatment process at the popular coastal resorts?

By the time the treatment works were built, UV treatment would be mandatory and YWS would be able to claim for the additional UV costs through the Ofwat regulatory cost-pass through mechanism. Call the East Coast treatment programme 'Coast-Care.'

She liked it and said she would take it to the YWS executive management team for discussion and potential approval. So fond farewells and after three weeks of supporting the Yorkshire cause, I headed home and joined the rest of the Smith family for a Christmas and New Year holiday with Clean Sweep friends in Jamaica (mon).

A longer stay in God's own country

We returned home in early January 1996, and there was a telephone message awaiting on the home phone. It was from Margaret at YWS. Could I ring as soon as I returned home?

"I have spoken to Trevor (Newton CEO YWS), and, if you are available, we would like you to return as soon as you can for a period of 3 months, say to the end of March," she said when I returned the call.

"During that time we want you to head up the press team, recommend any changes, and also help us appoint a new Media Relations Manager." Two days later I was heading back to God's own (parched) country to continue the work, but in a different capacity.

The water supply situation in January 1996 was still serious and Yorkshire Water and its West Yorkshire supplies were by no means out of the woods, but things were slowly beginning to improve. The massive £50 million road tankering operation had helped and we had begun to see modest amounts of something called rain beginning to fall in the right places – although January was still only 50% of the long-term average.

Reservoir levels were not much improved but importantly the combination of the tankering impact and the rainfall, had stopped them falling further, taking the controversial plan for rota cuts and standpipes off the agenda. In the same month Yorkshire Water announced the setting up and funding of an independent inquiry into the drought, to be held in Leeds and commencing in March, two months later.

The commission's chairman, Professor John Uff, publicly assured *"the complete independence of the inquiry and that Yorkshire Water is no more than one interested party in the proceedings. The company has stated that it would consider the inquiry's report, when published, to determine how it should influence the company's planning for water supply in the future."*

Meanwhile the full-time press team were supportive of my brief when I returned, and we set about doing some things differently, whilst keeping the good bits.

The most important, and arguably most difficult of changes, was the need to wean YWS off the well-practised and obliging internal attitude to press responding and in doing so, slowly take YWS out of the headlines and ultimately out of the press altogether.

Over the past six to nine months we had needed the press and media, and they revelled in the volume of storylines we were giving to them, both intentionally and unintentionally. It was easily sourced column inches.

A long way to go, but time to re-evaluate our press and media relations and communications. Getting out of the press and media circus rather than getting stuck in it was the strategy. A credible press enquiry deserved a professional response, as opposed to a third party trying to attract cheap publicity and profile at YWS expense.

We needed to make the distinction. Understandably YWS and the drought had made it easy to fill newspapers and air time, but we should not fall victim to lazy journalism. We began a review of responses to news outlets and adopted a more challenging strategy.

TV and radio, in particular, began to feel the impact of the change, and became disappointed, and sometimes critical, of our response.

On a particular occasion, a YWS press officer received a call from a BBC Look North Television journalist asking if we would put a spokesperson up for interview to respond to harsh criticism from a local councillor. Having looked at the councillors untrue claims, the press officer declined the interview invitation, and said that we would be prepared to give a written statement only.

Not good enough for the BBC. Fifteen minutes later my phone rang, and it was the News Editor of Look North. A rambling diatribe of complaint followed and "would we reconsider and put a spokesperson up?" No, I said, and line by line I explained to the Editor the ridiculous and false accusations being made by the councillor. There was a silence. The News Editor contritely added, " I am sorry to say Alan that you are a victim of a slow news day." The story was dropped.

A continuation of that tougher policy over the coming months led to a significant fall in press and media enquiries. However it was a two-way street. We stopped sending out proactive press releases unless they were essential and necessary public announcements.

The new approach brought some internal consternation. A belligerent engineer strode into the press office and demanded to know "who was in charge?"

"I am," I said.

"Well isn't it about time that we started shouting about all the pipeline and pumping station schemes we are carrying out across our patch, at record speed, to ensure water supply security?" he asked.

"Sit down a minute Andrew," I responded and went on to explain who I was and what I was doing there.

"Now," I said, "let me get this right. You want me to brag about the work you are doing for Joe Public to make sure that we guarantee he gets what he has already paid for nearly 12 months ago?"

I continued, "Don't you think that he, and a lot of others would say, about bloody time, and if you had done it 10 years ago, you wouldn't have frightened the arse off us with standpipes and rota cut threats."

Andrew sat back, reflected, and eventually said, "Good point! Will you come to the Institute of Water Officers meeting next week to explain the strategy?" A convert who became a good friend.

The new press and media strategy also included a commitment to holding monthly press conferences in Leeds, headed up by the Operations Director, to let journalists know the latest on operational and engineering improvement schemes, reservoir levels, rainfall data etc. Progress facts rather than "Wow, look at what we're doing."

We also introduced a computerized programme of approved company press briefing statements. Replacing the ad-hoc paper position filings. Policy positions in simple/press-speak; essential for quickly available and consistent messaging on everything from metering, drought latest, water and sewage treatment, to water mains, leakage, sewer flooding, 'fat cat salaries', and more.

In South West Water we had introduced a similar IT press package five years before and it saved significant time for the press officer and the journalist making the enquiry, and more importantly, ensured consistency of message.

One of the more bizarre internal meetings I was asked to attend was a Board committee which would be looking into the number of consultants YW had gathered during the previous 12 months.

Now that things were improving did we need them, and who should or shouldn't go? All very sensible but one snag. At the time I was a consultant. Nevertheless I was asked to go with a view to culling my own kind. John Layfield, Operations Director, chaired the first meeting.

I immediately declared an interest. I was one of the turkeys about to vote for Christmas.

"You're not a real consultant," he said in brusque Yorkshire tone, as near a compliment as you will get from a Yorkshireman and continued the meeting. John was a great guy, honest, pragmatic and a joy to work with.

Big time YW changes – above and below ground

Inevitable Yorkshire Water strategic changes and developments were happening at a fast pace. The momentum of change would reshape future thinking and management.

On Friday 15th March 1996, Yorkshire Water plc announced significant Board changes.

Sir Gordon Jones, who had been Chairman since 1990, was to retire in April 1996 and his successor was named as Brandon Gough, former Chairman of Coopers & Lybrand.

Trevor Newton, Group Managing Director, and Deputy Chairman, and Chair of Yorkshire Water Services Ltd, was to retire from both Boards at the end of May 1996.

Dr Kevin Bond, previously CEO of the National Rivers Authority, would become Chairman and Managing Director of Yorkshire Water Services Ltd.

On Monday 18th March 1996, the Uff Inquiry hearings began at Leeds Town Hall.

On the second day, Trevor Newton, was scheduled to attend and give evidence. I was asked to accompany Trevor and manage any likely press and media enquiries. He was in good form, but I sensed slightly nervous, as we set off. In the event there were only a handful of reporters and no rugby scrum.

I reflected afterwards that whatever had gone before it was a sad end to a career. A predictable consequence of the previous 12 months of criticism and chaos.

Sir Gordon and Trevor; two professional guys who had achieved a lot in their previously successful careers, falling on their swords, before the regulators and politicians inevitably reached for the blade. Wrong place? wrong time? wrong decisions? History will decide.

Publication of the UFF Report into the Drought - May 1996

As expected the Report was damning in a number of areas including:

- Lower YWS demand forecasts, combined with an investment strategy that put the emphasis on quality, meant the water supply system was already overstretched by the beginning of 1995
- Leakage levels – equivalent to the whole of daily water domestic consumption put into supply – needed urgent attention
- Yorkshire Grid incapable of supporting demand in West Yorkshire – investment needed to rectify
- Threat of cut-offs caused great distress and anxiety in the community and demonstrated that cuts in water supplies are not acceptable in a modern urban society - except in the most unforeseen and exceptional circumstances
- Lack of Emergency Plan - recommended for putting in place to deal with effects of withdrawal of supplies

At a press conference held at Leeds Town Hall on the publication day of the Report, Professor Uff commented, "The Inquiry revealed that this was a crisis waiting to happen. It might have been avoided but as a result of the drought it did happen."

133

Chapter 20. Should I stay or should I go?

My three months stint at changing things in the press office, including the appointment of a new Media Relations Manager was coming to an end.

And then Kevin Bond arrived. He asked me if I would sign a three-year contract and work with Margaret Stewart and others to begin to rebuild the company's reputation. And this had all started back in November 1995 with a 'let's see how it goes for one week and take it from there.'

A lot of things to consider. Family settled in Devon. Did I really want to be part of another high-profile slog to help turn around another water company with real and perceived reputation problems? Two days of consideration later I signed the three-year contract.

Why? The challenge and the adrenaline of working with others who were determined to change things. 99.9% of the people who worked for YWS were good people. Totally focussed and a pride in their work and the service they provided. In most instances they too felt let down with what had happened.

Many of them working in locations and carrying out activities that most would find undesirable or impossible. The national and international pantomime played out over the previous year was not of their making.

The fact that some had been told, at the height of the debacle, that they didn't need to wear their uniforms for fear of being harangued, was unforgivable, but at the time reflected the extent of the resentment and anger felt by many disillusioned and frightened customers.

"You can shove your standpipes up your arse" was heard by guys at the sharp end. Uncalled for but understandable. Appeals to save water fell on many deaf ears. The statistics proved it.

In the previous critical drought of 1976, similar appeals were heeded and water savings came. This time, and arguably with many more communication channels and press and media coverage, the community retort was "You're a private company, you save it."

So the challenge of turning the reputation around was huge for everyone connected with YWS and I wanted to play a part. But before moving on to the Kevin Bond era and my recollections, I am often asked where did I see the drought blame? This is my view.

Blame game

Was it God, Government, or a Gamble? A combination of the three, but all, with hindsight, have genuine cause for appealing the verdict.

God: and remember that most Yorkshire people consider the county to be the Saviour's own. He had not allowed the Pennines to be as dry as 1995/96 since records began. Walking on water was never a problem for him in the traditionally rain-soaked Pennines. However the historic facts were that it was the driest period since records began, either in public or private sector water ownership, and that scarcity, although not as severe, was generally county wide. Rainfall was less than 50% of the average for most of 1995/96 on the Pennines. In fact in the 18 months between April 1995 and September 1996, average rainfall for the region only occurred in three of those 18 months. However, blaming God may have longer term self-inflicted consequences.

Government; as with my experience in South West Water, the Government's hands were dirty.

At privatisation in 1989, the Government played their 'Get out of jail free' card liberally across the water sector so as to avoid threatened EU prosecution for failure to comply with new and tougher EU Directives. The very essence behind the idea and ultimate strategy of Margaret Thatcher's water privatisation.

As mentioned previously the Government had sat on its hands, and purse strings, through the 1980's whilst tougher EU Drinking Water and Environmental Directives from Brussels became law. The UK compliance delays were hurriedly built into the 'must do first' five-year regulatory economic and environmental capital programme priorities of the new, all-tails-wagging, privatised water companies.

No 'Get out of jail free' card for the 'tail waggers' though, just the consolation of allowed hefty increases in customer bills over the same period.

Question: So why was this pertinent to YWS and the drought?
Answer: fundamental. The majority of the newly privatised Yorkshire Water's first five-year capital programme (1990-1995) was, like other water companies in England and Wales, focussed on regulatory 'must do first' project priorities which included water quality and treatment, sewerage, and inland and coastal sewage treatment. Faced with this threatened European legal time-bomb, water resources was such a low

priority on the Government's and Ofwat's regulatory agenda in the early 1990's as to be hardly discernible.

In fact only 4% of the YWS five-year, regulatory allowed, capital programme was allocated to water resources. Also in the 1994 Ofwat Periodic Review, neither climate change, nor water supply planning, with a margin of supply over and above predicted demand (headroom), were considerations allowed by Ofwat and the regulatory boffins.

Few company submissions for resource expansion received Ofwat approval. And he still got his knighthood.

Gamble: so an act of God and Government appeared to absolve YWS. Not so.

Gamble 1 - Going into 1995, the very tight margins of demand versus water resources in West Yorkshire had been well known and understood at YWS senior management level for some years.

Gamble 2 – despite the above and a very dry spring and early summer, YWS management delayed the seemingly embarrassing introduction of hosepipe restrictions in West Yorkshire until July 1995. This avoidable delay further accelerated the depletion of already critically low stocks.

Gamble 3 – The YWS Board significantly misread the public mood and unprecedented level of fear and hostility from all stakeholders at the prospect of standpipes and rota cuts. Egged on by the lingering, overwhelming unpopularity of water privatisation.

YWS instead trusted that the Yorkshire character of grit, pride and history, and we will overcome together, would see the crisis through. Like the Yorkshire Tea advert.

They believed that the climate had conspired to cause a water crisis of a magnitude not seen before and that we had to grin and bear it and share the burden. Standpipes and rota cuts were part of the sharing. 'We are all in this together, we have no choice, and it is what it is.'

The Yorkshire public were having none of it. As previously mentioned enter John Gummer, Government Cabinet member and Secretary of State for the Environment and the 'no rota cuts and no standpipes' meeting with Sir Gordon Jones, YW Chairman.

The short meeting took place well before the planned Emergency Drought Order hearing in Dewsbury, which was set up to consider the application for the introduction of rota cuts.

From that Ministerial edict onwards, management focus switched dramatically to planning, implementation, and execution of the massive, and ultimately successful £50 million road tankering operation. It saved the day, but not the reputation or the blame. The damage was done.

The name's Bond, Kevin Bond

The four years working with Kevin were some of the most challenging but rewarding in my career. In May 1996 it was a new dawn.

Yes, we were still in the grip of a continuing drought and below average rainfall, but things were improving, and at last we were able to start looking forward, whilst continuing to apologize for the past.

Kevin began a whirlwind county wide handshaking, meeting and greeting campaign, that saw him talking to every nook and cranny of political, commercial, domestic, industrial, agricultural, religious, and community life, including representatives of many different and diverse Yorkshire organizations.

As you would imagine the biggest five letter word in the world, Sorry, was regularly employed during those many meetings together with an explanation of future plans.

By October 1996, and only one year on from the darkest days of critical water shortages, the extraordinary and fantastic work of the technical and engineering arm of Yorkshire Water, had worked miracles in laying 220 kilometres of new pipelines and building 26 new pumping stations across the county, costing over £170 million.

Also by October, reservoir levels had slowly climbed to just below 50%. The huge capital investment in the pipelines and pumping stations meant the Yorkshire water grid was now much more secure, robust, and flexible, with the ability to transfer water to areas of greatest need, should future conditions and weather patterns arise.

Hull and back

In the Autumn of 1996, Margaret wanted me to work on a long running saga on probably the largest single capital investment project in the company's history and at that time, the largest in the UK water industry.

Go and see a chap called Duncan Bennett. I did. At the time Duncan was 'Mr Hull'. Not of the Emu fame. Let me explain.

Hull is an east Yorkshire city, perched close to the mouth of the Humber Estuary. An English city that, in 1996, was discharging untreated human sewage into the Humber Estuary from its 260,000 population.

Yes you read it correctly, not 1896 but 1996. Raw sewage from two pumping stations, sited to the east and west of the River Hull, daily disgorging thousands of gallons of human excrement into the Humber Estuary. So in the era of private water company bashing, it is worth noting that this historical, medieval, unacceptable practice, both in Hull and in other parts of the North and South West of the UK, was approved and carried out by publicly appointed and elected local authorities.

A massive and unforgivable environmental legacy of public ownership. As many councillors were oft quoted, "there's no votes in shit." I digress.

Duncan's YWS unenviable mission was to clear all hurdles for the approval and construction of a new £200 million state-of-the-art wastewater treatment works in the Hull environs. This included establishing and agreeing local buy-in to a preferred site option and subsequent planning approval, clarifying treatment levels and Environment Agency discharge consent, and negotiating construction contracts prior to commencement.

A tall order, but perhaps the tallest was the site location. Everyone understood the need for modern sewage treatment, but no one wanted a sewage treatment works close to them. An echo from my Clean Sweep days.

The treatment levels conundrum which had rumbled on in Yorkshire for some years, was both bizarre and real. The fact was that if Hull (and its sewage discharge points) was deemed to be a coastal town, the level of treatment would be less i.e. more dilution.

Certainly the Humber Estuary was tidal which leant more to the designation argument as 'coastal'. On the other hand the reality was that Hull was not coastal, but just inland and therefore the argument being that it should receive the higher level of inland biological treatment. Representations to MP's and other key opinion formers, over a number of years since privatisation had achieved little.

I sensed that the frugal YWS preferred the cheaper coastal designation, but that local luminaries, including MP's and councillors, wanted the higher standard, despite the fact that they and their predecessors had sat on their hands for over 100 years, whilst raw sewage, with no treatment at all, had spewed into the Estuary.

The arrival of Kevin Bond, ex Environment Agency, as Managing Director quickly cleared the fog. The company-wide higher treatment standards approach, that I had recommended via Margaret almost 12 months before, had been adopted.

One long running problem for Duncan out of the way. That clarity also helped him with Environment Agency negotiations on agreed discharge consent parameters.

However, as expected, the tallest order would prove to be agreement of the treatment works location. The reality was that the city of Hull and its tight urban boundary offered little or no room for a corner shop, let alone a sprawling but necessary modern sewage treatment works site. By its very nature, a typical works needs a relatively large footprint to accommodate numerous stages of treatment.

Duncan liaised closely with both YWS appointed planning consultants and local planners in a clear and transparent way. We needed to deliver the works and meet latest European environmental legislation.

Equally the good people of Hull also needed to know, understand, and agree, or not, the thinking and proposals. After looking at nine potential sites, the preferred location was at Saltend, to the east of Hull.

But here was the issue. It was outside of the Hull City boundary. It was inside the boundary of the unitary authority of East Riding of Yorkshire Council. Problem. The relationship between East Yorkshire Council and Hull City Council was not the best. The diplomat might say constructive tension. More reason to be, and be seen to be, even handed.

This then was the background and rationale to our significant communications planning which was rolled out at the end of September 1996.

Over the coming weeks and months we talked to the planning authorities, local parish councils, MP's, local residents, and businesses, environmental organisations including the RSPB, Yorkshire Wildlife Trust, and English Nature. This included face-to-face meetings, local exhibitions, leaflet circulation and distribution, culminating in a very lively and packed public meeting at Hedon Town Hall.

Duncan and I were on the top table. Understandably the Hedon residents were concerned and had a right to be. The proposed Saltend site was around two miles from Hedon and was the nearest urban settlement.

139

I remember queuing, shoulder to shoulder, with many chattering and lively residents, to get into the Hall. Shuffling my way in and carrying the giveaway projector.

Low profile strategy immediately exposed. I was rumbled and harangued by comments including "here look, he must be one of the buggers from Yorkshire Water," and "no chance mate, you're not putting the bloody thing here."

I was unsure whether he meant the projector or the treatment works. However I took the view that a smart-arsed comment from a native of Derbyshire, and not the fatherland, would not go down well and might have meant Duncan was on his own.

Discretion was key, but the baying crowd was already baying. Tone and similar level of discourse continued in the Hall when the meeting got underway. We, 'the suits' made brief, but necessary, scene-setting presentations. Inevitably this irritated the crowd who couldn't wait to impart – never mind about 'slick fancy presentations.'

I had been there before. A veteran of many campaigns. As a water company representative at a local and packed public meeting anywhere in the UK, you are not there, on the podium, to receive a Formula One wreath and a magnum of champagne.

Simply, you are there for a roasting. Baiting of a water company official in public is a national sport and I was a practising professional.

The trick is (a) to expect it and remain calm with seemingly attentive demeanour and (b) let the pot boil.

Let them ferment. Steam and letting it off is democratic. They have a right to. Don't interrupt. Two ears and one mouth. Don't argue. Wait for the infrequent silence to answer.

As the pot boils so your time to answer diminishes. The level of over talking, argument, and interruption of each other in the baying audience causes tribal friction and factions.

The debate begins to descend into chaos, and amongst one another. The gathered look to the podium. You are suddenly thrust into the peacekeeping role.

From villain to virtuous. Some even begin to feel sorry for you and listen and/or urge others to listen. Sanity returns. Discourse is intelligent, if not agreed. Vesuvius has erupted but the lava is cooling down. Job done. That is just about how it happened that night. Coming away I thought we had earned the respect of many, if not agreement by all.

Twelve months later, in October 1997, YWS received full planning permission and the new treatment works, pumping stations, sewer tunnels, pipelines and other infrastructure was completed and fully operational by 2002.

The modern works now serves a population equivalent of over one million and complies with latest European wastewater treatment legislation. More importantly the good people of Hull and area have an environmental treatment solution of which they can be proud. Ending, at last, the centuries old and unsatisfactory public sector practice of dumping raw untreated sewage into the Humber Estuary.

We called it Humbercare, and Mr 'Hull' had done his job. Who needs an Emu anyway?

More Care on the way…

By Spring 1997 my contribution to the consultations in Hull had come to an end. Kevin Bond had been elevated and appointed to CEO Yorkshire Water plc and Jonson Cox, formerly MD of Yorkshire Environmental, the non-core arm of the Yorkshire Water plc, took over Kevin's former role as Managing Director of Yorkshire Water Services.

I was asked to head up the YWS communications team in Bradford, reporting direct to Jonson Cox, but with obvious dotted line to Margaret Stewart, Director of Corporate Affairs in the plc team.

Jonson's task was enormous. The rescue and recovery initiatives of the drought had taken its toll on many functioning areas of the water company. Not the least of which was the need to rethink and restructure the core business.

Ofwat levels of service performance indicators were bumping along the bottom of the league table of the English and Welsh companies, and regulatory operational budgets had taken a big hit. Kevin Bond's charm offensive was beginning to have an impact in the region, but the regulatory engine needed a serious overhaul.

The combination of Bond's charismatic external qualities and Cox's tenacity for under-the bonnet overhaul and reconditioning looked to be a marriage made in heaven. It wasn't.

Meanwhile I was looking at post 'sorry' and how we should communicate the many capital projects that were in the planning and design phase of a massive five-year capital investment programme.

Big benefits for customers tap water, wastewater, local river water,

 holiday seaside water. However the reality was these benefits were often flagged, either in press releases or construction sites as underwhelming

and boring civil engineering schemes. Nothing to indicate to the customer where the hard-earned water bill payment was going to improve his or her local lot. Time to talk to the local community in a local community way that could be understood and potentially be of interest. After weeks of planning and design we launched:

COASTCARE

TOWNCARE

RIVERCARE

HUMBERCARE

Each of the hundreds of annual capital projects would be identified and branded in one of the categories.

COASTCARE: new and higher coastal sewage treatment standards
TOWNCARE: upgrades to water treatment works, mains, and sewers
RIVERCARE: treatment improvements at inland sewage works
HUMBERCARE: new sewage treatment works for Hull and area

Richard Ackroyd, Engineering Director, was 100% behind the new and simplified capital programme articulation. The new look also drew external community and regional press and media interest. It was the first significant, proactive toe that we had dipped into press and media waters since the withdrawal strategy of 12 months before.

Equally important, it proved a fillip to the YWS project engineers working on individual schemes in terms of branding, profile, and their significant contribution.

The newly formed and motivated communications team under my guidance, including press, marketing, and capital scheme communications, settled well. All coordinated their different specialist inputs into a single and transparent offering, 'improvements in your local community', the when, where, how, and why. We were starting to leave the drought dark days behind but had a long way to go.

Around this time I decided to carry out a personal local communications initiative which failed miserably. I was living in a 5th floor apartment by the side of the River Aire in Leeds City Centre. I had parked the car and entered the building lift on the ground floor.

The lift door was just shutting when someone made a grab for the door and squeezed in. Small lifts and long conversations with strangers don't tend to go together. Most prefer to tolerate the uneasy atmosphere before exiting on chosen floor. However, on this occasion, instead of the customary eyes in the air routine, or looking aimlessly at the floor number change, I happened to glance across.

My fellow passenger was Alan Smith, this one famed for his soccer talent, rather than water board prowess, with England, Leeds United, and Manchester United. Too much of a coincidence to let it pass.
"Not very often you get two Alan Smith's in a lift," I remarked with a grin. Blank stare. I repeated, "not very often you get two Alan Smith's in a lift."

Half way through the embarrassment of explaining that I too was Alan Smith we arrived at my 5th floor stop. No time either for a truncated version of the new Care programme or to ask how he was getting on in the Premiership.

He was going higher, probably to see Rio Ferdinand who lived on the floor above. I exited with "good to see you" and he said "Yeah". Moral of the story? Keep your gob shut Alan when passing time in a lift. He did, why didn't I? Nor did he ask for my autograph.

A royal encounter

A meeting with Prince Andrew, Duke of York. I was asked to represent Yorkshire Water at a ceremony at the Royal Armouries, Leeds in June 1997. He was there to put a royal seal of approval to a James (not Kevin) Bond exhibition.

Along with about forty other local, name-tagged business representatives, we were dutifully lined up and told that the Prince, on arrival, would walk along the gathered welcoming line and may stop at anyone for a short conversation. I do recall that there was a professional lady standing next to me, who, to use modern parlance was "bricking it," and on several occasions muttered, " I really do hope he doesn't stop at me."

The prince and the pauper meet...

The Prince arrived and the gathered hushed. He stopped at the second chap in the line-up, spent a couple of minutes chatting before continuing to walk down the line. My nervous neighbours' wish was granted. He didn't stop at her. He stopped at me. With the obligatory handshake, glance at my name tag, and how are you, he proceeded to talk about an article he had read in "the Telegraph" on his train journey north.

I did not question whether it had been the Daily Telegraph or the Bradford Telegraph and Argus. That would have been too Yorkshire. The article related to the Environment Agency (EA) and a policy announcement.

If lady luck had not smiled on me that day, there might have been two in the line 'bricking it.' But, fortuitously, I knew all about the context. Earlier that day I had scanned our press office cuttings and picked up the EA piece and had already thought about the impact on the water industry and our reaction.

Not thinking for one minute that it would be raised later by royalty. I gave him my cogent view and off he went. A friendly chat with a friendly guy.

JC Super star?

By now I was getting to know Jonson Cox and his way of working. Change was very much underway, and we had Price Waterhouse Coopers crawling under every stick and stone of internal organization and business process, ably steered by a couple of ex managers from Jonson's previous environmental group business, along with 'Mr Hull' and other project managers.

Ofwat levels of service performance began to rise as some early improvements kicked in. Jonson asked for and got a £6 million investment approval from the plc into new technology – including the introduction of a new component, probably the earliest introduction of any UK water company.

Tough books. For the first time the interface between customer (call centre), works planning and scheduling, and technician at the sharp end, was seamless. This and other significant IT, operational, and customer service business change initiatives significantly improved the company's Ofwat positioning.

So much so that within 4 years YWS was to go from bottom to top of the league on Ofwat levels of service performance measures and indicators. No mean achievement for him and the excellent team he had gathered around him.

He was probably the sharpest intellectually gifted guy that I worked with in my career. I remember being at senior management team meetings where a succession of project managers would enter the room and present their case for specific project approval and funding.

They had probably worked on the project for the thick end of 3 months, and he had seen the papers a few hours before. They would answer the A,B and C questions, but by the time Jonson had got to pertinent question F they were floundering. An intellectual prowess not matched by many.

Did I trust him? No. Was he liked internally? Like all managers, some did some didn't. What was it about him? I am not sure. Fundamentally I think he was shy and as with many it tended to compensate itself as tough, at times terse, and often uncompromising.

Did he like me? I think he was wary of me. I had a couple of run-ins with him. The first was embarrassing. For him.

145

There had been a high-profile inaccurate news story on water quality in one of the Yorkshire papers. My recommendation was that I talk to the Editor, we take it on the chin, and forget it. The story had not run anywhere else and a conversation with their Editor would be sufficient to make the point and move on. Not so said Jonson.

We took advice from a top rated and well-known firm of London media lawyers who said we had a case. Jonson was keen to hire them and to go forward with a plan of action.

I repeated my advice to Jonson that we were in danger of winning the battle but losing the war. Our reputation with the media and local opinion formers was still shaky and recovering from the drought. This was a local and popular newspaper.

Bringing the case would encourage the rehearsing of past negative comments in the newspaper but this time to a much wider audience, even if the case went in our favour. He would not let it go. He insisted that it should be on the agenda of the next management team meeting with attendance swelled by YWS water quality experts.

In an atmosphere akin to a courtroom setting, he put his case and I mine. He asked for a vote around the boardroom. It was overwhelmingly in my favour of argument. Not the result he wanted. The embarrassment was self-inflicted and the exercise futile.

Jonson was the complete antithesis of Kevin Bond. That caused growing friction within the business. Kevin, open, creative, charismatic, and easily bored with detail. Jonson, cerebral, incisive, and structured.

I remember in the early days of working with him, he was keen to get media training. I wasn't so sure, but he wanted the experience.

We went down to a high-flying media training outfit in London. He was uncomfortable and not ideally suited to that environment. I knew it before we made the trip.

It was no shame. Being media savvy and coming across in a relatively relaxed and confident manner takes time and training but you can get there with the right basic essential of personality type and disposition.

But if the core of a personality is naturally shy, edgy, or the slightest bit uncomfortable, it is exposed in the forensic lens of the camera. No amount of training can polish that particular apple. It is no disgrace and I have worked with many who are of similar disposition.

Anyway our relationship was tolerable and professional for 18 months or so as the successful business process changes happened thick and fast. I was also chuffed at the way the communications team had developed in that time.

And then change came suddenly again to our unlikely hero. It was now the autumn of 1998. Margaret Stewart, Director of Corporate Affairs, with whom I had a great working relationship, came to see me at the YWS Bradford office.

After our usual catch up with how things were going she went over to close my office door. I had started to talk about my employ at YWS and future plans. She urged me to do nothing, and then, confidentially, let me know that she was about to leave YW plc and join National Grid in a similar role.

Her offer was almost finalised, and she would probably be resigning in the next two weeks. She went on to say that " when I hand in my resignation, I would not be surprised if Kevin wanted to talk to you about joining him as my replacement in the plc."

Two weeks later, she did, and he did. Just as Margaret had predicted I got a call from Kevin to go and see him in Leeds. We talked about Margaret's departure and was I up for a move to the plc? We talked about the many challenges, the pace of committed growth and acquisition of non-regulated businesses and activities whilst still ensuring that we continued the improvements that Jonson and his team were making in the regulated business.

We agreed terms and shook hands. Back at the Bradford office later that day, I got a call on a crackling car phone from Jonson Cox, returning from Hull.

"Alan, it's Jonson, it's likely that Kevin will contact you to offer you the Corporate Affairs Director role at plc. My strong advice is don't take it. We have got a lot of things happening in YWS and I want you to stay and be part of it," he said.

I explained that Kevin and I had met earlier, and I had accepted the role. Jonson didn't like coming second best at anything, so I knew I had to be aware of potential slings and arrows.

Chapter 21. Regular guy to Groupie

Me (left) & Kevin Bond CEO

In the Autumn of 1998 I joined Kevin Bond and the rest of the plc team. Kevin had an agenda for me that was both daunting and exciting. Amongst the shopping list of specific challenges we talked about the potential acquisition of a US water company and the rebranding of the plc. The latter was both complex and far reaching in terms of the differing stakeholders involved, from the City and Stock Exchange, the myriad of regulatory bodies, to all employees in the different businesses in the Group, and their customers and suppliers.

The name change was long overdue. I had seen the confusion it created, particularly with local customers of having almost identical names for the Group (Yorkshire Water plc) and the core regional water and wastewater business (Yorkshire Water Services).

The confusion wasn't confined to Yorkshire but also mirrored in my previous companies, Severn Trent and South West Water. Most times with group acquisitions, many local customers and bill payers wrongly, but understandably, thought we were using their money to "splash" out on new ventures.

We began working with a specialist London consultancy at the end of 1998 and started the internal dialogue of taking the Board with us in terms of name change options, process, and timing, early in the New Year. Now when it comes to naming anything, from babies to businesses, everyone has a view. The Board was no different.

Amongst others, I remember one director coming up with a Yorkshire reservoir name. It seemed to me to be an odd suggestion bearing in mind we were attempting to differentiate, not to replace one local name with another.

Midway through the name selection process we did have a huge slice of luck in NOT choosing one of the front-runners. Bear in mind that the stated Board strategy was changing, growing, building value, not only in the UK and Europe, but also North America.

The name Arken seemed to resonate. Firstly with ourselves and the consultancy we were working with, plus Kevin and a number of insiders working on the rebrand. Easy to say, read, and transatlantic friendly. As we got into the Spring we had a decision deadline to meet. The name, however subjective, was the easy bit.

The behind-the-scenes process which followed of imagery and artwork creation and rationale, practical rebranding preparation of a host of items including signage, buildings, stationery, vehicles etc. was extensive. Add to that the planning of a comprehensive suite of financial and other communications programmes and initiatives for the many different stakeholders in the UK, Europe, and the US.

Arken was still favourite. We were soon to press the no-going-back button when......the name Arkan, a Serbian Warlord, and the 'Butcher of Bosnia,' suddenly flashed across world news headlines along with the Balkans War conflict. And stayed there for weeks and months. Allegedly Serbia's most notorious war criminal and indicted by the International Criminal Tribunal for the Former Yugoslavia.

I did not need to be told. Back to the drawing board. The Gods of timing smiled on us, but only just.

The alternative front runner, Kelda, was now centre stage. Scandinavian origin and meaning source of water or stream. Again simple to say, spell, and recall. Neutral enough to be European and simple enough for the US.

Kevin and the Board approved, and we could begin to plan all of the different facets of delivery. It was also agreed that we would announce the rebrand to all stakeholders at the Group Preliminary Results on Tuesday 1st June 1999.

A positive date for the business in terms of growth, change, and confidence. Coincidentally, on the same day, the appointment of a non-executive director who would go on to see things very differently and change things dramatically. His name was John Napier.

Another royal encounter

I received another invitation to meet and greet a member of the Royal family. Could it have been that I had made such a good impression with Prince Andrew that 'Andy' (to his friends) had pushed his elder brother to invite me round for tea?

Err. No. This time it was a Seminar and Reception at St James Palace to

meet HRH The Prince of Wales, as part of his role as President of Business in the Community. I also got the chance to see the sumptuous surroundings of the Palace and to network with many of the great and good business colleagues who were avid supporters of the Prince and his incredible work in supporting local charities.

Expanding across the pond

The provision of water and wastewater services in the US was, and continues to be massively fragmented, outdated, inconsistent, and in many cases not fit for purpose. There are approximately 150,000 public water systems (PWS), ranging from handfuls of customers to large city water and municipal undertakings.

Most Americans are served by around 50,000 of the PWS, known as community water systems. Most are publicly owned with only around 12% from private (so-called "investor-owned") utilities.

A prime reason for the YW Board to be looking at potential expansion into the US market. The fragmentation has led to significant inconsistencies and lack of compliance on drinking water quality standards and water resource capacity and needs.

Often the smaller systems cannot afford the capital investment needed in new treatment technology and processes, leading to local regulatory derogations or lack of follow-up prosecution.

One thing is for sure, the US framework for the provision of safe drinking water and wastewater services, both in quality and quantity, lags many years behind that of the UK.

To take advantage of potential US water consolidation, and given our greater knowledge and experience of large-scale, regional water services, in early 1999 we started talking to Aquarion; one of the top ten largest investor-owned water companies in the US, and based in Bridgeport, Connecticut.

Aquarion served 500,000 population in Connecticut and Long Island, New York with a workforce of almost 400 employees. Sales agreement was reached, and the acquisition was conditionally completed. Plans were made to announce, as with the rebranding, at the Group Preliminary Results on Tuesday 1st June 1999.

If we needed reminding how we in the UK water industry are so far in advance of our US water cousins in terms of water industry organization and structure, here is a revealing set of facts.

Connecticut state is around 5000 square miles, has a population of approximately 3.5 million served by over 2,500 public water systems (drinking water only).

Yorkshire is around 4600 square miles, has a population of 5 million served by <u>one</u> water company providing drinking water services, as well as wastewater treatment services. Many years behind the UK and long overdue consolidation opportunities.

And finally one quirky, and very different contrasting disposition between the US water consumer and the UK equivalent.

Often in the sumptuous surroundings of the Waldorf, Savoy, Park Lane, or other palatial London hotels where the typical Uncle Sam vacationer stays, they will enquire at reception as to why they cannot taste the chlorine in the tap water? On the other hand the typical UK consumer will complain if they can taste the chlorine.

Moral of the story? Our transatlantic cousins want to taste the disinfection reassurance. Here we trust it.

Fall of soot

I guess for those of an ultra-conservative, hard-nosed demeanour, the following is going to appear ridiculous. And it is. However the chance to be jocular is rare in the hectic swirl of suits and corporate agendas.

One of the Yorkshire Water plc directors had a preference, dare I say obsession, to retain his jet-black hair in spite of distinguished grey flecks regularly appearing and multiplying in his mane. My wife calls it highlighting but in this case lowlighting.

Such dramatic overnight colour change was stark and obvious. It also became the subject of speculation in terms of timing, particularly with the Company Secretary and me, who shared a similar sense of humour. In many ways this was unfortunate. The 'blackout' saga began to gain a life of its own.

It would manifest itself at the weekly executive management team meeting held on Monday morning. In order that we did not enter the meeting and guffaw at the sight of a fresh cranium coating, we got into a slick early warning process.

It worked well. The executive meeting would start at 10 00 am and if I or the Company Secretary caught sight of the black-maned Director, beforehand, and he had been at the dye bottle over the weekend, we would quietly open appropriate office door and declare 'fall of soot.'

Before quick exit. The commitment was total. If either of us had a visitor in the room at the time we were still duty bound to briefly utter the three-word early warning code; 'fall of soot.'

From personal experience I know that on occasions my visitor would look at me as if to say what was that all about? I would pass it off with either "problems with the air conditioning" or " my colleague has been working very hard."

Tuesday 1st June 1999

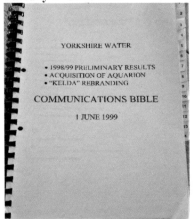

A huge communications exercise in the UK and North America – and all in one day. The coming together of three major announcements on the same day supported by comprehensive presentations and briefing information, tailored for UK and US stakeholders and financial markets. Preliminary Results for 1998/99, rebranding of the plc business, and acquisition of Aquarion US Water Utility

For around 4 weeks before the date I worked on the content of a 'Communications Bible' that included Stock Exchange announcements, executive presentations, press releases, letters to employees of YW and Aquarion, letters to key opinion formers in the UK and US, briefing notes, position statements, and more. Timing on the day was important, bearing in mind that we were 5 hours ahead of the US.

We had a team in London which included the Chairman, CEO, Finance Director and me, a team in Yorkshire, and an Aquarion executive team in the US. In London we began at 7:30 am and finished at 7:00 pm. The US team announced at 7:30 am (US time). All went OK.

The following day we flew to the US and on the next morning talked to all four hundred inquisitive Aquarion employees at a gathering in Bridgeport, Connecticut. Understandably they were thirsty for knowledge about the UK business and their new owner.

I remember an enthusiastic group of them seemingly disbelieving me that ONE water and wastewater business in the UK could provide a service to 5 million people whereas Connecticut needed over two thousand five hundred entities to provide water only.

"Put that past me again" was a regular retort. And, as if to rub it in even more, I said we only needed ONE operations control centre to manage the lot. I think they got the message that their new owners were genuine smart arses.

AGM Harrogate August 1999

No resting on laurels and on to the AGM in Harrogate. A chance for all shareholders, large and small, to quiz the top team on the activity of the past few months including branding and strategic direction. No massive dissenters. No demonstrations. Lively but constructive.

My concern was not of shareholders but one of the latest non executives to join the plc Board. As is the usual ritual, I briefed the plc executives and non-executives immediately prior to the start of the AGM agenda.

From Q&A's on brand change, US acquisition, Results, executive pay, water bills, and a myriad of current high profile operational or engineering issues likely to be raised. I had been around long enough to be aware of, and not like, a sullen stare from one of the latest non execs to join. John Napier.

It was the first time I had met him. He did not know me. And yet despite this, and throughout the briefing, I could sense a look of disdain and discomfort in him. It seemed he did not like me tutoring either him or, for all I knew, the Board. In short it appeared he had taken an instant dislike.

His disparaging look gave it away. Each to their own was my lingering thought. Onwards and upwards.

Aquarion corporate communications

Following our announcement of the Aquarion acquisition earlier in June there was a need to support our Connecticut colleagues with a series of meetings and greetings with key opinion formers in the US.

State politicians were taken aback that this almost unknown UK water company had the temerity to successfully launch a bid and win ownership of one of their prized and long-standing investor-owned water companies, despite the reassurance of the Aquarion President, Rich Schmidt, that we were the good guys. All very well but let's have a look at them was the native message.

And so, in the second half of 1999 I went backwards and forwards across the pond, sometimes with, and sometimes without Kevin, in a charm offensive to calm any fears of rape and pillage, meeting local dignitaries, organisations, and the press.

At the heart of the environmental concern was the protection of some 20,000 acres of 'watershed' land and the perception that we would attempt to sell large tracts to maximize the acquisition. Local Aquarion customers included Hollywood stars Paul Newman and Minnie Driver.

Mr Newman in particular was a passionate environmentalist and outspoken crusader of land heritage and protection. He need not have worried, but I understood his concern. The UK water companies environmental credentials and reputation on land and water catchment protection was second to none in Europe, and arguably in the World. I had seen and worked in magnificent watershed landscapes, Dartmoor in the South West, Peak District in North Derbyshire, the Yorkshire Dales, and North York Moors. Managed by custodians who enhanced as well as protected catchments. We did not need lessons on watershed protection but avoiding a mini–Boston Tea Party was key, and we needed to convey that message of reassurance.

I recall one particularly intense meeting with state political leaders in Hartford, Connecticut, capital city of the state. Kevin Bond, Rich Schmidt and I attended. After the usual niceties, the discussion got into the nuts and bolts of concern. Environmental protection was at the top of the agenda. They listened to the rationale of both Kevin and Rich as they sought to reassure. I kept my powder dry. For a while.

However, my intuition told me that we were being were too formulaic. The Hartford Chairman was courteous, but I could tell not altogether persuaded.

As the debate continued, I pondered that around that table no-one had the depth of experience on the subject than I had. Strains of the Magnificent Seven theme began to enter my head.

OK, I was no professional environmentalist, but had worked closely with scores of passionate and committed UK water environmental specialists on the moors and dales of our green and pleasant land. Speak or forever hold your cod piece. I signalled to the Chairman that I would like to add my thoughts.

I related my practical experience gained over thirty years and with three very different UK water companies, the behaviour and commitment at the sharp end as well as the Board room perspective, the age-old protection conventions, now backed up with tighter European environmental legislation (far tighter than the US).

Hartford's representatives were listening and nodding. Breathtaking arrogance here, but I think the input of a sharper-end practical view and realism pushed the reassurance credibility over the line. So did Kevin and Rich. I left the meeting believing that they thought they could trust us.

The Vikings are coming

ALcontrol, a subsidiary of the newly named Kelda Group, was a successful and growing international laboratory business with clients in the UK, Ireland, and the Netherlands.

The company owned and operated high-tech laboratories specialising in analytical services to the environmental, water, food, and emissions monitoring markets with 20 laboratories spread across Northern Europe.

In September 1999, ALcontrol completed the acquisition of KM Labs, a Swedish environmental analytical business with 13 laboratories and clients across Sweden and Norway. A total of 170 KM Labs employees would now be part of the wider Kelda Group.

Kevin Bond was unable to meet and greet the new arrivals at the acquisition presentation in Sweden, so I was asked to represent Kelda and welcome the new colleagues into the Group at what I was told would be a 'very different' location and event outside Stockholm, Sweden.

Intriguing. Armed with obligatory Kelda Group presentation, I was met at Stockholm Arlanda Airport to be driven to the event location. We drove for thirty or forty miles through remote hinterland covered in dense forestry. No vehicles, no people, no buildings. We came to a forestry turning and around a mile down a dusty agricultural track the trees parted to reveal a clutch of log cabins with a larger log building in the centre.

I was greeted by Gerard Baalhuis, ALcontrol MD, who I knew well, and shown to my log cabin. "Come and join us for drinks after you've settled in", said Gerard. I soon joined the gathering throng of new Kelda conscripts in the main building. In a couple of hours, I would be presenting.

But first, I was given a hessian sack to wear. Three holes, one for the head and two for the arms, together with a Viking helmet complete with horns. This was to be the historic garb of the day and evening sessions. Was it turning out to be one of those Swedish do's I had read about in my adolescent youth?

No. Admitted all were wearing the same unflattering, basic garb, and all were in very good spirits. But all were clever, knowledgeable, professional scientists. As expected most wanted to ask about Kelda, background, history, opportunities, and were eager to learn more.

Presentation over, and questions still coming thick and fast, we were shown to a series of benches with rough-hewn tables and "served" our celebratory meal. No cutlery. Just bare hands to take apart and devour the food.

Viking or what? Many conversations later it was time for my sack to hit the sack. The following morning I bade farewell to my new and extraordinary Kelda colleagues.

On the drive back to the airport, I reflected what a professional and enthusiastic lot they were. And one afterthought in particular. Although a 100% Swedish audience I didn't even have to think about one word of what they were articulating during my conversations. Perfect English – every one of them. Multilingual Vikings – not marauding.

Washington and Capitol Hill

In late autumn 1999 one or two of the more circumspect of US Connecticut Senators were asking for an audience with Kelda about the Aquarion acquisition. Could we come to Capitol Hill, Washington, meet with them and address their concerns?

I was assigned the task accompanied by Larry Bingaman, Vice President of Aquarion. He knew them. I didn't. I would do the talking about Kelda. After arriving in Washington DC we made our way to Capitol Hill to face some of the tightest security checks I have ever witnessed.

Once inside, we were ushered into a huge lobby area adjacent to the

Main Chamber in the House of Representatives of Congress.

We were told it was a busy day in the Main Chamber and the Senators would be taken out of one of the sessions for a brief discussion. We were told we'd have a maximum of

Senators and me (right) in Congress, Capitol Hill

seven minutes and no more.

A couple of Senators appeared. The main man, and asking most of the questions, was Representative Christopher Hays, a Connecticut Republican. Introductions over and a seven-minute snapshot presentation of Kelda later; the shortest in my career, I asked for any questions?

For the next 30-45 minutes they overshot their own deadline. All manner of questions but significantly, "you say you do wastewater treatment as well?" asked one of the Senators.

" Yes," I said. He went on, "we have chronic problems with sewage pollution around Long Island Sound (tidal estuary lying between the state of Connecticut to the north, and Long Island, NY to the south). "Do you think you can help us?" I assured them we could. They then hurried back to the Chamber, no doubt to resume the age-old Republican v Democrat political snarling in the House of Representatives. Job done. And more potential business.

Napier meeting No 2 and a one-to-one

Although I had seen John Napier at Board meeting presentations since the AGM, we had not had any detailed conversation. In early 2000 that changed. Brandon Gough retired as non-executive Chairman and Napier replaced him.

Shortly after, I needed to brief him on a relatively routine matter that as Chairman, he should be aware of. Directors remunerations were always of interest to the 'fat cat' inspired press and media and it was not unusual for newspaper owners and media outlets to purchase shares in the company to enable access to latest executive remuneration contracts.

As shareholders they were entitled to visit the office and ask to see them. Kelda's latest remuneration contracts had been approved and would be available for shareholder scrutiny shortly. Important therefore to agree a position statement to be used in response to any subsequent press enquiries. This exercise was routine. I had done it on numerous previous occasions at both Severn Trent and South West Water.

I asked to see Napier for a short one-to-one briefing so that he was in the picture and agreed with our press position. There then followed a surreal meeting which I wished I could have recorded.

He and I sat in a 3m x 3m box of a meeting room at Kelda corporate HQ Sovereign Street Leeds. I expected the atmosphere and was not surprised or disappointed. I briefly explained the meeting purpose and went on to show him the position statement.

"Why do we have to do this?" asked Napier.

"Do what John?" I said.

"Make directors contracts available. Why can't we say no to the requests?" he asked.

" We are required to do so under Company Law and Regulations, that's my understanding and has been for some time," I replied.

Irritated he said, "Let's get the Company Secretary in."

I summoned the Company Secretary and whilst awaiting his presence, the small talk was extremely small. Meanwhile a lady came in with a platter of sandwiches.

With an atmosphere resembling a scene from the Godfather I mumbled, "these are egg and cress and I have to watch my cholesterol," offering the platter in John's direction.

"I'm not bothered when I die," he responded.

At last we had agreed on something. Arrival of Company Secretary and the issue was further explained to him. The Secretary's view confirmed mine. It was company law and, if asked, we had to comply.

"Well my view is that we don't," Napier said. End of meeting.

New York and almost arrested

In March 2000, I organised a US Analyst and Investor briefing at the World Trade Centre, New York. Kevin Bond (CEO), Rich Schmidt (Aquarion), James Newman (CFO Kelda) and I were to attend. Meeting arrangements were finalised, including bulk printing of presentation hand-outs at Aquarion HQ in Bridgeport, Connecticut the night before.

I was in Bridgeport to manage production and take to New York. I was then driven to Times Square, NY where I was staying overnight, complete with two heavyweight boxes of print material. Scheduled to meet the other Kelda guys at the World Trade Centre (WTC) for early morning rehearsals the next day.

The following morning I took an early yellow cab journey to the WTC, heavyweight boxes safely in the boot. I arrived around 7:30am. Cabbie emphasised that he was not supposed to stop, but quickly dropped me and the boxes off immediately outside the expansive WTC main building doors.

Pandemonium at the time with early-bird New Yorkers cramming into the building from every direction. A sea of humanity with coffee cups, all focussed on getting into the building. Like an ant colony on speed. I looked for a doorman. No doorman. I looked for reception. No sign of reception. I looked for a helping hand. No takers.

Instead the single-minded mission of the worker bees in getting into the building first. For fifteen minutes I stood guard over the boxes, hoping against hope I could attract a doorman with trolley attached. No luck. So with shades of home-town boy Clark Kent, I decided it was time for action.

Taking on a Superman mission, I pushed the heavy boxes to a non-trip-over spot by the door side and made a dash to locate the main reception. Desk clerks by the thousand but no trolley and no doorman. In an impassioned plea, and bowels rumbling, I asked a clerk to find a doorman for me urgently and gave her my location.

She acquiesced. Praise the Lord. Now, morphing back to Clark Kent, I quickly returned to the entrance and the boxes. In my absence a large, and getting larger, crowd had gathered, and the messianic human flow had temporarily been halted. Three burly NY Policemen were managing an incident.

The 'incident' was two abandoned boxes. Forming a triangle around them the cops were shouting at the impatient commuters to stand back.

I stepped into the cordoned area feeling much more like Mr Bean than Clark Kent and claimed ownership of the boxes. They were not amused. After checking my ID and reason for being there, I was given a lecture by one of the officers.

Did I know you don't leave unattended packages here? Did I know the security risk? Did I know that terrorists tried to blow this building up a few years ago? (1993 – truck bomb in the basement). Did I not know the sensitivity?

After calming down, and listening to my grovelling apology, he agreed to wait over the boxes whilst I located a doorman and trolley. The cruel irony was that in 180 days on from the day of my conversation with the dedicated NY cop, there would be no sidewalk, no people, no doors, and no building. Only rubble. I hoped he was OK.

Holy hospitality – the Dean and the deal

Dean of York, The Very Rev
Dr Raymond Furnell

As I have mentioned before, Kevin Bond was the consummate hand-shaker and friendly face of the new look Yorkshire Water following the dark days of the drought. The benefits were enormous. The gradual return to an organization that could be trusted amongst the great and the good of Yorkshire was, in no small measure, down to his relationship building, understanding, and empathy in the local community and its representatives.

However, there was more than one occasion when Kevin, having been to meet a local worthy or organisation, would ask that I follow up on promises made.

Such was the case with a meeting with the Dean of York, The Very Rev Dr Raymond Furnell. Kevin said that the Dean was looking for a sponsorship donation for the upcoming York Minster Choir's Concert Tour of the United States and would I give the Dean a call?

Later that day I rang the Dean. He was an engaging character and we struck up an instant rapport. He talked about the upcoming tour.

"I think we were talking sponsorship of £2000," said the Dean, "and that would entitle you to the Kelda logo on tour brochures and programmes, including advertising material in the US."

160

I was underwhelmed and suggested we meet to discuss. A week later I was overwhelmed. I was sitting in the Deanery of York Minster. A

wonderful, architectural specimen, adjacent to the 7th century York Minster, one of the most magnificent cathedrals in the world and the largest of its kind in Europe. We sat in the Dean's study and negotiation was in the air.

The Deanery, York Minster

I was in the presence of a high-level negotiator who began by reiterating the offer. The Dean assured me that the concert programmes would receive wide circulation amongst US State key opinion formers in the six or seven concert locations. I was not convinced and had been working on a much more pragmatic, albeit ambitious alternative that would really give Kelda value for money.

Presumptuous and I guessed impractical for the Dean and the Choir. But in for a penny...I had noted that the final concert of the tour was to be in New York on the weekend of the 8th and 9th April 2000. I had been working with Larry Bingaman (VP Aquarion) on a Gala dinner for Bridgeport key opinion formers, customers, local officials, and their partners, on Friday 7th April in Bridgeport, Connecticut. A getting-together and getting-to know new owner and new customer. Was there any conceivable way that the Choir could squeeze one additional concert in before their final New York concert that weekend. A performance at the Bridgeport Dinner?

The Dean pondered. He wanted his £2000 and I wanted the value. After a few moments he said that he would have to consult with the Choirmaster to see if it was feasible. Certainly the location of Bridgeport, 60 miles from New York, made it practically feasible, but the choir boys vocal dexterity in terms of one further concert on an already busy concert schedule, might be too much.

The Dean would come back to me. Which he did, positively, a day later. We were on and the Gala dinner had a new and high-class momentum. I was convinced our American cousins would love it.

Chapter 22. A bitter sweet finale

In the couple of days before the Gala dinner I had meetings in Bridgeport and met up with Kevin in the hotel dinner venue late afternoon Friday 7th April 2000.

Also waiting in the wings, having arrived safe and sound, was the Dean of York and the Minster Choir. Tired from their tour exertions but delighted with how they had been received by the US packed audiences, they were in good spirits. The Dean in particular was his usual positive and humorous self. Cometh the hour cometh the Choir.

As I expected their performance was fantastic, and I felt proud to be a Brit that night. Standing ovations over, the Dean was pleased that we were so appreciative of the Choir and the part they had played in what was a memorable night.

With their help and positive support, I thought we had sowed the seeds of a future positive relationship and trust with our new transatlantic customers. Kevin thought so to. He thanked me for my efforts and said he would see me back in Leeds on Monday.

I reminded him that I was in New York briefing our US financial PR advisors on Monday followed by the rest of the week in Tampa on a short golfing holiday. Final pat on the back and "see you a week on Monday then." That was the last time I was to see Kevin.

Monday morning came and I made my way to the corporate offices of the financial PR company in the heartland of Wall Street. Several meetings later I checked my watch: 2:30pm. There were a couple of messages I needed to leave for my secretary back in Leeds before deciding to call it a day, get my things together and head off to JFK for the flight to Tampa.

It was 7:30pm UK time, and she would not be in the office, but I would leave something on her answering machine to pick up next day. Surprisingly the phone was answered. It was the PA of the Company Secretary. After greeting, I asked, "what are you doing there at this time?" whilst checking my watch again.

"Oh, there's been a Board meeting today," she said. I knew Board meetings never went on until this time, and I could tell she was hesitant and not her usual friendly disposition.

"I think I should put you on to my boss," she added.

And with that the Company Secretary came on the phone.

"Hi Alan, where are you?"

"In New York. You must have had a marathon Board meeting," I said.

"Kevin's gone," he said in a sombre tone. "Gone where?" I asked.

"Gone, he's resigned."

Silence on both ends of the phone.

"Napier is now Executive Chairman," he said. Silence again.

"Not a good time to be away from the company Alan" he advised.

"It's a great time to be away," I said, still gathering my thoughts and dealing with the shock.

"It gives me plenty of time to work out my negotiating position for an exit package," I said. "Couldn't work with that bloke for more than a day before wanting to hit him." The phone call ended soon after.

A week later, I was back in my office in Leeds. Relaxed, tanned, and more than ready for the anticipated Napier discussion.

As expected, his secretary came in and said that Mr Napier would like to see me at 10:00am.

The appointed hour and ironically back to the 3m x 3m 'Live and Let Die' meeting room. Napier sitting waiting. Serious expression. Mini small talk.

Napier. "Did you have a good holiday?"

Smith. "Brief but pleasant."

Napier: "Alan you will know of the news of Kevin's departure?"

Smith: "Yes"

Napier: "I don't think you and I will be able to work together. I will not be operating as Kevin did and therefore will not need your communications expertise and support."

Smith: "Understood John."

Napier: "You've done nothing wrong."

[I had already been tipped off that morning by the Chief Auditor that during my absence Napier had asked him to trawl through my past expenses looking for any wrongdoing or fraudulent claims – needless to say he had found none]

Smith: "I could have told you that John."

[recent annual appraisal showed all the ticks in the right boxes – which he also would have seen]

Napier: "So I would like to offer you 12 months' salary if you would agree to leave this coming Friday."

Smith: "Where do I sign John?"

Napier: "The HR Director will be in your room when you get back to finalise all the arrangements."

Back in my office I signed all the papers and momentarily sat alone, smiling, reflecting, and occasionally chuckling to myself at the outcome. Bloody fantastic! The reality was I was being paid over £100K to leave a job that I would have left anyway, simply because I could not stand to work for the boss. And by leaving quickly, avoiding a potential manslaughter charge.

Not long to be smug though. In the corporate world news travels fast. Later that day a small gathering found its way into my office. Fellow directors, and others who had heard of my Friday departure.

During the positive, informal wake, the cranium of Jonson Cox appeared at the door and was about to come in. Luckily I saw him.

"Johnson," I bellowed above the hubbub, "this gathering is for friends only." Embarrassed, he blustered a response which was somewhat difficult to hear and continued to enter.

"Did you hear what I said?" I shouted, "you are not welcome!" Red faced and obviously embarrassed he retreated. That was the last I saw of him.

The bizarre relationship with Napier had one more final surreal twist. Much against my better judgement I had agreed to a foot-shuffling farewell drinks 'do' on the Friday afternoon. Pineapple chunks and cheese-on-sticks had never been my forte.

However Napier had insisted, and for over 100,000 reasons I conceded. During the event he asked if he could have a quiet word with me in private.

" I understand you are going to set up your own business?" he enquired. "Go on," I said, "what is your point?"

" I may need your professional expertise to support various strategy announcements from time to time. Could you draw up a consultancy proposal based on a number of days in the year?" he said.
"Certainly John," I said.

Later I put together a one-page consultancy proposal and posted it to him. A £3000 daily rate should guarantee that I wouldn't see him again. It worked.

Kelda Requiem

And so the unique experience of the Yorkshire Water highs and lows were now behind me. Monday 6th November 1995 I came. Friday 21st April 2000 I went.

Reflections, many. Regrets, none. A roller coaster ride, not dissimilar to my South West Water days. Different issues, same hostility, and, at times, same chaos. One constant; the dedication of people who work in the industry. No difference between the commitment of an operative working in Launceston, Leicester, or Leeds.

The top 1% create the issue. The 99% manage them. Yes, the drought could have been anticipated. Hindsight is a wonderful thing. Foresight is even better. A monopoly supplier of life's essential resource has to have a surplus of the latter.

Did Kevin Bond turn the tide of public opinion? Yes. Certainly amongst politicians and many other key opinion formers. Was his exit premature? Yes. Was it welcomed internally and externally? No.

Did Kelda Group (and previously Yorkshire Water plc), founded and grown on a positive mix of complimentary and profitable water and environmental businesses, go on to become a shadow of its former self; with only a regulated business, and local customers money to maintain further shareholder returns? Yes.

Who was the architect of the latest model? A man who joined the Board in June 1999 as a non-executive when the clear corporate strategy was 'changing, growing, and building,' agreed at the AGM in 1999, and later communicated in the Annual Report and Accounts of that year.

A man who joined the Board when the Yorkshire Water Services business had been turned around post drought and was now top of the pops in comparison with other water companies.

In just 10 months this non-executive rose to Non-Executive Chairman, and then to Executive Chairman. Shortly after there was an embarrassing rejection by the Regulator (Ofwat) of the company's proposed mutualisation of the regulated business.

The profitable non-core businesses were sold. £750 million returned to shareholders in 2006 followed in 2007 by a £3 billion shareholder bonanza when the company was sold.

In 2008 the former non-executive resigned.

Chapter 23. The birth of Water-people

I was talking to Karen Moir, HR Director of Kelda on my last day at Kelda. Karen was one of the few HR Directors I had met who was pragmatic rather than process driven, and I liked her. A great professional. Too often 'Human Remains' Directors, or to continue the cannibalistic theme, 'Head of People,' use the mantra, 'don't let the outcome get in the way of a good process.' Not Karen.

"What are you going to do?" she asked.

" A lot," I replied, "I'm going to start my own business here in Leeds." She asked if I was going to take up the Coutts outplacement service which was offered in the severance agreement?

"No," I said firmly. "Don't need it. I know what I am doing and don't want any nurse-maiding."

"So Mr High and Mighty, where are you going to operate from?" she enquired.

"I'm going to get an office and kit it out," I said.

"That will take at least three months and in the meantime you could use Coutts as your virtual office,"she advised.

Smart operator that Karen Moir. Of course she was right. My pig headedness for not wanting to appear to be a wounded soldier attending rehab was way off beam.

And so I walked out of Kelda Group with a spring in my step and a windfall in my pocket. What was next? I had ideas. Plenty of them. I was wedded to the water industry, like it or not. And I liked it. Could I communicate?

A modest Yes. So knowledge of the water industry and a reasonable Derbyshire communicator. Did I want more of corporate communications? A consultancy business maybe? No, you can have too much of a good thing.

So what had I seen on the 'inside' provided by an external service to the water industry that I had not been impressed with?

Answer, recruitment. Did I know how a recruitment consultancy operated? No. But that was the easy bit. It had to be. There were many ten-a-penny consultancies in the market place.

Their blindingly obvious deficiencies were knowledge of the water industry and how it worked. As important what did individual animals look like? From junior technician to Board level, to expertise in scientific, operational, engineering, customer service, and regulatory activities, I knew the breed. Was that sufficient USP to start a business? I thought so.

Anyway, thanks to Ms Moir, I ended up spending 3 months in 'rehab.' Coutts was fantastic for me. About 200 metres from my Leeds city centre apartment and really invaluable in being able to use all the facilities, lap tops, phones, secretarial services, etc. I felt genuinely sorry for those redundant professionals that I saw that had, unexpectedly, departed their respective companies, many carrying the scars and still in obvious shock.

And here I was bouncing in each morning talking to design consultants, website, and advertising people etc about the essential foundations needed for the new business.

During this Dragons-Den-like early creative period, a canny individual approached me in Coutts and asked if I had 'signed on?' I had no idea what he meant.

"No, I am not wanting to claim any benefit," I said.

"Well you should still sign on," he advised, "if you don't, you won't have the required National Insurance stamps and contributions and it could affect your pension."

So reluctantly down to the local Leeds Benefit Office. Standing in a queue with unshaven ne'er-do-wells, and youths sporting reverse baseball caps and the latest gear, was like a scene from the 'Full Monty.' I felt distinctly uncomfortable and wondering what I was doing there.

Worse was to follow. After a long wait, I eventually arrived at a vacant booth to be quizzed on all the usual vital statistics, name, address.

"And when would you like to claim benefit from?" asked the bespectacled administrator, with eyes fixed on smoking keyboard.

"I wouldn't," I replied.

"You wouldn't?" she quizzed with upturned nostrils.

"No, I am setting up my own business and so don't need funds," I said.

"Are you sure you don't need funds?" she persisted.

"Yes, I am sure," I insisted.

"Have you been for any interviews?" she said.

"No," I responded, "as I explained I am starting my own business so not looking for employment."

There was obviously a digital box that had to be ticked.

"So where can we say you have been for interviews during the last two weeks?" she asked through the perspex of screen and specs.

I was beginning to think that she could not hear me. I decided that not wanting a financial hand-out, not attending interviews, was going to cause a software crash on the other side of the counter, and for all I knew nationwide, so I joined the charade.

"How about NatWest and Tesco's?" I said.

"That's fine," she said, followed by lightening clacks on her bouncing keyboard. "Is there anything else I can help you with today?" My sanity, I thought of saying, but didn't. Quit while you're winning Alan.

Every two weeks for 3 months I followed exactly the same balls aching ritual. Baseball caps, ne'er-do-wells, bespectacled administrators, same questions, same answers. Although creativity with interviews began to wane.

It was now June 2000. I had decided on the new company name; 'Water-people.' By saying it, reading it, or ringing it, the name told you what we were about.

At the same time a great guy called Phil Mayo (ex YW) was helping me set up and design the website, and the equally talented Simon Ingham (ex YW) was designing all the brochures and hand-outs.

I urgently needed an office and a full-time administrator. The office solution and location was pure luck and a tip from a friend. LCVS was an independent, not-for-profit company set up with finance from the Department of the Environment and Leeds City Council to provide small low-cost office and manufacturing units.

It's aim was to help small businesses to start up and survive in Leeds city centre. Perfect. £210 per month and 12 months lease. I decided at the outset that I would loan the new business £40,000 as a start-up fund from my recent windfall. If I spent that, and didn't make any return from recruitment placements, I would wrap up and put it down to experience.

Now the need for an office administrator. Back in the Coutts office, a fantastic office manager, Kate, had been helping me out with all manner of things including typing, letter circulations, setting up fit for purpose Word and recruitment documents etc.

Did she fancy joining me on this adventure? Miraculously she said Yes. I now had a company name, website, office, and office manager. But no revenue. Water-people Ltd began trading in September 2000 and by the summer of 2001, I had paid myself back the £40,000 and still had working capital in the Bank.

To coin a phrase Water-people was in full flow. The gamble had paid off and the grim reaper was a distant memory. How and why the success? Simple, and the rationale I had first considered when thinking about Water-people.

The market place was crying out for a recruitment agency that actually knew the water industry and its people. As I would very often say, and still do, it's exceptional to be ordinary. To do the job you are set up to do in a market you are supposed to know.

But we live in an age where customer service is often confined to a phrase in the Annual Report; where businesses are reluctant to put a telephone number on a website for fear of having to employ more people; where you wait 20 minutes for a Bank, Lloyds, NatWest, or others, to answer the telephone (because they've shut the local walk-in branch) but you are told, "your call is important to us" or "we are experiencing a high number of calls" when the reality is that they are experiencing a low number of people to answer them; if your company doesn't do any of the above, your company is exceptional by being ordinary. Sorry a Victor Meldrew moment.

Our early clients were engineering design consultancies, often known as framework partners, working on water industry capital investment programmes and projects. We quickly established preferred supplier status with many of these consultancies, including Atkins, Black and Veatch, Halcrow, MWH, Carlbro, Ewan, Mouchel Parkman, Arup, Entec, Babtie (Jacobs), Meica, KBR, and others.

Gradually we went on to work with some of the water companies, although their processes were often clumsy and not sharp enough for the market.

Support for international placements also grew and we were now operating and placing water industry professionals in many parts of the World including Europe, the Middle East, North and South America, Asia, and Australia.

The French owned Vivendi Environmental (later Veolia) became interested in what we were doing. The relationship grew and we were successful in placing numerous experienced senior professionals in their long-term Riyadh water and wastewater contract with the National Water Company of Saudi Arabia. ADWEA (Abu Dhabi Water and Electricity Authority) also came on board, and we helped them create ADSSCO, Abu Dhabi Sewerage Services Company with an MD and other senior placements.

Time for more resources and a really good guy who worked for me at Yorkshire Water was interested. Sean Tandy had a contracting background in the industry and knew the likes of Balfour Beatty, Morrisons, Clancy Docwra, and other contracting businesses and people, so was a natural fit. Sean joined us in 2002 and did a great job

A Yorkshire Brew

A little while later a bizarre local mini lottery gathered momentum in our multi-company office complex in Dock Street, Leeds.

It began entirely by accident, aided by a mercurial caretaker's Monty Pythonesque sense of humour. At the back of our building we were overlooked by the impressive Leeds HQ and operational base of Tetley's Brewery.

A vast, busy, and sprawling site with 24-hour activity. On top of the main building was a huge neon-lit sign, **TETLEY'S BREWERY**.

Every couple of weeks or so a neon letter from the sign would fail, and not go unnoticed by the occupants of the mini businesses in our complex. It became part of the jocular small talk at the coffee machine.

Until Roger, the caretaker, suggested that he organize a lottery draw, based on the next letter to fail. For the record, the apostrophe in Tetley's was also included as that, like the letters, had an irregular life, if not light, of its own. [am I really writing this?...need to get out more]

The lottery interest grew quickly and began to include occupants of other buildings and businesses on Dock Street. So successful was it that Tetley's Brewery management became aware of the phenomenon and articles appeared in local press and the company's employee magazine.

A couple of months later Roger let us know that we were developing a lottery surplus due to unclaimed prizes from transient letter gamblers and unclaimed winnings. What to do with it? Again it was mad-cap Roger, the lottery founder, who suggested we invest in a racing pigeon.

A racing pigeon. There was no sense in the suggestion but, equally, there was no sense in the original lottery suggestion, so we agreed. The pedigree pigeon was aptly named: **ETLEY'S REWERY** which went on to win several cross-channel events before, sadly, the lights went out.

Baghdad calling

The next three years continued to be profitable and in 2004 I received an intriguing call from Malcolm White, Managing Director at Mott McDonald. The Iraq War had come and gone and there was a relative, albeit insecure, peace.

The US inspired coalition was setting about the task of rebuilding areas of the badly damaged Baghdad infrastructure. In the carve up of who does what, the Blair Government had told the US that the UK would take care of the city's shattered water supply network.

The problem, unsurprisingly, was that the UK civil servants could not identify any experienced technical water engineer who was willing to project manage the scope and extent of improvement work needed to be done.

Baghdad was still a volatile city. Hilary Benn, Secretary of State for International Development and a Blair Cabinet Minister, had called a meeting of the MD's of the top five UK engineering consultancies with expertise in water.

Malcolm White was an invitee. He explained to me that Benn had said that the absence of a technical engineering professional was causing diplomatic embarrassment and could they help to find a qualified water professional. My understanding was that the consultancies had drawn a blank and that Malcolm had been recommended to talk to me.

The 12-month contract was financially lucrative as was the commission if I was successful. I asked how urgent, and the reply was 'yesterday.' I asked that Malcolm leave it with me, and I would come back in a couple of days. There were only four international professionals on our database of 5000 plus that I thought could do the job.

But would they want to, given the security issues on the ground? I made calls to all four. They were located in Moscow, Jordan, Dubai, and South America respectively. Three out of four gave an immediate No. The fourth was coming to the end of his contract in South America and was interested. For security purposes I will call him John.

Within a couple of weeks John signed up and was given an intense briefing on security before flying out to Baghdad. He was to live and work for much of the time in the 'Green Zone,' an extensive and heavily fortified complex which was originally the Baghdad palace of Saddam Hussain.

The US military had converted the interior of the palace into row upon row of stacked portacabin accommodation, for both military and civilian contractors. John would call me from time to time, in a very relaxed manner, to let me know how things were going. I remember that I was the more nervous on those calls, sitting in Leeds, than he was sitting on the edge of volatility in the Green Zone.

He explained that, occasionally, he would have to make site visits to survey the damaged water infrastructure. The miliary would provide armed-to-the-teeth Land Rover escorts on such dangerous missions. John was sharing his portacabin accommodation with a semi-retired Australian professional oil engineer, carrying out similar rehabilitation work but on oil infrastructure and pipelines. John had got to know him well.

Tragically he was killed by an explosive device strapped to the vehicle he was travelling in whilst out on a survey. After 6 months, and a continuing deterioration in security, John and many other civilian contractors were withdrawn.

America – you cannot be serious

By the mid 2000's we had bought a home in Naples, South West Florida and were operating part US and part UK thanks to the wonders of the internet.

During the US trips I came across what was to be a compelling learning curve of American behaviour and culture. Most Americans could walk and chew, but not necessarily at the same time. We had many American friends, but they tended to be the exception rather than the rule in terms of such multi-tasking.

A prime example of the former was the raising of the UK flag outside our US home. Stars and Stripes were everywhere in the four hundred home golfing development, so I thought we should give balance. After all we were allies in numerous volatile world theatres.

A week later, I received a letter from the General Manager of the complex. There had been complaints from residents that I was flying a 'Confederate' flag and that only the Stars and Stripes was allowed. I responded by correcting the Manager and the uneducated complainants and emphasised that as a coalition partner, I was sure that the management committee would support. I received a further letter to say that failure to take down the flag would result in suspension of membership to the club house and golfing facilities. A special relationship indeed. If Winston only knew.

The US use or misuse of the English language is legend. They also talk at, rather than to, one another. When we would go into a 'greasy spoon' restaurant, which was always a delight on food and cost, I would often hear a rotund overweight ignoramus shouting to the waiter, 'gimme the bill.' No please and no thank you.

On the other hand I would sometimes wonder if I was talking ancient Egyptian when requesting similar. "Could I have the bill please?" was often answered by "pardon me?"…"could I have the bill please?"…. repeat "pardon me?" OK, when in Rome…"Gimme the bill." - Answer: "coming right up."

Similar telegram talking at Miami International Airport when approaching immaculately dressed American Airways assistants, "Excuse me please is this the economy or 1st class line?" "Pardon me?" "Is this the….", you get the idea. Followed by continued vacant look.

Resort to command; abbreviated bellow, "ECONOMY OR 1ST CLASS?"

Instant understanding and response, "economy sir."

Regrettably this is how many customer service employees are used to being spoken to by the US walk or chew brigade. Poor Bill Shakespeare would still be at the check-in desk. "To be…pardon me?…or…not to be…pardon me?…that is the question…do you have a question sir?"

My entrance into America suddenly became problematic. In my Kelda/Aquarion US days there was never an issue but for some reason, there was now. From the early days of owning the Florida home, I struggled to get through the immigration gestapo and the dutiful, thunderously applied, immigration approval passport stamp.

The questions were always the same despite trying different personality approaches; from monosyllabic, mute, miserable, to cheerful, chatty, and charming. None worked and I was usually sent to the Sin Bin. This is how it played out.

I would hand my passport over to the uniformed, gun toting, badge-clad, non-smiling immigration officer and wait. A flick through my passport and a look at his screen. A second flick through my passport and a second look at the screen.

Question: "Gotta middle name? Answer, "No."
Question: "You sure?" (chew-only anal question). Answer, "Yes."
Result? Sin Binned.

The sin binning manifested itself by the immigration officer raising his hand and signalling to an equally armed, non-smiling, burly colleague who would escort me to a large, overcrowded room of multicoloured individuals who had also failed to pass Go and collect a violently stamped passport. Whether I liked it or not I soon got used to the procedure, but the first time was a hairy experience.

I was given an entrance ticket to the Sin Bin. Number 76. Which meant that 75 more individuals would be interviewed before me. I went up to the 'front desk' and, in typical colonial fashion, explained that I knew Jeb Bush, then Florida Governor, and had spoken at one of his colleagues conferences in New Orleans. (true about the conference and colleague. Stretching it about knowing Jeb). His uncompromising demeanour did not flicker. Unimpressed.

"Is this your signature?" leaning forward from his lofty podium and pointing to the green waiver card I had completed earlier.
"Yes," I confirmed.

"Then you have waived all of your rights and I could put you on that plane out there and send you back to the UK in the next 30 minutes. OK? Now sit down and wait your turn."

That did not go well. And no plan B. Two and a half hours later, and with a wife sitting on suitcases in a deserted baggage hall enquiring as to when my trial date was, I was summoned into a claustrophobic shoe box of a room behind the almighty podium to meet the next badge-clad, side-armed rottweiler.

"Take a seat," he said, flicking through my passport.

Question: "Your full name?"

Answer: "Alan Smith."

Question: "Gotta middle name?"

Answer: "No."

Question: "Sure?"

Answer: "Sure."

He asked when I was last in the US? why? where was I staying? The US home address threw him, and he left the room. I suspect to see, electronically, whose name was on the deeds of the house. 15 minutes later he returned. "OK you can go," he said, violently stamping my green waiver card.

"If you don't mind me asking, why the forensic check," I said.

"Because you have exactly the same name and birth date of a guy we are keen to talk to," he said. "And he's bad, he's bad."

"Does he have a middle name?" I said, pushing my luck.

"Can't say but you're likely to get stopped again until we catch up with him. Have a good day," he said, handing me my passport.

And I was stopped. Many times as we regularly criss-crossed the pond to and from Yorkshire and Florida.

Orlando International Airport, which we used from time to time, was no different. Other than the fact that I was usually the only one in the Sin Bin, so incarceration time was less, but no less humour-less.

I would be ticketed into the Sin Bin as Number 1. When a badge-clad burly eventually appeared, I would be sat on the front row of 60 empty seats waiting to be called. The burly would walk into the room, mount the podium and shout 'Alan Smith.'

As I was the only human in the room, apart from the burly, I had to own up that it was me. However I had to shout back, "here," with raised arm. I would like to have thought that it was obvious, but, as I had learned, podium protocol was sacrosanct. Job in HR for him, I thought.

One other highly embarrassing moment at Orlando Airport. On this trip we took my wife's elderly parents. We agreed that it was important that we briefed John and Eileen beforehand about my likely incarceration so that they would not be alarmed and explained the reasons why.

I would meet them 'on the other side.' They understood but were a little apprehensive as we lined up to face the badge-clad burly and his all-powerful immigration stamp.

I went first. Passport flick. Second passport flick. Middle name? Stamped my passport! Have a good trip! This was no time to climb on the desk, embrace, kiss, or offer warm thanks to the Gatekeeper. Keep cool and head for baggage. There's a T-shirt for it.

Father-in-law was next in line. There was a long conversation at the desk. Astonishingly, the officers arm was raised, and he was led away to the Sin Bin. Was I imagining this? No. As he was being escorted away, he gave a plaintive glance back to us, as if to say, 'with good conduct I should be out soon.'

At least he had a middle name. But so did the bad guy that they were after. In fact all three of father-in-law's names were the same as the wanted miscreant. The bad guy was apparently wanted for shady union agent activities carried out in New York before fleeing over the border to Canada.

So father-in-law was interrogated and asked if had ever entered the US via the Canada/US border? Was he an active union man? when did he last visit the US? No to all and first time visit to the US. However, he did innocently admit to them that he was a former agent but had given it up some time ago.

Where? And when? A news agent in Birkenhead but now retired. Good conduct and early release followed. He was free to walk and chew.
Water-people flowing and growing
Meanwhile Water-people continued to grow in the UK and overseas. Northern Ireland Water, who had not succumbed to any notion of water privatisation, needed new thinking and new ways of working. A new Chief Executive was appointed. Katherine Bryan was an excellent operator and knew the score. She had worked for both gamekeeper and poacher. I knew her from Severn Trent days whilst providing publicity

support for her ground-breaking work on reed bed wastewater treatment in Leicestershire.

We went on to place many interim experienced professionals from the mainland into NIW and the organisation was better for it. Bringing new thinking and replacing the 'we've always done it that way' mentality. Huge strides under Katherine's stewardship but after her departure, like all things Northern Ireland, politics got in the way, and NIW morphed back into local government mentality.

By now Water-people was dealing with most UK water companies but the experience generally was not good. Slow and beaurocratic HR internal processes, but we lived with it. In time the communications deteriorated further especially in dealings with Thames Water, Southern Water, and Severn Trent Water.

All three appeared to decide that they could save a few pennies on operating costs by appointing outsourced or embedded national recruitment agencies. The likes of Reed, Capita, and Pertemps got involved. Response times were poor. The embedded agency teams had, understandably, no clue as to how the water industry worked and acted as glorified post offices.

Taking little understood instructions from internal managers about a role vacancy, shipping the job description of that vacancy to nominated 'preferred suppliers,' and receiving back potential candidate CV's. Generally they struggled to answer role queries or judge technical CV's. Gradually I thought that this arrangement was not good for our reputation with candidates.

Things came to a head with Thames Water who were particularly poor. I had arranged with Reed, their embedded recruitment partner, that two candidates would attend for interview for a role vacancy at the Reading office on an upcoming Monday morning.

I received a call from Reed early that morning asking if I could tell them what role the candidates currently sitting in the Thames Water reception had come to be interviewed for? Bear in mind Reed had previously requested that we set up the interviews. I sent a letter resigning Water-people from the preferred supplier status.

It was not received well. In the recruitment world there is usually a dogfight to get on a potentially lucrative preferred list and so for a company to resign from it was unusual if not unique. I told them I was more concerned about our reputation than their surprise.

You can lead the horse to water…

We had another example of water company recruitment process effectiveness during this time. The mantra more and more appeared to be don't let the outcome get in the way of a good process. I was contacted by a a young 25-year-old, enthusiastic project manager, who had been recommended to talk to me.

After a conversation which included his stated aim to be a Managing Director by his mid-thirties, I was impressed and thought he had the right calibre and ambition for me to promote to a contact in Severn Trent. He was keen and agreed. My email to Severn Trent read,

Hello John, – we have just taken onto our books a bright project manager who is going places (see attached CV). He is currently with Ryans Utility Services operating in the North West. As you will see, for his age he has had significant practical experience…and has worked on a major Severn Trent scheme whilst at Ryans (achieving ST Contractor of the Year award).

Severn Trent interviewed him. The HR Manager was not impressed. After further encouragement he saw a senior Severn Trent Manager, but again was not taken further. About ten years later that bright young project manager fulfilled the commitment he made to me earlier. Steven Fraser was appointed Managing Director of United Utilities.

NAV's are neat…

Only Ofwat could come up with the catchy description of an alternati water and/or sewerage services provider for a particular geographic site or area. "New Appointments and Variations" or NAV's. Simply, developers are now able to choose to replace the existing local monopoly supplier for particular site with a NAV. Could be residential or commercial. Subject to Ofwat appointment and DWI and EA scrutiny.

The embryo of competition. Water-people began working with Brookfield Utilities and its subsidiary, IWNL, a newly licenced NAV in i early years. Today we now help several with specialist water sector recruitment needs.

Quick on their feet NAV's are making a mark. How quickly, efficie and sustainably they develop is for the future. Bizarrely the more success they are, the more the water model will need to change. The jury is still o The energy market is not a shining and encouraging utility example of lo term successful competition.

Chapter 24. Water-people on the move

It was now six years of profitable and sustained growth. But things change and you go with the change. Both Kate and Sean had progressed into other career opportunities, and I wished them well. For me I was lucky to have had their support and commitment whilst starting and growing Water-people.

I had two choices; to replace them or manage the business single-handed. If the activity stayed roughly the same I thought I could manage on my own and accept or reject other opportunities, depending on available time.

I also remembered talking to a really good IT professional who had started his business five years before me. He had taken on about thirty people and wished he hadn't. Far happier he said managing himself rather than spending his time managing and changing nappies. And his profit margin versus overheads had not changed significantly.

So with some melancholy and gratitude, I relocated Water-people from the Leeds city centre office to our home near Wetherby. Home office kitted and sorted, the bonus of daily end-of-day dog walking, and business as usual. Around that time I taught myself a good lesson.

A reputable engineering design consultancy and very good client contacted me. I had placed many technical professionals in the company and knew them well. They were looking for a civil design engineer for their Mumbai, India office. And quickly.

I carried out the usual search and eventually recommended a candidate who went on to be appointed. I had assumed that the salary would be broadly in line with his UK colleagues of circa 35K. After doing all the leg work, including India phone expenses, I was told that his salary would be £4000 pa.

My commission £600. In terms of time spent, telephone costs, definitely a loss leader. In terms of lessons learned, never assume. In terms of economic, if not broader moral education, an understanding of why consultancies have design offices in India.

Another highly respected and valued client was Berlin Wasser International AG (BWI). The overseas arm of Berlin Water who provided water and wastewater services to over four million Berliners in Germany.

We placed internationals professionals in many countries on their behalf including Europe, the Middle East, and Asia. Amongst them

Kathmandu, Nepal, and Albania, eastern Europe were particularly challenging but successful. As with all these things we were 'exceptional at being ordinary' and they thought a lot of us. Our reputation with them also paid longer term dividends and took us to the US working for one of the richest men in the world.

We had liaised regularly with BWI's top management team, one of whom was Karl-Heinz Zorn, Group Finance Director. He had left BWI and was appointed CFO Global Operations with RWL Water in New York, US.

A few months later I got a call from him. He explained his rationale for the move and told us about his new employer. RWL Water was one of the fastest growing water and wastewater solutions companies in the world, with customers in more than 70 countries worldwide.

It was founded by Ronald Lauder, son of Estee Lauder, who created the world-famous perfumery brand; and one of the wealthiest family dynasties in the United States. Lauder also has one of the largest and most valuable art collections in the world. A former US Ambassador to Austria, he set up set up RWL in 2010 with the philanthropic commitment to provide water solutions in developing countries across the globe.

So what could I do for Ronald and Karl-Heinz? They were looking for a Global Vice President, Sales and Marketing, with significant international water sector experience. I knew the man. Experience at a strategic business development and operating level in Veolia and previously worked in Europe, North and South America, US, Australia, and the UK.

However he was living south west of Paris. Could RWL be flexible? Could he be flexible? Yes. They liked each other. Two interviews later and to finally tie the knot, Ronald arranged to see our man in Paris at Lauder's sumptuous Parisian apartment in a chic quarter of Paris.

After a constructive two-hour discussion, with maid-service high tea and refreshments, the positive hand shake happened. Perfect. But not quite. The final question… "and what perfume does your wife wear?" enquired Ronald, as the French marketeer was leaving.

"Chanel No 5," came the answer (a rival brand). Who says the French lead the world in diplomacy? He still got the job. Thank the Lauder.

180

Water-people on the islands

Now operating across the world, we were placing people in many exotic locations as well as helping others who were leaving faraway island places. The Falkland Islands and St Helena to name but two. The Isle of Man did not come into the exotic category, but an enquiry from a Manx world-leading product company was nonetheless intriguing.

I got a call from a Director of Strix. I had never heard of them. "We are in hot water," he joked. I knew the feeling. He went on to say that they were the largest electric kettle element manufacturer in the world. Still puzzled as to why Water-people?

"I was told that you know all about experienced water quality professionals, and equally important, professionals who are familiar with tight regulation and compliance." he said. He went on to explain that Strix was a global company with IOM HQ and manufacturing and laboratory bases in China.

The majority of electric kettles manufactured in the world were fitted with a Strix element. Adhering to global quality regulations was fundamental in the Strix business sector. Regulators were present in all countries of the world and Strix was interested in individuals who had experience in quality, compliance, and regulatory reporting and relationships. We went on to forge excellent relationships with the company and, needless to say, we were in our 'element.'

Ironically, at around the same time, we were asked by Guernsey Water in the Channel Islands, to support the placement of a Water Quality Manager and this successful assignment led to a recommendation to near neighbours, Jersey Water, and their new CEO, Helier Smith. A number of water professional placements later, and the relationship continued to grow. Island business life had suddenly been very good for our mainland Yorkshire business.

In 2014 we upped sticks, this time to South West Devon and the beautiful South Hams. Oh! the convenience of the internet and the dog and bone in running your own business from home. Now located in a metropolis of 25 souls in a sleepy hamlet on the Salcombe Estuary.

Dealing with water and overlooking it. Little did we know that the upcoming coronavirus and its implications for working life would give a perception that we were already ahead of the game.

Rubbish of course but a really fortuitous coincidence. 'Lockdown' for us was business as usual. Very lucky.

US shooting and a close call

In November 2016 we took a US break to Florida. By now we had sold our SW Florida home in Naples and were visiting friends in the area. Our base was a hotel located on the harbour, and close to the beautiful local beaches.

We had been there for about a week and venturing out on a balmy Friday night for customary early evening meal with our 3-year-old daughter. We were driving slowly towards the car park exit when all hell broke loose. Two police cars with sirens screaming and lights ablaze pulled across our exit path, and four armed officers with guns drawn, flung open vehicle doors and ran into a section of the car park.

Although obscured by a tall hedge, we were three to four metres away from the action unfolding. Amidst desperate shouting, four gunshots rang out. Our vehicle was boxed in with no means of escape and seemingly in the middle of a gun battle.

A few seconds later, deathly quiet. Emergency lights from the police cars still reflecting in our car interior, one frightened little girl and two equally scared parents.

A police officer approached us, confirmed that we were witnesses to the incident and took our names and room number. We were held for an hour on the spot before being told we could go, but to expect contact from an investigating officer the next day.

Around the small hotel pool the following morning talk was rife about the incident. From a combination of employees and guests we got the detail. A couple had spent the day on a nearby beach, drinking heavily and arguing. They had got into a pick-up truck, continued to argue, and then pulled randomly into our hotel car park. The girl stormed off with shouts from boyfriend that he had a gun, and she should stop. A hotel guest heard the threat and called the police. The subsequent four gunshots were from the police, the man was hit twice and helicoptered to hospital in nearby Fort Myers. Wounded from the gun shots but not fatal

End of story? No, the start. Initially the cops had said they were going to interview me but by Saturday lunch, no sign of any contact. Perhaps it wouldn't happen. Anyway a little later I bumped into a hotel employee we knew and got on with well and had known for some years.

We spoke at length. I will not name the individual or his/her sex. The employee had met the armed police on arrival, pointed out the pickup truck, and witnessed all of the incident. In fact the employee was by the side of the officer who fired the shots.

The employee had also witnessed the officer's command for the driver of the pick-up truck to get out of the car with his hands in the air. The driver did exactly what he was told. Hands in the air, unarmed, bare chested, and wearing beach shorts. Two of the four shots fired by the officer had then hit the driver. The hotel employee had subsequently been interviewed by the police and made a statement confirming this eye witness account.

Late that afternoon I returned to our hotel room. A message was taped to the TV screen. I still have that message:

11:15 A. SATURDAY.

MR SMITH

WHEN YOU ARRIVE BACK AT YOUR ROOM
WOULD YOU KINDLY GIVE ME A CALL.

SPECIAL AGENT ED C
FLORIDA DEPARTMENT OF LAW ENFORCEMENT

(239)

IN REFERENCE TO LAST NIGHTS INCIDENT.
THANK YOU.

I called and arranged to see Special Agent Ed from the Florida Department of Law Enforcement (FDLE) on the following Monday in our hotel room. Apparently he was "independent" of the local force and asked to investigate and report on incidents of this type. A regulatory animal.

We sat on the room balcony. Really friendly guy, lots of small talk and banter about our respective lives. Cutting to the chase we started a taped interview. I related all that we had seen that Friday night. After about an hour we had concluded the main business and I saw him to the door.

More small talk. He went on to say we had got on well and suggested that we should meet up some time for a beer and gave me his personal email address. Job done. Almost.

The final couple of sentences of our conversation were to radically change my perception of the previous hour, including the friendly exchanges and atmosphere.

Almost as a throw-away remark, I asked if the pick-up driver would ultimately be charged. Bear in mind, during our meeting, I had made no mention of my knowledge of the trusted employee's version of events. Special Agent Ed said it was too early to say, but, he said, he had brandished a weapon, a knife, at the incident.

I knew he was lying. For over an hour we had greeted each other, eye to eye, until this moment. His comments on the knife and weapon were articulated with his eyes firmly fixed on the floor. Both uncomfortable and unconvincing.

Later on the same day, I caught up with the employee and briefly told the individual of my meeting. The employee was reflective but reaffirmed strongly that no weapon of any kind was shown or threatened to be used by the truck driver at the incident. As confirmed in the employees signed statement to the police.

I said we should go to the local press and media. I could get guarantees on anonymity to protect the employee and me, but the employee said that the job and family were more important and did not want to jeopardise either. I respected the individuals wishes.

The justice process had, apparently, been served; the seedy and often corrupt American way. Ironically 17 days prior to the Cove Inn shooting incident in Naples, the optional chew or walk brigade had elected probably the biggest liar of all as President.

As for Ed, he was an engaging personality, and I knew why. No further contact.

We want your name

From 1st April 2017 the water industry non domestic business market was to be deregulated in England, opening up to a form of competition. Prior to then there was no choice for businesses, who were restricted by geographic location, as to who provided and billed them fo water services.

Now new animals were to be born. Business water retail services companies. Very similar concept to gas and electricity. For the first time the business customer was going to have a choice.

Severn Trent was ahead of the game and about to set up a business water retail company through a joint venture with United Utilities. The JV would be based at Stoke on Trent.

Early in 2017 I got a call from Severn Trent. They talked about the JV and the fact that they liked my name. Alan Smith? Surely not. OK it has a certain resonance to sport, but no middle name, and 10 million others in the UK, one of whom is bad, very bad. The representative went on to explain.

"We like Water-people as a business name. At a high level we have been given the go-ahead to approach you to see whether you are prepared to share it. We could put 'The' in front to differentiate" she said.

"How much would you pay me for the right to use it? I enquired.

"£5000," she said.

"Pardon?" I exclaimed?

"£5000,"she reiterated.

"You have got to be joking," I scoffed.

"What would you be looking for?" she enquired.

"£50,000," I said.

"We wouldn't pay that," she said.

End of conversation. I reflected that, even at £50,000, it could have led to hassle that would not have made it worthwhile. How many would get the telephone numbers and websites of 'Water-people, the recruiter' and 'Water-people, the business retailer' confused? Potentially leading to misdirected and unwanted calls day and night. The deal was not done.

Instead Severn Trent went with the name 'Water Plus.' After five years of operating, their 'Trust Pilot' rating was 2 out of 5 stars, with 2/3rds of the reviews categorised as 'bad.' Google reviews were worse with ratings of 1 out of 5 stars. Water Non-Plus maybe.

There is a simple reason. The margins to be made versus the operating costs to make it work efficiently don't add up. Therefore operating costs are screwed down resulting in poor service performance.

Was introducing competition for the business retailer worthwhile? As so often happens, a free marketeer's dream and a practitioners nightmare. Look at the free market disaster of electricity and gas in the UK and US.

The Aga Saga

Now well embedded in our Devon home, and placements happening at a steady rate, life was good. However one assignment would prove to be the most bizarre in our business history. One morning the phone rang. "Hello, could you tell me how long you place people for?" said the enquiring voice.

"Well, it depends on the role," I said. "Permanent is obviously longer term but temporary or interim can be anything from, say 4 weeks to 18 months or more. It just depends on employers needs and the role. And how long do you need someone for?"

"Two hours," she said.

"Sorry," I said, "did you say two hours?"

" Yes," she said. "We are an Aga Cooker retailer. Tomorrow we are coming from the North West to deliver a new Aga to an address in the Kingsbridge area."

The rationale of the Water-people contact was still lost on me. But so were kettle elements so I retained my professionalism and patience. She continued, "the problem we have is that one of our three-man crew has reported sick and we need a three-man gang to unload the Aga. Health and Safety regulations require it. So we need a fit, handy man for a couple of hours. When we googled recruitment agencies in the Kingsbridge area, you were the only agency that appeared to be operating in the area," she said.

I explained that we were a specialist water industry recruitment consultancy, not a local agency, and operated across the UK and worldwide.

"I do apologise," she said, "I don't suppose there is a local agency you could recommend?"

"No, sorry," I replied.

"OK thanks," and with that the interim placement searcher was gone.

Fifteen minutes later I still felt a conscience. Could I have helped her? No, not really. After all we were renowned for placing professional water industry operations and engineering managers, environmental and analytical scientists, water and sewage treatment plant specialists…but cooker lifters…no…not within our international portfolio….

But what if I asked Darren? Darren was at the top of a ladder outside my window. A Yorkshire painter and decorator who was currently painting the outside of our farmhouse. Between brush strokes and, craning my neck upwards, I shouted to Darren the dilemma faced by the Aga company.

"Cooker lifter? I've been called some things," he muttered…

"I just wondered if you might want to take a couple of hours off and earn a bit of beer money?" I said.

"Where's the delivery to?" said Darren.

"East Portlemouth," I said, "a little village about 3 miles from here at the mouth of the Salcombe Estuary. Not that easy to find but I could take you there."

"Alrate, jobs a good un," said Darren, in true Yorkshire fashion.

So we had our interim Aga Unloader. I got back to the Aga company.

"I have been able to secure someone for you. His name is Darren and he's available tomorrow afternoon to help you out," I said. "He is very reliable, practical and fit so I am sure he will do the job for you."

It was the first time in Water-people's history that we had given a formal reference for a two-hour placement.

"That's great," she said. "Thank you so much. What would Darren be looking for in terms of payment?"

As newly appointed agent of Darren, the phlegmatic P&D, and now Aga Carter, I hadn't a clue. So to save another stiff-neck-of-a-conversation with the game Tyke, I blagged "£60 cash and no commission."

"OK, that will be fine. I will email you the delivery address in East Portlemouth. Can you ask Darren to be there at 2:30pm tomorrow please and tell him to ask for Steve? He is our lead delivery man. And thank you once again for all your help," she said.

Aga day arrived. As arranged I drove Darren, complete with bib and brace overalls, through the narrow and winding tidal estuary road to East Portlemouth. Dropped him off outside the resplendent and very grand sea-view house of the soon-to-be Aga owners and told him we would relax and wait on a nearby beach, until the cooker-carrying-caper was complete. Forty-five minutes later Darren strolled on to the beach counting the readies in a plain brown envelope. That was mighty quick. Had anything gone wrong?

" No, straight forward enough" said Darren, "although initially I got a hell of a chuffing fright."

He went on to explain that after I had dropped him off, he had entered the gate of the palatial premises, found his way down the drive to the front door but got no answer.

The Aga pantechnicon lorry was parked close-by. So he wandered into the back garden and, stooping there, admiring the flowers, was a frail, bowed man in his late 80's, walking steadily with the aid of a stick. Darren had said hello and that he was looking for Steve. The man had responded "I'm Steve."

Darren went on, "looking at him I thought, bloody hell, this might be the last Aga he lifts off any pantechnicon before joining the clever cooker carriers in the sky," and was not sure what to do. He didn't want to insult the man. Decorating suddenly seemed much less complicated. Couple of minutes of unsure small talk later and a burly delivery man bustled his way round the house corner.

"Are you Darren?" said the burly. "Yes," said Darren.

"Hello, I'm Steve. Shall we crack on?" A different Steve, this time resembling Atilla the Hun. Conscience cleared and a win-win. Steve, the octogenarian house owner got his cooker and Darren got his beer money. "Good deed for the day Darren" I said." You should be decorated."

Verdict on Water-people experience

We have been ploughing the water recruitment furrow worldwide for over 20 years now and worked with many good and not so good companies on most continents. At the same time supporting excellent water sector professionals in their career development.

Did I think it would be so successful? I hadn't got a clue, but I do think not wanting to fail generally leads to success.

If I was to give any modest tips to a would-be business starter or job-changing candidate, firstly it would be never underate or underplay what you know or have learned.

At every change of my career the daunting challenge of a new, relatively unfamiliar role or business, turned out to be matched by something I unwittingly brought to that role or business.

That surprise soon expanded my thinking from hope I don't fail, to contributing something positive and rewarding for both parties. But never forget my Mothers poem of earlier.

Secondly common sense. A rare commodity. Rejoice if you have it – it's not 'common' particularly at Board level.

Chapter 25. Our Rivers - natures drains

During the writing of this book, the issue of river water quality, wild swimming, and sewage dumping, has gone bananas. The stuff of legend. Like many legends there are a lot of fabricated myths, half-truths, and fake news swirling around. Social media has, as usual, played its part together with a bandwagon of uneducated politicians and a section of cynical and uninformed press and media.

Time to set the record straight from a river anorak of many years standing. You should know by now that I am not an advocate for the current crop of chief executives of water companies.

However, we owe it to the many thousands of hard-working and dedicated water industry people who in reality really run the industry, to spell out the true facts.

These individuals work around the clock, skilfully operating and maintaining sewage treatment works and sewerage networks across the country.

To get the truth out and to rubbish the fake stuff – the latter often pedalled by ambitious self-serving politicians with a propensity to say one thing and do another or more likely do nothing, we need simple facts. Here they are:

Water companies credibility and culpability in river water quality

Q. Prior to the restructuring of companies and ownership in 1989 was river water quality poor?

A. Yes. Many major rivers were toxic graveyards with river water quality declining.

Q. Why?

A. Industry, farming, and inadequate and outdated poorly performing sewage treatment works (oft quoted political reality "no votes in shit").

Q. At the sewage treatment works was it a capacity or process problem?

A. Both

Q. Why?

A.(1) processes - additional processes like secondary and sometimes tertiary treatment were required. The more effective the treatment, the more improved river water quality.

A.(2) capacity – boom in home and industrial development (population growth almost doubled since early 20th century) leading to treatment under-capacity at many works.

Q. Is that the position today?

A. Generally No. Partly because of £30 billion investment in inland and coastal sewage treatment by water companies since 1989 and partly because of a tougher regulatory stance by the independent Environment Agency.

Q. So why is it that rivers are still polluted and only 14% are achieving 'good' ecological status? Wasn't the £30 billion a waste of money?

A. No. The £30 billion investment programme was catching up on many years of inadequate funding and has achieved significant improvements with 70% of pollution load removed at sewage treatment works since the 1990's including significant reductions to ammonia and phosphate levels, and toxic metals including cadmium and mercury.

Q. OK but that still doesn't explain why rivers are still polluted and only 14% are achieving 'good' ecological status?

A. River pollution comes from many sources, the largest polluter is agriculture. Over 40% of today's pollution comes from fertilisers, animal waste, pesticides, and other farming practices. Highway drainage and other surface water direct run-off also contributes.

Q. Do water companies dump sewage from outfalls without treatment?

A. Water companies don't dump anything. If they pollute by operational incident or mismanage they are prosecuted by the EA (£500 million in fines 2010-2020). See more detailed explanation of outfalls and how they work below.

Agriculture credibility and culpability in river water quality.

Since time began streams and rivers have drained the land, before journeying to the sea and a return to the water cycle. As the water travels it picks up minerals from rocks and soils as well as faeces and urine from all manner of creatures who live and thrive in or around rivers and have done so well before humans populated the earth.

Some impurities are fed on by tiny creatures and invertebrate; some finds its way to the oceans. Minerals and other impurities washed from the land pollute the oceans and have done for millions of years – one reason why the sea is salty. In later centuries as man began to live on land close to streams and rivers, livestock used as a food source, would urinate and defecate close to streams and rivers.

Fast forward to the last hundred years or so. The human population of the earth exploded. The UK population doubled and all needed feeding. Farming adapted and quickly developed to keep pace with the increased need for greater and speedier volumes of essential food produce for the table.

More foodstuffs, more agricultural chemicals draining into streams and rivers. More livestock, more farm animals urinating and defecating on land draining into streams and rivers. Run-off from agrichemicals used to produce larger crop yields, quicker, and disease free, including insecticides, herbicides, fungicides, and fertilisers, found their way into the aquatic water ecosystem.

This is today's agricultural pollution, for which society is responsible, either directly or indirectly, with farmers on the front line.

We all need the produce in ever greater quantities, and this is the unintended consequence. But a consequence it is. And it needs to be addressed. Successive Governments have prevaricated and done little else. Perception of the water companies and their negative higher-profile image has provided the perfect smokescreen for agriculture. Fat cat focus sells papers and fills airtime.

However, as mentioned previously, the greatest percentage of river pollution today – 40% - comes from agricultural sources. Tougher farming pollution legislation was introduced in 2018 but despite five hundred violations by farms and other agricultural concerns being recorded by the Environment Agency in the past two years, no agricultural prosecutions have been brought to date.

This issue needs to be taken more seriously and urgently addressed, alongside other actions.

Discharges to rivers – bunking the dumping

The sewerage system in England and Wales, that is the sewer network of 571,000 km (or 355,000 miles in old money), which if laid end-to-end would encircle the earth 14 times, transports poo, pee, kitchen, bathwater, and rainwater to over 6000 sewage works for treatment.

The clever Victorians were the pioneers of sewers, particularly in urban areas. Before sewers, sewage was thrown out of windows onto streets, or collected from over-run household cesspits, ultimately leading to mass cholera and other deadly diseases in major towns and cities.

The sewers got rid of the problem and eventually sewage treatment works were built on the end of the sewers to treat the foul and waste water before returning treated water to local rivers. In most cases the sewers were combined sewers.

They not only took foul and waste water from homes and dwellings, but also rainwater from roofs, streets, and other urban centres. Another clever Victorian engineering 'insurance policy' was to create overflow pipes in the sewerage system to avoid the sewers 'backing up' during heavy rain and flooding homes, streets, and urban centres with foul pollution.

These were called combined sewer overflows (CSO's) and discharged excess flows of rain diluted sewage direct to local rivers and watercourses. They worked well for many years and, because of more than adequate sewer capacity and therefore infrequent operation, were largely unseen and unnoticed.

Just like much of Victorian engineering they were built, or even over engineered, to last for many generations. Until climate change that is, and the almost doubling of the population since the 1900s.

Today's extreme weather patterns, with heavier and more persistent rainfall, means that the sewerage system is often, rather than rarely, at over-capacity which in turn triggers the CSO's into action many more times than was originally intended or designed. It is a current and developing capacity problem with a massive price tag to put right.

It won't be solved by cheap political jousting, blame, or points scoring. There are currently over 20,000 CSO's in England and Wales and hundreds of thousands of miles of sewers, many undersized and lacking today's capacity needs.

Even the capacity of storm storage tanks at some sewage treatment works, designed to store excess flows, are now often unable to cope, triggering the works overflow, and acting in the same way as the CSO's. In summary, three big points:

Firstly, it is not spills from CSO's. It is overflows. Spills are accidents like when you drop some tea on your Grandma's new carpet. Overflows are when there is not capacity.

Secondly, it is not dumping. It is not Sam the Sewageman from the local Water Board, reversing his tanker lorry in the dead of night and "dumping" a load of shit into the nearest convenient river.

Thirdly, it is climate change, an act of God, dictating that CSO's, instead of overflowing due to heavy rainfall once, twice, or three times in a year as originally designed, are now doing that in a month, or sometimes a week.

Remember that since many of the CSO's were designed and built, the population has not only doubled but also doubled the water it uses. Climate change has simply accelerated and significantly added to the capacity issue.

If you started your starry-eyed married life in a tiny bedsit flat with a Reliant Robin, they both may have been fit for purpose. Three kids, carry-cots, pushchairs, and a decade later, the roost and the Robin is not big enough.

That's the over-simplification of the problem in a three-wheeler nutshell. But the family issue is easier to solve than trading in a sewerage system no longer fit for purpose. About a £100 billion more of an issue.

Cries of dumping, dividends, and dereliction are not going to solve this one, arguably the biggest issue facing water companies and the water environment going forward. The solution? See next chapters.

Chapter 26. Wild swimming

The advice I would give for those who would swim in rivers is, by all means go ahead, but do it at your own risk. That risk is significant in terms of health and safety.

As I mentioned before rivers were, are, and always will be natures drains. Ducks, swans, mice, rats, voles, badgers, otters, bats, beavers, fish, and many more UK wildlife creatures enjoy a life by or in our rivers. They also pee, poo, and reproduce in the rivers. This means that swimming or paddling in rivers runs the risk of picking up germs like leptospirosis (Weil's disease), cryptosporidium, giardia, shigella, norovirus, and E. coli., causing gastrointestinal illnesses with symptoms such as nausea, vomiting, severe diarrhoea, and abdominal cramps. A risk to understand and for individuals to make.

So if we could magically airbrush out the significant man-made issues of agricultural chemicals, livestock pollution, treated and untreated sewage effluent discharges and surface water from roads and other urban pollution, there is still a real health risk of swimming in rivers.

But airbrush out we can't, and their presence only heightens the problem and the risk. A minor graze or ingestion of river water may well have nasty health consequences. I am a parent of five children and would always encourage my kids to swim in the sea but never in natures drains. I know what's in there.

But who talks about drowning from unseen currents, unexpected rapid river flows, and cold cramp inducing water temperature.

The latest report from the 'National Water Safety Forum' (NWSF) dated April 2022 shows that there were 277 deaths from accidental drowning in the UK in 2021 – a rise of almost 10% on the previous year.

The Report points out that "inland waters, such as rivers, canals, lakes, and reservoirs…continue to be the leading locations with 62% of the (drowning) deaths."

Tragically a spike in more deaths by drowning in rivers has occurred during the hot summer of 2022. The frightening reality is that the idea of legitimizing swimming in rivers, borne from a small minority of genuine enthusiasts, risk takers, and latterly band waggoners, is now being trumpeted by powerful advocates.

Like the irresponsible Parliamentary Environmental Audit

Committee (EAC). First though, a health warning. They are politicians. Second health warning. Like all good politicians, they want to be popular. Third health warning. They are naïve yet thick skinned, which is why they are politicians.

Experts in everything depending what week it is. Also talking the 'let's be popular' river bathing talk are some press and media outlets, and a few headline-seeking water companies and their CEO's, and surprisingly Water UK, the trade body, and the Rivers Trust.

The aim, amongst other things, is to create and increase 'Designated Bathing Water'* status for certain river stretches across the UK. Designated bathing waters are currently only designated on coastal waters, with one river exception [See more detail at the end of this chapter]. Here are poorly thought-through extracts from the Parliamentary Environmental Audit Committee Report on River Water Quality published in early 2022:

"Every community in the country should have access to waters— whether coastal or inland—that are safe for people to swim in without running the risk of falling ill…"

Are they planning mass extermination of river wildlife? Also…

"We recommend that the Government actively encourage the designation of at least one widely used stretch of river for bathing in each water company area by 2025 at the latest…"

This is utopian, misguided and naïve, but of course superficially popular. The classic case of cart and horse. Well somebody has to tell the King that he has not got any clothes on.

You cannot turn the clock back to Adam and Eve's environment in five minutes or indeed in a generation. Since A&E's time, nature and man has used rivers for umpteen practical reasons. We have learned the hard way that many of the reasons, in hindsight, were fundamentally wrong. Rivers have been mistreated. We are where we are.

The cost of raising river water quality standards fit to safely bathe in are enormous and almost impossible to consistently sustain and maintain given natures input and fluctuations in urban and rural drainage. As a minimum:

- the EA will have to revise and enhance sewage treatment works permits which will mean significant capital investment in higher levels of treatment, leading to higher water bills

- new and upgraded sewers and CSO's, requiring significant capital investment and higher water bills
- new and more intensive sampling and monitoring, for both treatment works and CSO's, meaning the EA will need significant additional Government funding to meet higher levels of operating expenditure
- Acceleration of plans to reduce agricultural pollution, the biggest polluter, leading to greater subsidies to farmers and/or higher produce prices
- Schemes to treat and better manage surface water drainage direct to water courses, from roads, private drainage, and open spaces leading to significantly increased costs for local authorities, highways agency, and private land owners.

These activities are the horse. The cart will be the progressive introduction of designated bathing waters for river stretches followed by stringent monitoring to ensure compliance.

Introducing designated bathing waters on river stretches before this happens is a recipe for disaster. We are already seeing the folly of a bathing water designation introduction on the River Wharfe in Yorkshire, whilst the river quality is deemed 'poor' by the Environment Agency.

And who is going to pay the bill for all of this? The Environmental Audit Committee say the water bill payer. Will the 96% of water bill and taxpayers who don't swim in rivers want to pay significantly higher charges to fund the pleasures of the 4% of wild swimmers?

The answer may be 'Yes' but until someone has put the horse first and asked and answered the huge financial question, there are two options. Either understand the risk, understand the issues, and continue river swimming or use the local safe swimming pool where there are lifeguards, water quality testing every few hours, and no dangerous currents or diseases. That's why they were invented.

Finally, the most glaring and shameful example of political pronouncements and activity, this time aided and abetted by a clutch of water company chief executives. And this, even for politicians, is bewildering. As mentioned earlier the Parliamentary Environmental Audit Committee during its RWQ proceedings suddenly became an overnight champion of river swimming. Not courting popularity of course. Not catching the wave of recent popular campaigning. How dare we suggest such a thing? Of course not.

However whilst falling over themselves to be the superficial, popular, cool guys, there was a fundamental omission that would have insulted the thinking of a primary school pupil.

Astonishingly whilst giving the impression of already wearing their woolly bathing trunks under their M&S underpants and preparing to jump off Westminster Bridge for a quick dip and infection, they omitted to discuss, or address, or talk to, or summon, any expert from any water safety organisation, lobby, or the like.

So no ROSPA, no National Water Safety Forum, in fact no questioning of any independent safety expert to balance their new found 'wild' recommendations.

Despite record open swimming drownings recently announced. Despite inland waters, such as rivers, canals, lakes, and reservoirs being the highest percentage of those tragedies.

On the contrary, perhaps the most banal of questions was asked by Committee Chairman, Philip Dunne, of each of the water company chief executives who attended the Committee's oral evidence session 13th October 2021. The opening question.

'In the light of what we now know is the state of the rivers, with not a single river in this country in good ecological condition, and in the light of the public recreation that has happened in an enforced way through Covid over the last 18 months, would you swim in any of the rivers in your area?

Answer from four of the five chief executives, YES. Surprise, surprise.

However during the whole session the fundamental question of the need for care and safety, the dangers of currents, cold water, potential drownings, was neither emphasised or raised by anyone on both sides of posturing debate. Scandalous, unforgiveable, but typical of the breed.

What are designated 'Bathing Waters'? The UK has over 600 designated Bathing Waters – sites that are popular for swimming and paddling and have been designated under the Bathing Water Regulations 2013. They have been put in place thanks to the EU Bathing Waters

Directive that was first introduced in 1976. UK designated Bathing Waters are mostly coastal, with only 16 lakes and only one stretch of river.

How are Bathing Waters monitored? Water Quality standards have been set for Bathing Waters based on World Health Organisation research into the incidence of stomach upsets in people bathing in waters with different levels of bacteria. Water is tested for two types of bacteria, E. coli and intestinal enterococci. Tests are carried out regularly, usually weekly, by government environmental agencies between 15 May and 30 September in England and Wales, and 1 June and 15 September in Scotland and Northern Ireland.

Bathing Waters are categorised as 'excellent', 'good', 'sufficient' or 'poor' on the basis of bacteria levels. Sites are rated annually, and on a short-term basis in response to temporary pollution. By law, the local council must display information, online and on signs at Bathing Waters, about water quality and pollution sources during the bathing season. If there is a temporary pollution incident they must explain the nature of the problem and how long it's likely to last.

If a Bathing Water is classified as 'poor', an 'advice against bathing' symbol must be put up on site and online, along with information about pollution sources and what action is being taken to clean it up. This doesn't mean you can't swim – the sites remain open – but there might be an increased risk of getting ill.

198

Chapter 27. Running water today

Time to look at what this Derbyshire lad's 60 years' experience of publicly and privately operating in the water industry in the UK and overseas has brought to the surface. The journey has given me enough insight and opinion to reflect on where we are today, the good, bad, and the ugly.

Equally important, in the next and final chapter, to see where we should be heading to meet the challenges of tomorrow. To get a wider view, I have been in touch with many water industry professionals who I either worked with or respect, and who know the industry intimately.

I have not been in touch with the many transient carpet baggers and asset strippers, who plague the industry, for personal and corporate short term financial gain. The trash-can of history awaits these non-entities.

One more point. The following views are not driven by any political persuasion but by practical reality, borne from experience of lessons learned and doing it right or getting it wrong.

Running water today - Joe Public's view – and the fat cats

Let's start with well-known basic facts. Water companies operating in the private sector does not sit well with the public. It didn't in the lead up to privatisation in the 1980's, it didn't during privatisation in 1989, and it doesn't today [Survey carried out in 1989 -79% against. Survey carried out in 2017 - 83% against. Despite £200 billion investment since.

Two reasons; one fundamental, the other self-inflicted and aided and abetted by the boardrooms of water companies. The fundamental is easy to describe and impossible to shift. The public cannot be convinced that the 'simple' matter of gathering water when its rained, treating it and piping it to customers taps should be considered a profit-making business.

Even less when flushing it away. Despite the water companies investing many millions of £'s into a multitude of local, regional, and national communication initiatives over 30 years and more, their message has largely fallen on deaf ears.

Why? Because tap and toilet was always there. When he or she was born, when he or she went to school, when he or she got married, when he or she had kids and grandkids. When he or she watered the garden or filled the paddling pool. The tap still flowed drinkable water, same colour, same taste, same shower, same bath. The loo still flushed.

So what changed to suddenly bring profits into the equation, said Joe Public? Enter a new Board room animal to help Joe confirm suspicions.

A plump feline strain began breeding and multiplying and taking over in water company boardrooms. More commonly known as 'fat cats' they confirmed Joe's suspicions. Splashed all over the news and drowning rationale. Joe had sussed it.

The communicator had no chance. Hence the rationale behind the title of this book. Joe still thinks it's the Water Board when he cares to think about it. And that's the problem, he doesn't.

He is content in the belief that the Water Board is anonymous until something goes wrong. An anonymous water company is a good water company is the mantra. That will do for Joe.

Until, that is, he hears about the obese moggies. During the writing of this book I had no intention of going fat cat hunting, but the strain was all over the news as I wrote. I could not in conscience avoid researching and commenting.

The Moggie Magnificent Seven and the Annual Remuneration Roadshow

Severn Trent   'Making a difference together'
CEO LIV GARFIELD   **£2,807,800**
(see note 1 below)
STOP PRESS: Update 2021/22   **£3,913.400**

United Utilities   'Being purpose led'
CEO STEVE MOGFORD   **£2,940,000**

Anglian Water   'Love every drop'
CEO PETER SIMPSON   **£2,074,647**

Thames Water   'Delivering Life's Essential Service'
CEO SARAH BENTLEY   **£1,230,000**
(see note 2 below)

(NB. When SB joined TW in September 2020 there was agreement that she would receive £3.1 million "buy-out" award over the next three years to compensate for loss of bonuses /incentives that she could potentially have been paid at Severn Trent over the same period)

South West Water   'Bringing water to life'
CEO SUSAN DAVY   **£1,724,000**

Southern Water   'Water for life'
CEO IAN MCAULAY   **£1,082,400**

Yorkshire Water   'The future of our water is in safe hands'
CEO LIZ BARBER   **£1,316,000** (retired May 2022) (total remuneratio

NB 2020/21 published water company accounts – unless stated)

The numbers speak for themselves. What is even more bewildering is that there are reams of Annual Report gobbledegook, jargon, pie charts, and the like, from remuneration committee chair-people and so-called experts, that seek to justify these outrageous numbers. However, volume and vacillation rarely convince. On the contrary only testimony to corporate self-delusion.

NOTE 1

Liv Garfield CEO Severn Trent.

It is estimated that Liv Garfield at Severn Trent has had total remuneration of over £20 million since joining the company eight years ago in 2014. It is also worth noting that in October 2020, just 6 ½ years after beginning her water industry career in April 2014, she was awarded the CBE 'for services to the water industry.' A Commander of the Order of the British Empire.

Over £20 million and a Gong for less than a decade of unstinting and loyal service. This, despite being accused of being 'disingenuous' in October 2021 following an appearance with other water company Chief Executives, in front of the House Of Commons Environmental Audit Committee. The Committee later commented, as follows, as part of its **'Report on Water Quality in Rivers'** publication dated 13th January 2022:

Paragraph 147.

The chief executive of Severn Trent repeatedly claimed that the company did not discharge raw sewage. She said that, because storm overflows discharged a mix of sewage 'heavily diluted' with rainwater, the contents of any discharge were 'pretty much already rainwater.'

Paragraph 148.

148. While this claim may have been intended to reassure us about the discharges from overflows on the Severn Trent network, we do not find it convincing. Levels of pollution in combined sewer overflows are not routinely monitored.

Paragraph 150.

The public are rightly shocked when they discover that untreated or partially treated sewage is regularly dumped into rivers and streams in England. We have heard that the rainwater washing into storm sewers can contain microplastics, industrial chemicals and hydrocarbons. It will then mix with human waste from homes and businesses containing harmful bacteria. In some cases, the only 'treatment' that such discharges will have received will have been to pass through a mesh grill.

Paragraph 151. We therefore found the claim made by the chief executive of Severn Trent that its sewer overflow discharges were 'pretty much already rainwater' to be disingenuous. As water companies do not routinely test the quality of the discharges from storm overflows, they are in no position to make this claim. Discharges from overflows can be highly contaminated with raw sewage and other pollutants. To claim otherwise shows a disregard for the public's concern about water quality in rivers.

CBE for 'services to the water industry' did I hear? I rest my case.

NOTE 2

Sarah Bentley CEO Thames Water

I found the Sarah Bentley case equally fascinating. Sarah joined Severn Trent in December 2014 and left in August 2020. It does not appear that she had any other water sector experience prior to that time. And yet the following statement appears in the Thames Water Annual Report 2020/21 and on the website:

> *" A multi-disciplinary executive with extensive water industry experience…"*

Let's stop a minute. Are we missing something? December 2014 to August 2020. Five years and eight months described as "extensive water industry experience." Not much longer than an apprenticeship. Methinks a gong could be long overdue.

Also we have another remuneration gem from the fat cattery playbook. Sarah agreed to join Thames Water from September 2020. Presumably she was very receptive to the idea, which is why she agreed to join.

Equally Severn Trent was sorry to see her go but wished her well. As a result of her decision to leave it would mean, presumably, that she would forfeit future Severn Trent bonus and incentives remuneration over the next three years.

Not rocket science, just common sense, bearing in mind she was no longer there. The same treatment, for example, as that which might be afforded to an NHS worker, or policeman, or fireman, or rail worker, or

202

care-home worker, or anyone who might leave or retire today, but would not expect, for example, holiday pay to be paid for the next three years.

But No. Enter the cattery compromise. It's called having your Kitekat and eating it. Thames Water Annual Report 2019/20 – under 'Remuneration for Sarah Bentley' is the following additional and incredulous paragraph:

'In addition, and consistent with the provisions of our Remunerations Policy, the Committee agreed to replace *in-flight incentive awards that were forfeited by Sarah on her joining Thames Water. Details of the buyout award will be finalised in due course and disclosed in next year's Annual Performance Report.'

…fast forward to…"next year's Annual Performance Report…" which reads, Thames Water Annual Report 2020/21 – Sarah Bentley's remuneration for 2020/21

'As reported in last year's report, Sarah was granted awards to replace unvested awards which were forfeited as a result of her leaving Severn Trent. The payment of around £447,000 in the table includes £314,935 which relates to Sarah's 2019/20 annual bonus forfeited and £132,014 as compensation for the proportion forfeited for the 2020/21 annual bonus.'

My understanding is that, in total, the Severn Trent 'unvested awards' that were forfeited by Sarah Bentley and agreed to be paid to her by the Thames Water buyout, totalled £3.1 million, comprising of potential bonuses, deferred bonuses, and long-term incentives.

Thames Water said it (her total remuneration) "was benchmarked against other water companies and other London and south-east utility companies".

I think that the vast majority of Thames Water employees and customers would say that those who did the bench marking had not only lost the plot but did not know there was one. Pie charts in the sky…

As a former spokesperson in the water industry I have often tried, and failed, to defend executive salaries but none as grossly out of all proportion and comprehension as those in the Moggies Magnificent Seven list above.

At engine room level there are 50,000 fantastic and dedicated people who have worked for thirty or more years in the water industry, often in trying and unsociable locations and conditions, who will have earned less than a fat cat's annual salary in a lifetime.

Neither will their 30 years of commitment and loyalty have earned them a gong, more likely a duplicated HR certificate and no more. There can be no moral or logical justification for obscene financial awards for a regulated monopoly business.

*As for "in-flight incentive awards," a real beauty and surely a worthy Pulitzer Prize winner from the prolific pie chart producers of remuneration rhetoric. In flight from whom? I confess that on family holiday journeys my young children had in-flight incentive awards – jelly babies – for being good. But only after they had delivered – and not before.

Running water today - a dose of reality today

There are regular cries from political parties, politicians, trade unions and others to return the water companies back to public ownership, more for reasons of private ownership distaste than public sector practicality. It is a nonsense and would never work. For two key, undeniable, reasons.

First, a public monopoly providing an essential public service, particularly a public water service, will always be at the mercy of short-term political thinking, priority, and finance.

The 70 years prior to 1989 gives us all the evidence we need to prove the point. It teaches us not to make the same emotional and political mistake again. How many times do we need to witness the lack of investment and the consequences in the public sector? Today's demands on Government and the public purse are there for all to see. Whether we like it or not, and I don't, water and wastewater services are way down the pecking order when it comes to Treasury funding priorities. We have seen it before, and we would see it again.

Second, any newly elected Government threatening returning the industry back to the public sector, would have to look at the current market capitalisation of the water companies. Consequently the large compensation price tag that the Treasury would have to find to pay off shareholders. A political priority non-starter. But the first point above is the key.

I have already rehearsed the critical shortcomings of investment whilst in the public sector. It's easy to say under-investment, very jargony. What was the practical reality of life in the public sector in pre 1989 days and before privatisation? Been there, seen it, done (or not) done it. Worth repeating examples from earlier in the book.

- Drinking water discolouration and contamination from ageing iron pipes
- Leaking water networks across the UK with 60% losses in some areas
- Sewage treatment works inadequate and struggling to cope with increased flows from local domestic and industrial development. Many failing consent standards with river water quality on the decline
- Sewers undersized and no longer able to cope with flows from domestic and industrial development
- Little or no coastal sewage treatment. Hundreds of crude outfalls pumping raw sewage onto popular beaches and bathing waters. Over 200 in the South West alone
- Cities like Liverpool and Hull, with populations of over 1,000,000 and 300,000 respectively, discharging raw, untreated sewage into the Mersey and Humber estuaries.
- Collapsing sewers, inherited from the Industrial Revolution in the Manchester/South Lancashire conurbations. Adjacent houses often destroyed by collapses
- Non-compliance with EU Directives on Drinking Water standards. UK threatened with European Court action
- Non-compliance with EU directives on Wastewater standards. UK threatened with European Court action

I was there in the thick of it, often having to explain what we were not doing and why, and using the lame, but true, reasoning about lack of investment, and how low the water industry's ranking was when it came to successive Governments' public sector investment (PSBR). Was Joe Public really bothered ? No.

Over 30 years and £200 billion of record investment later, there has been a tidal wave of improvements across clean water, wastewater, and environmental improvements to rectify many of the issues above. Is Joe Public aware No. Do rival politicians want to know and endorse and shout about the industry achievements? No. Do the press and media really want to know? No. Unlike the high-profile coverage of fat cat stories.

So what does Joe Public know? He knows his/her water bill has risen significantly. In a single generation he/she has footed the bill for historic public sector neglect and under investment in the early/mid-20th century; implementation of new EU standards - agreed but not delivered in the 1980's; future planning capacity for anticipated growth and demand in the 21st century.

A triple whammy. Does he know that NO. Does he blame privatisation and profits? YES.

Having worked for 30 years in the public water sector and the same in the private sector, there is only one obvious conclusion of where the real and significant improvements have been made. Ask any other geriatric water professional and he/she would say the same.

Of course the delivery of improvements in the private sector, thanks largely to funding availability, was far ahead of anything I had seen or experienced before in my career. Almost on a par with the clever and farsighted Victorian engineers and philanthropists of the Industrial Revolution.

From 1989 the shackles were off, the finance was available, and the delivery was both chaotic and exciting. To those that enjoyed the thrill of the chase, a great opportunity. To those that were unsure, the prospect of early retirement. To those in the middle, a chance to retrain, learn new skills, be encouraged to take on new technology and greater job satisfaction.

To those joining, a career with the promise of environmental satisfaction, recycling, innovation, sustainability, just at the time when the environment was beginning to take centre stage.

A thrilling prospect for environmentally aware, super charged graduates to make a difference. Equally important the employment boost that the new investment created in the local and wider economy.

Thousands of new jobs and security of employment for project managers, designers, modellers, scientists, contractors, product, and service suppliers.

Has any of this cut any ice with Joe Public? No. Not a stitch. By 2022 the negative needle of public unpopularity of water privatisation has moved little.

A privatised monopoly providing an essential public service, particularly a public water service, will always be illegitimate in the eyes of the customer. To think otherwise is an act of delusion. 30 years of transformation and improvement has done nothing to move Joe Public's view. Unpopular it was – unpopular it is.

But Alan, however unpopular, you are obviously a big privateer believer are you? No, far from it.

Here's the bad and the ugly of private ownership. The current water company model is driven by short term profit and not by long term environmental and sustainability goals.

The key announcements in the current company calendar model are financial results. Profit and dividend forecasts. And beating the Regulator. These numbers drive the primary focus and attention of the Board – shareholder and ownership interest come first.

The model dictates this approach and the way it is meant to work. Fine for private sector, market driven, competitive companies, but not a provider of a monopoly essential public service.

When I had learner plates on, my mentors would continuously stress that the water industry was a long-term industry and had to plan and think long term. Not for short-term spivs looking for short-term returns.

Today, significant water company internal focus, activity, and time is spent planning to outsmart the regulator at the next 5-year Ofwat Periodic Review. Internal non-productive machinations, paid for by Joe Public. Planning for the next 5-year cycle submission as the current deliberations are completed and announced.

Chief Executive appointments are made to reinforce and support this short-term financial demand and culture. Many are now helicoptered in with no water experience, flitting in and out, but with a common reputation for slimming down, reducing, creating efficiencies, all of course returning shareholder value and pleasing the financial fraternity.

And all of course whilst slurping in the fat cat saucer with monster remuneration rewards and unearned solid gold pension contributions.

Traditionally, and where I nod positively to the past, home grown chief executives made their way through the ranks and knew the business intimately, with different mind sets and a bottom-up, closer to the wheel, approach and understanding.

Not surprisingly most of the current water company boards are packed with non-executive accountants, economists, legal, and regulatory experts. There is an exciting answer to the public v private conundrum. See Running water tomorrow…next chapter.

Running water today….the Regulators
Environment Agency

One of the key, and applauded, positives from the privatisation process was the establishment of an independent 'guardian of the environment' body.

Initially set up in 1989 as the National Rivers Authority, but in 1996 becoming the Environment Agency also taking on wider responsibilities including those of Her Majesty's Inspectorate of Pollution and local authority waste regulation, as well as the aquatic environment.

Billed as one of the most powerful environmental regulators in the world. It was. However, like many public sector bodies, it has suffered greatly from a lack of investment and under-funding. Ironically the precise same curse as the water undertakings pre-privatisation.

The result? A guardian of the environment with its' hands tied. Not the fault of the thousands of many dedicated and often over-worked professional environmental people who work there but restricted by the tight purse strings and lack of foresight of Government.

An agency that has the mammoth and increasingly difficult task of protecting our communities and countryside from the ravages of flooding. But a lesser focus on other statutory duties simply because of the critically small annual budget.

Greater flood protection prominence and scale thanks to the elephant in the global room; climate change. From warnings to prevention and protection, to aftermath support and reinstatement. This reality has meant that the greater policing of the water environment and monitoring of the poacher; the water companies, agriculture, and industry, has been a secondary task to the primary focus.

I emphasize, not a dereliction of duty, but of cash, and desperately trying to spread too thin resources of manpower across too fat a brief. The Chief Executive of the EA recently said that "our ability to protect our waters depends on us having the powers and resources to do that, and that hasn't always been the case." A touch of the 'Sir Humphrey' but we know what he means, despite the deliberate tense obfuscation in the phrase.

There is also a cultural nervousness within the EA. There should be more proactive, higher profile growling than the public perception of playing second fiddle to the fat cats. The starved EA budget psychologically encourages this reticence to take pole position.

A good example of this was my attempt to get a senior EA professional to talk to me for an off-the-record briefing of where he/she thought we were in terms of progress, achievements, challenges, for inclusion in this book. I was told that things were "a little sensitive at the moment" and so declined. Growl or a whimper? More thoughts about EA future recommendations later in the following 'Tomorrow' chapter.

Running water today…The Regulators The Drinking Water Inspectorate

 - the super silent regulator

The Drinking Water Inspectorate (DWI) was formed, following privatisation in 1990 to provide independent reassurance to Joe Public in England and Wales, that his/her public water supply was safe and drinking water quality acceptable. The smallest of the regulators, operating with less than 50 staff, they have done a superb behind-the scenes-job with a myriad of responsibilities.

Too many to mention but including, **technical auditing of water companies, assessing water company sampling and data, policing drinking water quality incidents, water quality complaints, agreeing water company programmes for improving drinking water quality, Ofwat liaison re quality and price impact, enforcement, local authority oversight re private water supplies enforcement, and much more.**

As part of managing sharp-end external communications in all three of the water companies I worked for, I came across the DWI, often in less than positive circumstances. Although never dealing directly with them, I did work closely with top class water company quality scientists who did.

In Severn Trent, South West Water, and Yorkshire Water, the two way relationships were both professional and constructive. That was in no small measure down to the gifted professionals who work in UK water quality, whichever side of the fence.

Without doubt, the very best in the world. The cynics would say, from a water company corporate strategy risk perspective, water quality was the number one priority, and they would be right, compared to, say wastewater treatment. But that should not underate the water quality scientists and their professional capability in both organisations.

Bear in mind that in the UK over 14 billion litres of wholesome drinking water is used every day, and yet major water quality incidents are extremely rare. Comparisons with other countries in the world, particularly the US, are interesting and should make us thankful.

So in terms of the DWI performance since its formation in 1990 would I change anything going forward? No, only get more journalists to shout about their unseen, dedicated, work. Although, given its coy track record, I don't think they would appreciate headlines like *"a super Inspectorate – we're gonna' tell the electorate!"*

Running water today...The Regulators   Ofwat

Of w at   A customer champion. I think not.

Forcing down water company bills? Encouraging and monitoring efficiency? If you look at the statistics, Yes.

Least cost strategy success? Grip on fat cat pay? Grip on profit? Grip on shareholder returns? No. Clarion, proactive voice on standards v costs pace on behalf of the customer? E.g. choice, priority, preference, No. Proactively explaining to the customer how the water companies are funded? Bill revenue? Debt? Equity? Creating a fair balance? What is the fair balance? No.

Often esoteric economic formulae introduced to determine service performance, customer service measures, and more, which generate cerebral jousting with water companies and their consultants but do little or nothing to improve the actual front line service delivery to Joe Public.

An opaque, cold fish of an organization that gives no empathetic signals to the master he serves. Unless you read Government and Whitehall and not customer as the master. Let's take a look at some examples of least cost.

Ofwat – Least cost – the customer

Certainly been welcomed in driving down bills but has that efficiency drive, measurement, and purpose tended to backfire on the very customer who allegedly benefits. During research into this book, many contributors either to industry past strategy or future ideas, wanted to share recent personal sharp end "customer service" experiences or those of friends or relatives in their local community. I wasn't looking to address that level of detail, but they were more than sufficient in number and concern to warrant examples.

Example 1. Reported leaking stopcock outside house. Low priority, easily resolved, simple, and oft repeated, common report, from diligent customers throughout England and Wales.

On this occasion a visit by a water company inspector, two months after being reported. Two weeks later repaired. One year later – same stopcock leaking.

One week later repaired again – but customer's internal washing machine stopped working. Filter blocked with blue plastic from external stopcock repair. Customer unblocked filter. Sometime later, same stopcock leaking again.

Contractor arrived to repair, customer advised contractor of previous blue plastic blocking. Told by contractor not to worry. Repair completed whilst customer was out.

Customer returned to find no water to house or internal heating – for 5 days – despite four phone calls to water company advising 90 year-old mother living in customer's cold house. Month – February. Taps, Combi Boiler, thermostatic showers, washing machine, dishwasher all blocked with blue plastic fragments. Fifth day a private plumber arrived and not surprised to find the situation.

Plumber remarked that "this happens all the time and keeps me in holidays abroad several times per year." Sixth day. New thermostatic valves, and replacement parts for boiler, installed.

Water company denied liability and said it was a private side issue. No compensation. Customer complained with photos of offending pipe. Eventually £50 offered and rejected, £150 and then £600 offered and rejected. Finally, after independent appeal, £1000 compensation paid.

Example 2. Blocked sewer. Again straight forward and common complaint. Water jetting easily and quickly resolves.

Young family moving into house. Belongings left on driveway whilst move took place. Sink gully blocked, and household customer inspection showed that blockage was backing up from the adjacent public sewer.

Water company contractor attended and set up jetting unit. Before commencing the contractor was advised by customer not to attempt clearance from driveway (on the private side) because any backing up could result in sewage flooding and pollution contamination to household goods still on the drive.

Customer advised contractor that it may be more sensible for jetting un-blocking to take place downstream of the property on the public sewer side so that excess water could run freely away and be contained safely and hygienically within the public sewer.

Advice ignored by contractor. Sewage flooding and pollution of drive took place. Baby car seats covered in sewage, along with several other items. The water company agreed to have seats professionally cleaned but returned with sewage still stuck to the seats.

Company eventually agreed to replace with new. The householder replaced much of the other drive pollution damage at their own expense. The retired senior water industry professional I spoke to commented that, *"all of this was totally avoidable. So now the water company have another family who have not got a good word for them. Most customers never communicate with a water company. An incident, in this case a blockage, is a great opportunity to impress. Turn up quickly, resolve effectively and leave. In this case the opportunity was lost."*

Example 3. Planning consideration. Plans to build a conservatory in the rear garden were sent by customer to water company. Company refused permission because the conservatory was planned to be built over or near underground sewer pipes. Actual water company plan submitted to the customer as proof of their decision showed sewer was abandoned years ago. Permission should not have been refused and was later granted. Unneeded hassle for the customer following unprofessional advice.

Example 4: Leak reporting. A Midlands couple reported a leak in Langley Mill, Derbyshire. The water company call centre operator tried to convince the reporter that Langley Mill was in Wales (the operator was spelling it with double 'L').

These examples are a drop in the bucket. My view is that the Ofwat least cost strategy, whilst fulfilling one aim, seemingly reducing bills, has led to clumsy and bungled outcomes of customer service similar to above. The squeeze is obvious. Ofwat tightens the screw with minimal five-year billing increases or, more recently, billing reductions in its 5 year pricing review.

In turn, the water companies attempt further reductions in already reduced sharp-end operating costs, employ more external contractors, or to use the latest jargon, 'framework contractors,' at next-to-nothing margins. The contractors, in order to earn their meagre margin, need to maximise number of jobs in a day, often using inexperienced operatives, and "bingo" you have the customer service you ultimately deserve.

Outsourcing to contractors on water mains repairs, sewer maintenance, metering, leakage, and other sharp end activities undoubtedly reduces water company operating costs, but the loss of local network knowledge, and reputation, is never regained.

The impact is not seen in the Ofwat Fawlty Towers of esoteric statistics, not in the feline-furry boardrooms, but in the customers stopcock-ups and sewage spraying fiascos. What price £10 off your bill? The company that manages the wrongs, not the statistics, will top the pile.

Least cost has also, in my view, increased risk and impacted employee motivation. When water companies fit the operating jigsaw into the latest least cost regulatory template, manpower is a critical and obvious focus.

Hence the constant navel gaze at structures and restructuring. At privatisation the cost reduction fruit was so low, managers could trim its rich pickings whilst horizontal. Not now. Yes we have new technology, bringing with it obvious staffing reduction opportunities and re-training. However we are at a crossroads of 'complacency versus concern' on what is the optimum level of risk. Through Water-people and our activities, I regularly talk to a variety of employed water industry professionals on a regular basis. The upwardly mobile will tell me that current staffing levels are OK, and, because of technology and training, there is no cause for concern.

Others, and a growing number, will say that the paring down in key operational areas of experienced wise heads has left generational knowledge gaps which is a real cause for concern, particularly when things go wrong. I would like to be in the former camp, but experience tells me that the latter should be listened to so that 'least cost' doesn't triumph at the expense of someone else's cost.

Ofwat – least cost – the contractor

Contractors working for the industry are like marmite – you either do or don't like the attitude, skill sets, and experience of contracting culture. Whatever your view, they come under great pressure to deliver quickly and efficiently on tight margins.

Whilst talking to a leading contractor recently he volunteered a simple example of how client 'least cost' had recently permeated to economies on water mains repairs and renewal – a critical part of capital maintenance, and not one for short term thinking. This was his story.

Electrofusion couplings are designed to connect two ends of polyethylene underground piping together. Not easy to fit, and can fail, unless conditions are ideal. They often pass pressure tests post fitting, but the weld can give way at a later date because it's plastic and not ductile (i.e. metal).

Recommendations were put forward by us, the contractor, to use hydraulic fittings, which largely overcome potential unreliability, but cost three times the amount (£6 vs £2). Bear in mind that this was one of the largest water companies and was a huge contract. Considering longevity, the amount of time saving on site, and reduction in asset risk and leakage it was a no brainer. However, it was not adopted because the water company procurement team could not see past cheapest cost versus whole life cost and reliability. Worshipping at the altar of the shareholder. Short-term thinking for a long-term industry...

Ofwat and fat cat remuneration

As previously mentioned, this issue is top of Joe Public's irritation list and the one most likely to get his/her back up, to continue the feline metaphor, in terms of negative perception of the industry. The same irritation goes for just about every other stakeholder, particularly politicians and the press and media. Lame cries from chastened water company press officers of 'market rates' for a private company operating an essential monopoly public service cut no ice.

So what has Ofwat done to regulate the source of this high-profile customer angst? Nothing. Absolutely diddly squat.

Despite Michael Gove (then Environment Secretary) in 2018 attacking the water industry over high pay and dividends and saying, " unless water companies take action, pressure for renationalisation will grow." In the same hot-air rant Gove went on to say, "I will give Ofwat whatever powers are necessary and back them in any action they need to take." Since then no new powers and no action. But plenty of action from the fat cats.

FACT: Liv Garfield CEO Severn Trent plc   2018/19 total remuneration **£2,395,400**   (at the time of the Gove rant)

FACT: Liv Garfield CEO Severn Trent plc   2021/22 total remuneration **£3,913,400**   (4 years after the Gove rant)

Where are you Mr Gove?...What went wrong?...

Fresh from the Fat Cat failure, Gove went on to be the Secretary of State of Levelling Up. I can only assume that he may have suffered from vertigo and couldn't face the levelling down.

Up or down he was sacked by Boris in the dying throes of the Boris bundling saga. Sacked by the sacked. In fact since 2018, dividends and moggie pay have increased significantly.

Ofwat's latest weak, ineffective cry was that fat moggie pay-outs should be linked to environmental performance. That took a lot of strategic contemplation bearing in mind weeks of incessant headlines on river water quality.

Bandwagons and jumping on come to mind. Too little, too late, and too feeble. The damage is done. A howler of a missed opportunity to even get near to being a customer champion.

A 2013 quote from Jonson Cox, then Ofwat Chairman, is interesting. Asked how he would implement reforms, Mr Cox said: "It is better to improve corporate structures and behaviours by reasonably firm encouragement now, rather than being forced to take stronger action later." We're still waiting.

Ofwat and dividends

The Ofwat website will tell you *"We have no formal powers to control dividends"* and *"* w*e have no formal powers to control profits."* So what does Ofwat do? *"We set price controls, which control the revenue the companies can collect from their customers in bills. In setting price control we must make a judgement on what is a reasonable rate of return on the capital investors have provided. This return must be sufficient for the company to attract investors and lenders to finance the investment programmes."*

True, Ofwat has used the levers to bear down on key financial parameters which are designed to squeeze or eliminate the practice of excess returns to shareholders. But has it? A bit more from the Ofwat mantra…

The balance between debt and equity varies between companies. Our approach to setting price limits seeks to create conditions where the funding for additional investment can come from either debt or equity. We do not decide on the capital structure of the sector, but we think it is important that each company's structure is sustainable in the long term...

Do I hear the whimper and not the growl? Like the fat cat issue, by common consent from most neutral financial observers, the regulators dividend restraining efforts have, at best, been marginal and more likely inadequate. Extract from:

"Fair rate of return for the regulated water industry in England and Wales."
Report prepared for Defra: Final report 2018 Vivid Economics Ltd (now McKinsey)

…the (water) sector has nonetheless taken on more debt and paid out higher dividends than Ofwat expected, and companies have so far not provided sufficient evidence in viability statements to show how financial stress might affect customers or taxpayers. Many companies have significant pension fund deficits, whose repair could have been funded using returns that were disbursed as dividends...

Jonson Cox was Chair of Ofwat from 2012 to 2022. His tenure was interesting, with few indelible marks, particularly on recommendations on the two key areas that Gove highlighted in 2018: dividends and executive pay.

I thought his was a surprise appointment. In 2010 he resigned from Anglian Water after a 6-year spell with an alleged £9.5 million salary, bonus, and pension pay-out.

An important point of interest here, and not as trivial as it may seem. There are inaccuracies in his CV which are of concern, particularly as it was placed before a House of Commons Committee.

It relates to his time with Yorkshire Water. The CV was circulated on 4th July 2012 to the House of Commons Environment, Food and Rural Affairs Committee Pre-appointment hearing: Chair of the Water Service Regulation Authority (Ofwat), prior to confirmation of the Cox appointment.

The published CV 'Summary Career history' states that Cox was Managing Director of Yorkshire Water Services from 1996 before resigning in March 2000.

In fact he did not take on the role until April 1997. I was there. Companies House records also confirm 1997.

Why is this important? The Yorkshire drought crisis was 1995-1996. Kevin Bond was appointed Managing Director of Yorkshire Water Services in April 1996.

As referred to earlier, Kevin worked tirelessly across Yorkshire to apologise to many key customers groups and other important stakeholders, at the same time as working to ensure the delivery of a massive water infrastructure improvements programme on the Yorkshire water network. All of this largely carried out by the end of 1996.

The CV inaccuracy therefore could lead to a misunderstanding that Cox was at the helm in the teeth of the operational water crisis recovery that faced Yorkshire Water in 1996. I am sure that this was not intended, and that Cox would see it as an oversight.

However placing it in front of the House of Commons with the inaccuracy and it being perpetuated later on the Ofwat website with additional narrative, as well as other sites, is unfortunate.

I spoke earlier about talent and trust working with this individual in the 1990's. My instincts remain the same. He was awarded the CBE in 2020 for services to the water industry (not to be confused with the rail industry).

Chapter 28. Running water tomorrow...time for change...new water company model needed

Is the current model, introduced in 1989, to provide essential water and wastewater services in England and Wales fit for purpose for the challenges lying ahead? No.

Here's the rationale for change. Over time, as each generation has developed and grown, so has water usage and the need for it's safe disposal after use. Lessons have been learned and changes made.

Sir Winston Churchill said that "the longer you can look back, the farther you can look forward." As I mentioned earlier, we owe a lot to the Victorian era and its clever engineers and scientists for recognising the critical importance to community health and well-being of providing adequate clean drinking water and safe sewage disposal.

Town halls continued the good work but lacked the funds to maintain the water challenge, particularly away from major towns and cities. Financial commitments on other urgent growing community needs held the sway.

The decades of the 1950's, 60's and 70's saw a reawakening of the importance of managing water and the river environment, with significant legislation and reorganisation taking place. Catchment Boards, to River Boards, to River Authorities, to Water Authorities.

Creating the ten regional water authorities in England and Wales from the previous cast of hundreds of smaller water undertakings in 197 was a master stroke.

Its principle of one entity managing the whole water cycle, on a river catchment basis, from source to tap and its return to rivers and oceans, led the world and still does compared to other developed countries.

You only need look at the US and see the fragmented, disorganised and chaotic situation of over 100,000 water and wastewater treatment providers. Shortages and quality issues are common place. Uncle Sam has got nowhere near attempting consolidation as was successfully achieved in the UK 50 years ago and they are paying the price.

As ground breaking as the new water authority concept in England and Wales was, it suffered the same critical issue as many of the town halls before them. Lack of funding. Right vehicle but little fuel to drive the engine.

Capable of delivering but constrained by Government purse strings. Threats of imminent EU prosecutions was the Thatcher Government stimulus leading to the 1989 water privatisation. However unpopular, the new model was right in 1989. The years before in the public sector with scant and inadequate infrastructure investment or priority was undisputable proof to demonstrate why.

Now in 2022, with over £200 billion invested since 1989 from private funds, larger debt, and increased water bills, we witness higher drinking water quality standards, upgraded inland and new coastal sewage treatment works, thousands of miles of water mains and sewers replaced or relined, and more infrastructure improvements on the way.

So why change? There is a man for a season, but not for all seasons. The same applies to monopoly water services. The advent of a private company providing an essential public service in 1989, however unpopular, was a necessary evolution. A shake-up and incentive for a sleeping, underfunded, life-essential giant. Bringing greater funding, focus, and exposure.

However, the impetus of the private model has now served its useful purpose. Many of the issues and challenges of 30 years ago are not the issues of today and tomorrow. Time to move on.

"Not for profit but for people" model - the way to go!

I first started hearing about the Welsh experiment in water in the early 2000's. To me it sounded quirky but then again the Welsh have always been different, and I paid little interest.

I did know that Hyder (the previous Group name) which owned Welsh Water and a significant electricity business, had run into financial difficulties, thanks mainly to the combination of Blair Government's windfall tax and Ofwat's significant cuts in water bills happening at the same time.

The double whammy resulted in a break-up and selling off of the Hyder Group businesses, and the creation of Glas Cymru, a single purpose company, who would own Welsh Water. The new not-for-profit company would be limited by guarantee, with no shareholders but a significant addition of unpaid members of the of the local community.

The 'little interest' I had grew. From what seemed a curious way to run a huge business, one of the largest in Wales, the 6th largest water company in England and Wales, and with over 3 million customers, it appeared to be going from strength to strength.

Now, and twenty years on from the start of the experiment, it has proved to be a resounding success. Its performance across a range of industry comparators is either better than, or almost equal to every other measure.

Gone are profits, gone are shareholders creaming off inflated dividends, gone are fat cats. Instead the annual 'surplus' i.e. income over expenditure, that the company makes is either distributed back to the customer in the form of billing reductions or ploughed back into capital investment improvements to local treatment works, water mains and sewers.

Their proud proactive line: *" Glas Cymru has no shareholders and is operated solely for the benefit of the customers of Welsh Water"* is music to the ears of those who believe that a monopoly supplier of an essential public service should not be in private shareholder hands - the overwhelming view of the vast majority of Joe Public in England and Wales.

They also appoint over 60 independent unpaid 'members' drawn from all parts of the Welsh community, who ensure that the business remains focused on its primary purpose of providing high quality water and sewerage services to the local communities served by Welsh Water.

The members carry out an important corporate governance role. Their role is not based on representing a particular group or stakeholder interest, only that of the local community. They do not receive a fee and the company welcomes and gets applications from a diverse and wide range of community backgrounds. Appointments are made on the advice of an independent membership selection panel.

The refreshing success of the model is compelling. Market research shows that the community believes that Welsh Water is now of, and serving the local community, returning to being part of the essential fabric that knits society and its social and environmental needs.

Not remote, distant, and distracted by an obsessional need to generate and maximise short term profits and dividends. The big question is could this model work across the English water and sewerage companies?

The answer is Yes – although it would require a significant political push and likely legislation from an incumbent Government wedded to the philosophy. Boardrooms with shareholder domination are unlikely, like the turkey, to vote for Christmas.

But my view is that, as well as the strong moral argument of adopting a proven and successful 'mutual' model for an essential use provider, it would also be a strong vote winner with an electorate irritated by fat cats and profits.

Yes, there would be the significant issue of shareholder compensation, but a firm manifesto commitment supporting a 'not-for-profit' model would probably ensure more realistic water company valuations.

Anyway financial restructuring is for the bean counters and way beyond my pay grade. Put simply, the much more complex 1989 public-to-private process was managed with great success so I am convinced the Welsh model implementation could be equally well delivered.

Politics and people coming together gives me confidence that it could be achieved and relatively painlessly.

[See: Welsh Water – A Model for the Purposeful Ownership of a Utility case study 2021- Oxford University – Said Business School]

Greater Local Community Involvement…mine not theirs..

Adopting the not-for-profit - but for people Welsh Water model would bring much more local community focus and involvement in local water and wastewater services, sadly lacking and almost invisible with the outdated English water company model of today.

Just look at the following backgrounds, drawn from a cross section of non-executive English water company board members profiles - highlighting the classic and transient interloper animal.

…extensive experience of financial and corporate reporting, delivering major transformational change….a former non-executive director at Ladbrokes Coral PLC…a wealth of commercial, financial, and high-level management experience…30 years' experience in the automotive industry… working in a regulated environment in the financial services industry…involved in large projects and the production side of Royal Dutch Shell's business…project management and information solutions to the oil and gas industry….career in the regulated finance industry….roles in banking and technology…business, finance and technology leadership…financial management, M&A and business transformation expertise…experience in financial and general management….substantial advisory and regulatory experience…brings experience from sectors including medicine, bioethics, financial services…extensive strategy, corporate finance, risk management and M&A experience….transformational change, performance improvements and the development of renewables….highly experienced chartered accountant, with

global financial and governance experience...strategic business management within a regulated, highly dynamic environment....advised regulators and companies in a range of countries and sectors on regulation, market structuring and competition issues...expertise in driving efficiency and embedding innovation to deliver performance...and more...and more...of the same thing...

Where are the regional and local customer service champions who can tell management how it really is, local priorities, issues, choices? Where are the experienced ex regional water company professionals? Where are the regionally and locally based professionals?

The not-for-profit Welsh model would bring the appointment of non-paid members drawn from all areas of the company patch. More attuned local knowledge leading to more attuned improvement programmes and local services.

You would then get local objective views on priorities and choices; river water quality improvements and the pace and cost, including inland designated bathing waters, sewerage improvements and the like. More bottom-up input, preference, and choice from local Joe Public rather than a suit in London or Birmingham.

A superb example of fantastic regional and local cooperation is the clean-up of the River Mersey. Forty years ago the Mersey was an open sewer, with a deadly cocktail of raw sewage and toxic chemicals. In typical Liverpudlian humour it was said that if you fell in the Mersey you wouldn't drown, you would be poisoned.

Many billions of pounds later and the Mersey today is a river transformed, one of the cleanest in Europe with whales, porpoises, dolphins, octopus, squid, crabs, shrimps, and other sea creatures returning at the mouth of the river.

As well as the massive investment (over £8 billion on sewage treatment alone) from local, regional, national, and European sources, the overriding key reason for the successful clean-up was the creation of the Mersey Basin Campaign with water companies, local authorities, and significantly, local people living near the river, working together in a common cause.

A network of many unpaid, local action coordinators, working with volunteers, schools, and businesses, on a wide range of local improvement projects brought the community's aspirations into reality.

That local fabric of cooperation could be created again in England in the interests, and for the benefit of, a cleaner river and water environment. But the current water company model has to make way to make it happen.

Ofwat abolition

I can almost hear the murmurs of derision. What? The customer watchdog? The water bill controller? Surely this man's lost the plot. OK, so here's the rationale. Give or take a few millions, Ofwat costs the tax payer around £40 million per year to run.

When it was devised in 1989 as an economic regulatory governor on price limits, comparative competition, and other efficiencies, it was an essential and fundamental player in the checks and balances of water company life in the private sector.

However, like the current water company model, it has now passed its sell by date, particularly if the not-for-profit-but-for-people model was to be adopted.

Price proposals and limits would be set and approved by each individual regional company. This would not be revolutionary. Many regional entities and organisations have been doing the same for many years. The most obvious example are local authorities providing not dissimilar public services who have proved more than capable of setting and collecting local rates and there has been no rioting in the streets.

The new water company model would have the added safeguard of local and regional member input to ensure reasonable funding whilst ensuring that local spending is kept to an acceptable community level. In the event of intractable disagreement a national body could be nominated to adjudge the issue and resolve. Like the National Audit Office or Defra.

The Ofwat abolition would eradicate the need for the greatest paper chase ever known to man since Adam and Eve got it together. I refer to the Periodic Review process. Supposedly a business case required to be presented by the companies and approved by Ofwat every five years which sets out plans, obligations, costs, performance, and suggested price limits.

Realistically this Everest of information and data is worked on back-to-back before, during, and after each Ofwat deliberation. A continuous and costly process of industry navel gazing. Water companies spending millions of pounds, millions of man hours, millions of internal meetings, and employing what seems like millions of consultancies, laying out the business case.

And Ofwat similarly spending millions of pounds, millions of man hours, millions of internal meetings and what seems like millions of consultancies, on second guessing the millions of pages submitted by the water companies, and eventually making a subjective judgement on future price limits.

Imagine the masses of time and manpower that would be freed up in the new model - new look regional water companies to better focus on community benefit and support. A no brainer.

Comparative competition – an essential and useful tool introduced in the Ofwat armoury in 1989 to compare water company with water company in terms of performance and efficiency – including operations, capital expenditure, customer service and other parameters.

It has done its job and the water companies have responded with significant improvements in the last 30 years. The margins of performance are now so close and comparable in these areas as to not warrant further time and effort in over regulation of diminishing returns. As one reputable, and independent economics and finance consultancy has said,

"The restrictions on mergers to preserve the comparative regime, and the historical success of the comparative regime, have, paradoxically led to less need to maintain comparative competition to the same extent going forward. Debt financed models do not necessarily sit easily with comparative competition, and significant convergence on cost and service levels across the industry means that comparisons are in any case less valuable than they once were."

Ofwat has done its time. Like the curates egg, the regulator brought benefits and blunders. No regulation of profits, no regulation of dividends, combined with a least cost mentality, has not served Joe Public well at the sharp end.

An economists esoteric strategy of determining theoretical customer service performance may have supported the box ticking brigade but cut no ice with real service at the customer coal face. And as for controlling fat cat remuneration, Ofwat has never been at the races. Missing 'inaction.'

Stronger Environment Agency

One of the key positives coming out of the 1989 reorganisation was the separation of gamekeeper and poacher in terms of regulation of the water and river environment. The creation of the National Rivers Authority, a few years later to be subsumed into the Environment

Agency (EA), was fundamental and timely, bearing in mind the impact of regulatory and political changes of privatisation.

Its positioning as a public sector body responsible for air, land, and water quality, including water resources, fishing, and navigation was common sense, as was the bringing together of all key aspects of environmental policing and regulation.

As mentioned previously there has been one huge flaw in the strategy, and ironically it is the same issue that blighted the water industry in the public sector; funding. It is chronically underfunded and has been almost throughout its 30-year tenure.

As one senior manager reflected to me from one of the key consultancies who work for the EA, *"their resources and budgets are so thinly stretched that the pressures of climate change and the understandable priority of flood prevention, investigation, and support, takes up so much of their time, budget and effort, that they are morphing into concrete pourers".*

The principle of an environmental, regulatory one-stop shop leads the world, and the model is the envy of many. However unless the politicians get their act together and properly fund it, the Agency will always come up short in its role as an effective and efficient 'guardian of the environment' across all of its key responsibilities.

The people that work for them are top class, dedicated environmental professionals. There just aren't enough of them. When they were first formed climate change was perceived as 'iffy.' That iffy is in the dustbin of history and now reality.

The importance of the Environment Agency and its current and future impact cannot be understated. If it means we all have to pay a bit more tax to help police and preserve our kids future environmental legacy, then so be it.

Another critical issue for the Agency and its future operation and success that urgently needs addressing is profile. Too often it is a shrinking violet in terms of proactively grabbing hold of a high-profile environmental issue and properly leading the debate or explaining the facts to an easily led public.

More often than not it is behind the curve of a current story and responding rather than leading. Again that may simply be priorities and resources but in an age of fake news and conspiracy, the profile needs addressing.

The river water quality debate, wild swimming, and designated bathing waters are examples where others, often the misinformed, have grabbed the headlines.

The most exciting future opportunity for a stronger, more influential, and higher-profile EA, could come if the not-for-profit-but-for-people water company model was to be adopted in England.

The concept of a more focussed grass roots agency in local community partnership with the new regional not-for-profit water company, its members, and local groups, would fit well and be an exciting prospect.

The EA is already well attuned to listening and working with local communities on flooding problems and solutions but with increased funding and resources could also do more on local river partnerships, improvements, choices, and cost.

These issues are often debated in the round and from afar at political or economic levels. More would get done and more preferred local improvements would be delivered for the benefit of all.

The Mersey experiment is tangible proof. A joint ownership of the local environment. Multi-faceted guardians of the environment. The kids want to do it – why can't we?

Final thoughts

So was the decision of the 15-year-old Derbyshire lad to opt for an employer that "paid you when you were off sick" a good one? My mother would say so.

From Nottingham to Mansfield to Leicester to Birmingham to Devon to Leeds to Montego Bay to Stockholm to Connecticut to New York to Washington DC and back to Devon. A life in the often hot water industry taught me a number of things.

It isn't about boardrooms, Chairmen, Chief Executives, Directors, or shareholders. Those elite few represent much less than 1% of the water industry, even though they get most of the profile, and a treasure trove of remuneration.

The rest, the 99%, who really run the industry, are dedicated engineering, operational, scientific, and customer service professionals in the engine room. The engine that provides essential-for-life daily water and wastewater services to over 50 million domestic and industrial customers in England and Wales.

Having spent over 60 years working with them in the public and private sector these are the guys who deliver, come rain come shine, with little public profile but, like me, are proud to be part of it.

The antics of the thin sliver of posers and politicians is of little concern to the engine room. The engine will perform whatever the letterhead says.

However, as the industry has changed, as new technology has been introduced, as climate change has become a reality, so the know-how in the engine room has changed.

There are now more graduates with a career passion for the environment and the adrenalin to relish and take on fresh environmental challenges. The engine room is up for it. The 1989 model is not. Climate change doesn't do short term. The City and financial owners do.

Time to change the model - and plan for the next 50 years - not 50 months. Come on politicians, surprise us!

A new water agenda – the next generation

Company	**Not-for-profit-but-for-people company (limited by guarantee)** no shareholders – no dividends – no fat cats - community driven, regional price setting
Customer	**Greater local community involvement** local members – local company consultation, decision-making, working closely with the EA
Regulation	**Ofwat abolition** not fit for purpose - done the job – time to go
Environment	**Stronger Environment Agency** increased funding – more effective/proactive – more local input - partner with new WC

(all of this water has been passed by management)

THE END

Acknowledgements

During the writing of this book I spoke with many water industry professionals. Some retired and some very much in the thick of it, running the essential water and wastewater services of today.

Some very much continuing to progress their careers, thoughts, and ideas, some coming to the end of a career dedicated to such an essential and worthwhile cause.

Thanks to all of you for the time and the consideration you afforded me. I know some will think my recommendations are plausible and others not. Above all you should always have this one overriding thought, they pay you when you are off sick.

Thank you Mother

Radio postscript

BBC Radio Cornwall – phone in
,,,,,done many times before....
Bills, metering, leakage, sewage, hosepipe bans, fat cats
1st caller: why won't my dog drink your water?
Lesson: never think you've heard it all before
